# Untangling Organizational Gridlock

Also available from Quality Press

*Quality Service Pays*
Henry L. Lefevre

*Deming's 14 Points Applied to Services*
A. C. Rosander

*Implementing Quality with a Customer Focus*
David N. Griffiths

*Quality Dynamics for the Service Industry*
W. F. Drewes

*Quality Service—Pure and Simple*
Ronald W. Butterfield

*The Customer Is King!*
R. Lee Harris

*The Quality Revolution and Health Care*
M. Daniel Sloan and Michael Chmel, M.D.

*Quality Assurance in the Hospitality Industry*
Stephen S. J. Hall

*Quality Management in Financial Services*
Charles A. Aubry II

To request a complimentary catalog of publications, call 800-248-1946.

# Untangling Organizational Gridlock

## Strategies for Building a Customer Focus

Michele L. Bechtell

ASQC Quality Press
Milwaukee, Wisconsin

*Untangling Organizational Gridlock:*
*Strategies for Building a Customer Focus*
Michele L. Bechtell

Library of Congress Cataloging-in-Publication Data

Bechtell, Michele L.
　　Untangling organizational gridlock: strategies for building a
　customer focus/Michele L. Bechtell.
　　　　p.　cm.
　　Includes bibliographical references and index.
　　ISBN 0–87389–147–3 (alk. paper)
　　　1. Total quality management.　2. Customer service.
　3. Organizational effectiveness.　I. Title.
　HD62.15.B43　1993
　658.5'61—dc20　　　　　　　　　　　　　　　　　　　　　92–46118
　　　　　　　　　　　　　　　　　　　　　　　　　　　　　　　CIP

10987654321

ISBN 0-87389-147-3

Acquisitions Editor: Susan Westergard
Production Editor: Annette Wall
Marketing Administrator: Mark Olson
Set in Optima and Galliard by Montgomery Media, Inc.
Cover design by Dorothy Wachtenheim.
Printed and bound by BookCrafters, Inc.

Distribution of this title to trade bookstores and libraries by AMACOM Books, a division of American Management Association, 135 West 50th Street, New York, NY
10020. ISBN 0-8144-0203-8.

For a free copy of the ASQC Quality Press Publications catalog, including ASQC membership information, call 800-248-1946.

Printed in the United States of America

  Printed on acid-free recycled paper

 ASQC
Quality Press
611 East Wisconsin Avenue
Milwaukee, Wisconsin 53202

*To B. Koval,*

*who showed me the way*

# Contents

# Acknowledgments

This book is about people—how they grow, how they learn, how they work together and change. And so it is fitting to thank the people who influenced this work.

*Untangling Organizational Gridlock* began while I was on the faculty of the Arthur D. Little Management Education Institute, which awards a masters degree in international management. Many of my students, following completion of their studies in the United States, returned to quasi-public or government positions in Africa, Southeast Asia, Europe, and Latin America. The presentation of the material in this book was strengthened by their objective and critical review as managers and students of total quality.

What began as a text for the classroom subsequently found a wider audience. Many thanks go to my clients, both here in the United States and overseas, who, over the years, allowed me to work with them to implement large-scale organizational change for performance improvement. Their willingness to listen, experiment, and reflect provided the inspiration to share our experiences with others.

Of course, all the ideas and experience in the world do not necessarily make a good book. That requires the ability to create a document that speaks in an easy fashion and keeps the reader moving through not just 10 pages but through 250 or more. To this end, Peyton Petty provided invaluable editorial assistance throughout this project. A talented editor, Peyton identified flaws in structure and the inevitable redundancies that appear in an initial written work, helping to make this the fun book that it came to be.

Matt Loeb at Quality Press provided considerable support for both the technical and managerial issues described in this book. His confidence in, and enthusiasm for, the messages presented here gave me the energy to keep at it, despite a busy consulting schedule.

Annette Wall, production editor at Quality Press, did a superhuman job in reviewing, coordinating, and finally converting the manuscript into a real book. Her valuable suggestions and attention to detail made the difference between good and great.

Thanks go to the many others who reviewed and/or influenced this manuscript in its early and intermediate stages: Sandra Arangio, Freed Bales, Don Barth, Marcia Bartusiak, Michael Bergman, Alan Brache, David Braunschvig, Kathleen Lusk-Brooke, Chip Caldwell, David Couper, Patricia Dannielson, Jay Darby, Alison Farquhar, Louise Firth, Henry Frechette, Randy Goodall, Richard Hackman, Aleta Holub, Dan Kim, Brian Kreutzer, David Kreutzer, Don Mattes, Joe Posk, Michael Pugh, William Rogers, Donald Schon, Marge Srabian, Phillip Stone, Roger Ward, and Deborah Woog.

Final thanks go to my sister Cynthia B. Wood for her continued love and support.

*Here is Edward Bear, coming downstairs now, bump, bump, bump, on the back of his head, behind Christopher Robin. It is, as far as he knows, the only way of coming down stairs, but sometimes he feels there really is another way, if only he could stop bumping for a moment and think of it.*

—Winnie the Pooh

# The Service Gridlock

Today, service organizations are under the gun to change, and to change radically. Once-complacent consumers and taxpayers demand that managers stop viewing their organizations as mere pass-through mechanisms and instead take control of issues that have long been concerning them. They insist that both private and public sector organizations simultaneously improve quality and reduce cost, a task that many managers and administrators rebuffed as impossible in the past.

In the health care industry, for example, employer frustration with soaring medical costs has led to a dramatic growth in private, state, and federal fixed price contracts. Employers are scrutinizing their health care costs and services like never before, and they are expecting their health care providers to do the same. Patients, too, are reviewing costs. Carrying an increased share of health care costs, they increasingly demand active involvement in the health care decision-making process.

The property and casualty insurance industry is also being forced to manage its costs more aggressively. Abandoning the free market approach to setting insurance rates, an increasing number of states regulate price as well as terms. In California, for example, consumers outraged by rapidly escalating auto insurance premiums pushed a landmark referendum, Proposition 103, through the state legislature. The referendum imposed a rate rollback of 20 percent, effectively setting a ceiling on auto insurance rates, and also forbade insurers from exiting the state in defiance.

Consumer discontent has also hit the public sector. Taxpayers no longer accept tax increases as automatic pass-throughs of rising expenses. Instead, they demand more cost-effective delivery of services. At the federal level, many agencies attempt to survive the largest budget cuts they have experienced in more than 40 years. At the state level, anti-tax initiatives are on the rise. In Massachusetts alone, nearly one million signatures were collected in less than three months opposing a proposed $2.8 billion tax increase for 1990.

Churches and other religious institutions, too, face changing "customer" expectations. These service organizations whose very survival depends on the willing financial and time contributions of their members are increasingly "competing" for donations with other charitable organizations and for time with recreational activities.

The stories go on and on. Customers have raised their expectations. If a service organization is not meeting their needs, they switch suppliers or revolt outright. No matter which service business you are in, you probably feel the wrath of your customers' ire and the pain of confusion. Few organizations have been spared.

## CHANGE OR DIE: NO MORE "BUSINESS AS USUAL"

What happens if you don't respond to customer concerns? What happens if you do not provide quality products and services at affordable prices? The answer is simple. You die. A Royal Dutch/Shell survey reported that in a little over a decade, one-third of the firms listed in the 1970 Fortune 500 had disappeared.[1] The survey went on to estimate that the average life span of the largest industrial enterprises is less than 40 years. According to Peter M.

Senge, director of MIT's Center for Organizational Learning, there is a 50 percent chance that the company you are working for will disappear during your lifetime.[2]

Whether you are in the manufacturing or service sector, these are ominous statistics. For the United States, where the service industry represents over 60 percent of the GNP, they are especially foreboding. Why should we be concerned? The United States has at least two white collar workers for every blue collar worker. If white collar productivity does not improve, our national productivity cannot rise. In the last 10 years, blue collar productivity rose by close to 30 percent, yet, despite technology investment, white collar productivity is falling.[3]

What led one of our most promising industries to its current demise? Changing demographics? Special interest groups? Tough foreign competition? Do available resources of people, time, funding, or knowledge make the difference? No! If your organization is suffering poor performance, the answer does not lie outside your organization, but within. The poor performance running rampant in the service industry today is directly related to the management of the service organizations themselves. Whether it be due to oligopolist history, regional concentration, or protected, regulated positions, many service organizations today display a traditional operating style that promotes inefficiency, waste, and poor quality. They are tangled in their own known and intended internal policies and procedures, a snare of their own making.

How did this happen? Many organizations have unknowingly contracted certain organizational diseases which threaten their long-term health. Specifically, four plagues render many service organizations weak: organizational gridlock in the form of constricted processes, management anorexia in the form of self-inflicted ignorance, addiction to the immediate high of the quick fix, and selective amnesia regarding management failures.[4]

Is your organization in gridlock? When information, activities, and critical processes are in gridlock, despite good intentions, nothing is accomplished without extraordinary effort. Is your management system anorexic? When managers reject valuable knowledge offered by others, plans end up being unworkable. Are you and others in your organization addicted to destructive behavior? When managers reach for the quick fix, be it a three-day training course, or keeping large inventories to hide deeper problems, they delude themselves into thinking that they have their disease under control. Does your organization suffer from amnesia? When individuals and organizations do not take the time to acknowledge and learn from their past, however traumatic the experience, they miss opportunities to make significant long-term improvement.

Until recently, service organizations could get away with being reasonably unhealthy. But today, the situation is different: If you do not change how you operate, soon someone will be writing your organization's obituary. Whether your business is in insurance, banking, health care, travel, consulting, or public service, the mandate for change is clear. You and your organization must radically change the way you do business. It will not be easy. Improving the health of your organization means taking time out to examine your basic operating assumptions and replace those that are dysfunctional with more competitive ones. But it can be done. Others have courageously tackled the quality problem in their own service organizations to achieve dramatic and measurable improvement. Yes, Winnie the Pooh, there is a better way of coming down those stairs. We call it companywide continuous quality improvement.

## CUSTOMER-FOCUSED QUALITY: A PRIORITY ABOVE PRIORITIES

Today, more and more service organizations are choosing a single strategy for change from which all other strategies follow: customer-focused continuous quality improvement. The conventional understanding of quality is that inspection and rejection are the only means of achieving high quality in products and services. But total quality management goes beyond that, connecting customer perceptions of timeliness, accuracy, and responsiveness to all aspects of an organization's behavior.

What exactly is this strategy? It is a management approach to business that aligns the activities of all employees in an organization with the shared objective of creating delighted customers through continuous improvement in the quality of all processes, goods, and services. Managing for quality in this context does not mean "inspecting in" quality. Instead, managing for quality improvement means "building in" quality to all products, services, and processes on an ongoing basis.

## IS IT WORTH IT? YOU BET! QUALITY PAYS

"But isn't improving quality going to cost me?" you might ask. Improving quality does take time and money, no doubt about it. Failing to improve quality, however, will cost you much more. Responding to customer complaints or reworking something that was not done right the first time is very costly. And, if it is "too little, too late," the cost skyrockets with the damaging long-term effects of lost accounts, legal suits, and bad publicity.

Striving for quality isn't just good for business, it's good for everyone. MBNA American, a credit card company in Delaware, knows this well. With a reputation for quality service and over 95 percent customer retention, MBNA recently received over 12,000 applications for 500 job openings.[5] In the same period, a competitor experiencing a 12 percent customer defection rate was leaving the state due to its inability to find employees. It is human nature—people want to be on a winning team. Providing quality service is a benefit to organizations as well as to the people in them.

## UNTANGLING ORGANIZATIONAL GRIDLOCK

This book is about performance improvement. It describes an approach to business that is both financially rewarding and personally challenging. But it will require that you prepare yourself and those around you for change. One thing is certain: You cannot correct your problems by doing better what you already know how to do. Significant improvement cannot occur until you realize that your poor performance is directly connected to the very criteria by which you define effective performance.[6] To make significant progress, you and others in your organization must challenge your past visions and fantasies about what it takes to run a successful business.

## PART I: THE STRATEGY

For those just beginning this journey, Part I of this book describes a customer-focused quality improvement *strategy* to untangle organizational gridlock, leverage your existing resources, and radically improve performance. It will help you answer the following questions.

- Does quality improvement have a payoff for my organization?
- How can it help me build a competitive advantage?
- How is customer-focused quality different from the way we operate now?
- How can I begin the continuous improvement journey?

The distinguishing characteristic of a customer-focused quality improvement strategy is that it requires you to look deep within your organization to discover and leverage more natural talents and capabilities of which you and others have been unaware. It is a means to identify and develop previously hidden resources into practical skills and competencies to achieve superior performance. What are the special elements of a customer-focused quality improvement strategy that create these benefits? Part I describes the four cornerstones of total quality management (see Figure I.1). In brief, they are as follows.

### Chapter 1. Can You Hear Your Customer Murmurs? The Need for Customer Focus

How can managers function amid the cacophony of voices that scream out to be heard every day? Who is right? Which voice has priority? Who should set the direction? The answer is simple: Make your *customer* the traffic cop. Organizations that listen the hardest and respond the fastest to their customers are the ones that succeed in today's competitive environment. In this chapter, you will learn how to identify your customers, their needs and expectations, and

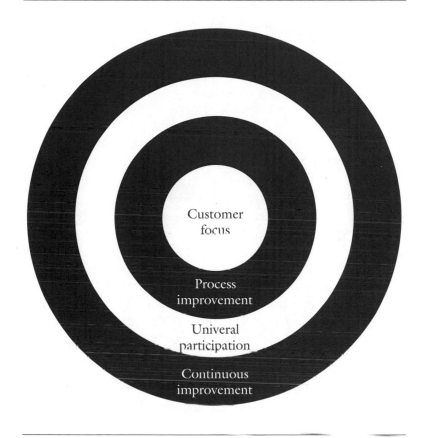

**Figure I.1:** The strategy

how building personal, long-term relationships with your customers is critical to continuous quality improvement.

## Chapter 2. The Secret Is in the Wiring: The Need for Process Improvement

How does information flow in your organization? In many service organizations, information and task requirements flow vertically, winding their way down the organization chart from one boss/subordinate group to another. Yet products, processes, and customer issues usually run horizontally *across* functions. What happens when information from a vertical path rams into the needs and requirements from a horizontal path? You get a short in the electrical system, the lights go out, and important customer issues fall through the cracks. The solution? Since an organization is only as strong as its weakest link, you must build quality into every operational link. The secret is in the wiring.

## Chapter 3. Management Anorexia: The Need for Universal Participation

Most service organizations have more resources and raw intelligence than they can ever use. Yet too few managers adequately tap those resources. Like the anorexic who exercises control by refusing to eat food, many managers who come from the traditional school of boss/subordinate relations exercise control by refusing to ingest the information in their employees' and peers' heads. The result is self-inflicted ignorance. In today's competitive environment, you cannot afford to waste valuable knowledge. Instead, create *expressways* for shared knowledge and talent. Learning how to learn from others requires new skills and beliefs on the part of managers.

## Chapter 4. A Physical Workout: The Need for Continuous Improvement

Are you in a rut? Are you stuck in a viciously repeating cycle of working the same problems over and over again? In today's rapidly changing business environment, moving in fits and starts or even standing still can actually mean going backward. Organizations which strive for continuous improvement know that the quick fix, while it may appear attractive in the short term, can be more costly and ineffective in the long run. So they take a little more time up front to get behind the problem symptoms and eliminate the *root cause* or causes behind their recurring problems. They work together in a disciplined way to collect data to understand the situation, search for the underlying contributing factors, and monitor their solutions over time to verify that corrective action has eliminated the problem forever.

## PART II: THE PROCESS OF BECOMING

The operating principles in Part I make common sense in the end. So, once informed, most people are eager to convert theory into action. In the spirit of change they do similar "good" things: They spend money on training. They collect data on customer needs and expectations. They create cross-functional problem solving teams. But only a few service organizations successfully make the transition. In fact, three out of four fail to break the stranglehold of their dysfunctional work habits. Even among the most successful service companies, few have created a culture of total quality excellence that permeates every cell of the organization.

If customer-focused quality improvement is the competitive strategy of choice, then why are so many organizations failing to reap the benefits promised? Why aren't these principles and practices taking hold and sprouting everywhere? The answer is simple. Many people do not know how to manage organizational change. A commitment to continous customer-focused quality improvement requires changes in many aspects of individual and organizational behavior. And making the transition from old ways to new ways can at times be slow and painful. Skill in managing this delicate process is critical to success.

Whereas most of the existing quality improvement literature emphasizes the operational aspects of quality, namely, how to improve quality at the procedural level, Part II of *Untangling Organizational Gridlock* additionally addresses the dynamic cultural and managerial processes surrounding organizational change. Specifically, it will answer the following questions.

- How can I accelerate the speed with which I and my organization adopt new perspectives and learn new behaviors?
- How can I anticipate critical junctures in the change process?
- What am I doing that may be getting in the way of my effectiveness as a leader?
- How can I maintain the gains?

As you will discover in Part II, the speed with which an organization can change its culture is related as much to what it does as to the order in which it does it; in other words, its ability to think in terms of dynamic processes of change rather than simple events. So what are the cornerstones of a successful organizational transformation? What are some common management traps that can sabotage the improvement process? How can you ensure that you will be a successful change agent? Part II of this book describes five key elements of strategy implementation (see Figure I.2). In brief, they are as follows.

## Chapter 5. Making the Transition: Battling the Immune System

How do you rewire a house with the electricity turned on? How do you fix a 747 in midflight? How do you make significant organizational changes amid the complexity of an ongoing enterprise? If only we could freeze-frame the world, make our organizational changes, and then press "go." But this is not possible. When you attempt to improve quality, you launch a process of organizational change amid a dynamic set of management systems, policies, and norms that already keeps your organization in balance. You and your people may want to change, some even desperately so, but often the "system" will conspire against significant change. To improve your probability of success, approach the change process as a systems thinker rather than as a systems "tinkerer."

## Chapter 6. Unity of Purpose: Consolidating Good Intentions

What led to the internal traffic jam in the first place? Too many people going in too many directions at the same time. Many people attempt to clarify direction by telling others what to do. However, taking the time to issue rules and policy statements is a luxury most service organizations can no longer afford. What is the alternative? Internally engineer the organization's mission, vision, values, problems, and opportunities in the mind and heart of each employee so that everyone has a common framework upon which to act. When all are aligned with superordinate goals and objectives, coordination improves, competing activities are minimized, and creativity is maximized.

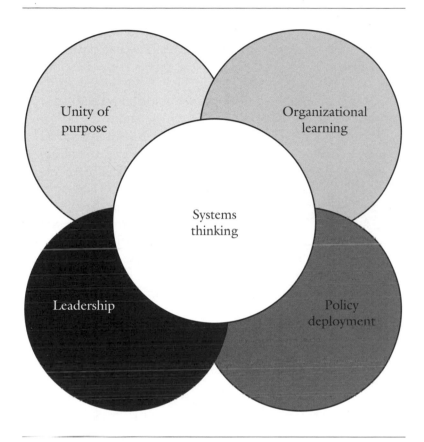

**Figure I.2:** The process of becoming

## Chapter 7. Organizational Learning: Recovering from Organizational Amnesia

Why do so many organizations seem to work the same problems over and over again? Aren't they learning from the error of their ways? In an era of rapid technological innovation, changing global markets, and new regulations, service organizations must have the capacity to learn quickly so that they can respond appropriately to new situations, no matter how traumatic. Many people believe that individual training and education will ensure organizational learning. But individual learning is not the same thing as organizational learning. While individual learning is necessary, it will not ensure that organizational learning will take place. Connecting individual learning to new organizational policies and procedures requires radically new levels of coordination, commitment, and knowledge.

## Chapter 8. Management, Learning, and Leadership: Are They Different?

In an era of consent, how do leaders lead? If an individual can no longer direct, give orders, coerce, or force intelligent employees to accept orders blindly, how can he or she influence direction? Many say that leadership concerns shared vision; others say that leadership concerns learning and teaching. This chapter shows that leadership is neither. While shared vision and learning are essential for continuous improvement, leadership is uniquely concerned with that ever-important moment of *choice*. The trick is to know which choices and choice processes create enough critical mass to move you and your people from inertia to initiative.

## Chapter 9. Policy Deployment: Focus on the Critical Few

Even the best of efforts to improve the quality of our products and services can sometimes fail. And so, in the spirit of continuous · improvement, we need to discover what worked, what didn't, and why. The problem is that many management teams do not know what went wrong, let alone why, until it is too late to be useful. To avoid surprises and ensure positive results, more and more organizations use a rigorous and disciplined planning process to tie lessons from their quality improvement efforts to key long-term business issues. By focusing the entire organization on a few vital issues rather than the trivial many and taking the time to learn from miscalculations and faulty assumptions, you can make quality improvement a *reliable* strategic process.

## SUMMARY

Why do so many service organizations suffer from poor performance? It's not for the lack of resources—people, time, funding, or knowledge. Virtually every service organization has far more resources than it can ever use. Instead, most service organizations suffering from poor performance are tangled up in a snare of their own making: their own internal operating policies and procedures.

The good news is that, if you take a hard look at your operating assumptions and replace dysfunctional behaviors with more competitive ones, then you can make significant progress. Organizations are, in the end, only collections of people, so organizational change for performance improvement is a very human process. The following chapters will bear this out.

## Notes

1. Arie de Geus, "Planning as Learning," *Harvard Business Review*, March/April 1988, 70–74.

2. Peter M. Senge, *The Fifth Discipline: The Art and Practice of the Learning Organization* (New York: Doubleday Currency, 1990), 17.

3. Keki R. Bhote, *Next Operation as Customer (NOAC): How To Improve Quality, Cost, and Cycle Time in Service Operations*, AMA Management Briefing (AMA Membership Publications Division, American Management Association), 111.

4. Three similar plagues are described by Brown University president Vartan Gregorian when outlining the challenges facing the United States in the 90s.

5. Frederick F. Reichold and W. Earl Sasser, Jr., "Zero Defections: Quality Comes to Services," *Harvard Business Review*, September/October 1990, 105–112.

6. Chris Argyris and Donald A. Schon, *Organizational Learning: A Theory of Action Perspective* (Reading, Mass.: Addison-Wesley, 1978), 22.

*The customer wants solutions, not institutions.*
—Edward R. Kirby

# PART I

# The Strategy

Today we live in a volatile environment. Rapid changes in technology, customer expectations, and strategic alliances can often make managers feel as if they are dancing on moving ground.

In such a complex environment, traditional organizations are struggling to survive; they are being eclipsed by more lithe and responsive organizations. How are high-performing organizations responding differently to the same turbulent environment? If you are already feeling the pain, know that there is no technological miracle to save you. Paving the cow paths with the latest technology will only compound your problems, not mitigate them. And any geographical advantage you may have leveraged in the past simply no longer exists. Today, success requires a radically different competitive weapon: *a commitment to customer-focused quality improvement.*

"But my organization is suffering," you might be thinking. "We do not have access to immediate and abundant resources to invest in quality improvement." The good news is that dramatic improvement in performance can be achieved by leveraging your *existing* resources, by simply working smarter, not harder. What the members of the organization focus on, how they work together, who they partner with, and how they spend their time emerge as critical features that differentiate a high-performing organization from others. So what are the key elements of a customer-focused quality improvement strategy? How is it different from traditional business practice? What is required from top management and others to make it work? Part I answers these questions and more, starting with a look at how we define that elusive concept of *quality*.

— ✧ —

*Like most marital problems, most problems in client relations can be captured in the complaint, "We don't talk anymore."*

—David Maister

— ✧ —

## CHAPTER 1

# Can You Hear Your Customer Murmurs?

## The Need for Customer Focus

Not too long ago, I telephoned the CEO of a large insurance company to ask about its quality improvement initiatives. Much to my surprise, the CEO's secretary had no idea what I was talking about. "You must have the wrong company," she said. "We're an *insurance* company, not a manufacturer, so we don't have quality control." When I pressed her further, she said in exasperation, "No offense, but I don't think your question fits here." Unfortunately, too many people in service organizations, from CEOs to front-line staff, share this person's attitude. To these people, quality control only pertains to organizations that produce solid objects—things you can touch, hold, or see.

If more people who work in the service sector understood the full meaning of quality and its importance to their customers, they would sing a different tune. Day in and day out, customers "vote" on their favorite services and products every time they buy something. The organization which offers the highest quality in its products and services, as perceived by its customers, wins.

Lately, a lot of service organizations have been losing some important elections. In Sydney, Australia, an employee of an insurance company knows this well. Awaiting a large payment in transit from the other side of town on a Friday afternoon, she called the branch of her bank next door, a branch that usually closes at four in the afternoon. "I have a $50 million deposit arriving at five minutes past four," she said. "Will you keep your doors open for me so that I can run this deposit right over?" The answer? No. The consequence? The woman's company lost $21,000 in interest between Friday afternoon and Monday morning!

This is not the only instance of poor service that customers receive. Insurance customers complain about policies that are difficult to read and understand. Air travellers bemoan delays, the poor quality of food, and poor service during domestic flights. Taxpayers question costly bureaucracy in many government services. The list goes on and on.

Why is there so much poor quality out there? As a member of your organization, don't *you* care about quality? Do you deliberately set out to provide poor service to your customers? Of course not. The answer, instead, lies in how you and others in your organization define quality. In many service organizations, management decides what quality means. Prior to divestiture, AT&T "knew" that it was providing quality service if customers didn't have to wait long for a dial tone when they picked up the telephone receiver. AT&T worked hard to get that dial tone just right, instituting all sorts of measures and reports to record and monitor its performance. Many insurers "knew" that a quality insurance policy addressed the company's actuarial exposure, cost structure, and administrative requirements, even if customers were unhappy with the terms. At Blue Cross/Blue Shield, management "knew" that it offered quality health care coverage by providing rich benefit packages, even if these were costly to its corporate clients.

Now how did AT&T come up with the formula that a quick dial tone equalled quality? How did Blue Cross/Blue Shield determine that rich benefit packages for its corporate clients equalled quality? How did the branch bank in Sydney, Australia, determine that good management practice meant maintaining accurate banking hours? Decisions like these were made amid a cacophony of voices rivalling that of the New York Stock Exchange on a typical day. Representatives from finance, sales, marketing, and operations shouted, "Listen to me—it's got to be done my way." Depending upon the industry, particular voices would tend to prevail. In the telecommunications industry, the voice of engineering usually won. In health care services, historically the physicians won. The actuaries invariably won in the insurance industry. The saying "The squeaky wheel gets the grease" could never be more applicable.

The only voice you didn't hear was that of the customer, if only because the customer was not in the room. The customer, or any other outside perspective, never had a chance. Small wonder that 10 to 30 percent of customers will defect from the average U.S. company this year.[1] It never occurred to the folks at AT&T prior to divestiture that customers took it for granted they wouldn't have to wait long for the dial tone. Customers showed more interest in a variety of other products and services. Out of sight, out of mind— the customer's voice was never heard.

## QUALITY RESTS IN THE EYES OF THE BEHOLDER

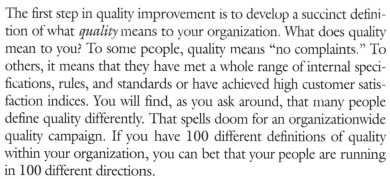

The first step in quality improvement is to develop a succinct definition of what *quality* means to your organization. What does quality mean to you? To some people, quality means "no complaints." To others, it means that they have met a whole range of internal specifications, rules, and standards or have achieved high customer satisfaction indices. You will find, as you ask around, that many people define quality differently. That spells doom for an organizationwide quality campaign. If you have 100 different definitions of quality within your organization, you can bet that your people are running in 100 different directions.

Was the customer part of your definition of quality when you answered the question just now? Individuals who bypass the customer when defining quality often confuse conformance to specifications with perceived quality. They are so intent on listening to the voice of the hierarchy and on "looking good" from above that they completely forget the customer. How do you get out of the gridlock of competing internal voices? The answer is to focus on the customer. The voice of authority, the voice above all other voices, must be the voice of your customer. Jan Carlzon of Scandinavian Airlines explains:

> *Last year, each of our 10 million customers came in contact with approximately five SAS employees, and the contact lasted an average of 15 seconds each time. Thus, SAS is "created" 50 million times a year, 15 seconds at a time. These 50 million "moments of truth" are the moments that ultimately determine whether SAS will succeed or fail as a company. They are the moments when we must prove to our customers that SAS is their best alternative.*[2]

Today, managers in high-performing service organizations recognize that they have customers and are letting their customers do the talking. They understand that it is up to their customers to judge the quality of their products and services, and that each customer may perceive quality a little differently. In short, they practice customer-focused quality improvement. Customer-focused quality is the commitment to continuously meet or exceed your customer's expectations. Let's look at this statement more carefully.

First, customer-focused quality means recognizing that you have *customers.* Some service organizations are barely aware that they have customers. Other service organizations keep their customers at a safe distance. These are the entities which call their customers "rate payers," "voters," "policyholders," "passengers," and "patients." Getting beyond these labels is a critical first step toward quality improvement.

Second, customer-focused quality means just that: focusing on your customers' *actual needs and expectations,* not on what you think they should need or want. Customer-focused organizations let their customers do the defining because they know that only their customers know what is right for them. "But we're already conforming 100 percent to specifications," you exclaim.

"We're doing great." This may be true, but whose specifications are you following, yours or your customers'? What if your specifications are wrong? Despite good intentions, the company may not know best.

Third, customer-focused quality means striving to *meet or exceed customer expectations*. Meeting your customers' expectations is only the beginning, a first step that might help you survive. The true route to long-term survival, the step that will gain you that important competitive edge, is to exceed your customers' expectations.

Finally, because customer needs and expectations are always changing, your job is never done. To stay in business, you have to be able to delight your customers time and time again. Quality improvement requires *continuous improvement*.

To improve quality in the eyes of the customer, the entire organization must be committed completely to focusing on the customer. Customer focus is the first step to untangling organizational gridlock. When the customer's voice can be heard clearly above the cacophony of other voices, then you are well on your way to becoming a total quality organization.

## IS IT WORTH IT? YOU BET! QUALITY PAYS

Some people worry that being customer-focused, while sounding good in theory, will actually cost them more money than the benefits are worth. But this assumes that what is good for the customer is not also good for your bottom line.

Quality pays. In a series of studies that spanned 18 years, researchers at the Strategic Planning Institute in Cambridge, Massachusetts, analyzed the profitability of over 3000 strategic business units covering a wide variety of industries. Those with high-quality products and services had an average profit of 12 percent, compared to profit of 1 percent for those with low quality.[3] Other studies show that by increasing customer retention rates by only a few percentage points, insurance brokers, bankers, health care providers, and other service organizations can increase their profits by 25 to 100 percent.[4] Consumers not only demand quality, but as these studies suggest, they will gladly pay for it.

MBNA American, a Delaware-based credit card company, knows this well. When MBNA American discovered that many of its customers had shifted to the competition, it launched a major customer retention strategy. Within 8 years, MBNA reduced its customer defection rate to 5 percent, half the prevailing rate in the industry. The firm's industry ranking went from 38 to 4, and its profits increased sixteenfold![5] Why? Among other reasons, it can cost five times more to attract a new customer than it does to retain an old customer.[6] And profits increase commensurably with the length of your relationship![7] As more and more service organizations are finding, strategies which focus on satisfying the customer, thereby stemming defections, are vastly more effective than traditional cost-cutting strategies.

Times have changed. It used to be that executives could shrug off their customers, if only because there were "always more where that one came from." In today's fast-paced, competitive environment, however, it pays to make customer satisfaction a strategic focus. If you choose not to treat your customers well, the organization down the street will gladly do your job for you. Successful organizations know that it pays to listen to customers. Here's why.

• **Listening to your customer tells you what business you should be in.** One of the lessons brought out by Peters and Waterman in *In Search of Excellence* was that excellent companies are better listeners.[8] When you listen to your customers, you often reframe your products and services. A health care facility may discover that it needs to consider the "hotel" side of its business as well as its medical services. Insurers may discover that easy-to-understand instructions and consolidated billing are just as important as the terms of the insurance policy itself. Airlines may discover that how their customers are treated at the ticket counter carries as much weight as the quality of the in-flight service.

• **Listening leads to talking, and talking leads to knowledge exchange.** When organizations do not listen to their customers, they rely solely on knowledge *transfer,* a one-way communication from management to customers. They miss the enormous benefits that can come from knowledge *exchange*. When your customers exchange knowledge of their problems and perceptions with your organization's knowledge of a possible solution, it is easy to identify creative solutions and discover unique opportunities for competitive advantage.

• **Listening allows you to gain control.** High-performing organizations design with an eye toward the future. Such an action-oriented stance helps them meet their customers' changing needs, often even before their customers know that their needs have changed. By being ahead of the game, they gain strategic flexibility. Listening to customers also helps them identify and retain profitable customers who are vulnerable to defection rather than discover departures after the fact.

• **Listening to customers is cost-effective.** Many people believe that increasing product and service quality in the eyes of customers is costly. But this ignores that fact that the very problems that customers complain about, such as time delays, lost paperwork, or incorrect bills, all cost money. What is good for your customers is good for you, too. Keeping your customers happy can lead directly to increased revenues, increased referrals, high repeat business, and larger market share.

• **Listening builds common focus.** Customer focus provides the means to align members of the organization. It helps people see the link between what they do and success in the marketplace. When customer satisfaction becomes the objective above all other objectives, you can significantly reduce internal squabbling, competition, and conflicting departmental objectives.

• **Listening is energizing.** Nothing can be more motivating than a dialogue, one-on-one, with a person who is in need of help. While customer data are informative, they lack the human element. Encourage yourself and others to go face-to-face with your customers. The benefits? Increased attention, accountability, and innovative solutions.

## KEYS TO CUSTOMER FOCUS

In today's competitive service environment, customer focus is the key to long-term success. The objective is to capture and maintain customer enthusiasm. The strategy is to dedicate all management resources and processes to meet or exceed customer expectations. The road map is the delineation of customer needs and expectations. Sound like common sense? That's all it is. Then why do many service organizations fail to reap the full benefits that customer focus can bring? They fail because they labor under some false assumptions.

• *We already know what the customer wants.* This attitude, otherwise known as the "company knows best" syndrome, reveals management's detachment from customers. Management lacks objectivity.

• *No news is good news.* This is the belief that if you don't hear customers complain, then they're happy. Looking into what customers really think seems to take too much time, energy, and courage. Management lacks initiative.

• *Take care of the product, and the service will take care of itself.* Management fails to understand that customers perceive and judge each service experience in its entirety, not as an unconnected episode or feature. Management lacks an appreciation of service as a total experience.

• *Customers state what they want.* Customers often make statements about a product or service when they actually mean or wish to say something entirely different. Getting at the underlying meaning requires that you pose questions designed to reveal the truth. People lack skills to acquire relevant and accurate customer information.

• *Many customer complaints are due to events beyond our control.* This myth is frequently expressed another way: "It's not our fault" or "The customer is being unreasonable." People lack a sense of responsibility for their actions or non-actions.

• *Customer data belong in the sales and marketing departments.* In many service organizations, what little data exist on customers remain a closely held secret. Management fails to saturate the organization with the voice of the customer.

These myths lead to inefficient management decisions based on false assumptions. They cause otherwise intelligent people to miss market opportunities, misread customer desires, grossly overestimate customer satisfaction, compromise rather than emphasize customer needs, and waste resources on activities of no value to the customer.

If you examine the flip side of these management myths, you can begin to see how customer focus is different from traditional management practice. Here's how managers in customer-focused organizations approach their business.

• We evaluate performance in objective terms.
• We take the initiative to seek out our customers' complaints and to determine their needs.
• We focus on our customers' total experience.
• We strive to enhance our knowledge acquisition skills; we really do want to know what our customers think.
• We openly discuss our customers' concerns.
• We take responsibility for finding solutions to customer problems.

Let's explore each of these statements in more depth.

## Be objective

Too few managers in service organizations take the time to systematically identify their customers, let alone listen to them. Many people find themselves promoted or transferred into a department characterized by hard and fast rules, performance measures, and specifications or by preexisting organizational problems which may require immediate attention. They frequently get so caught up in putting out fires that they never take the time to figure out who their customers are or to discover their needs and expectations. The result? Missed market opportunities, unhappy customers, and lost business.

Customer focus requires an objective view, however uncomfortable or painful it might be, of your organization. The challenges? First, put aside your own preconceptions. Second, believe what your customer says. Employees at West Paces Ferry Hospital in Atlanta, Georgia, know these challenges well. The Institute of Medicine's report to Congress in March 1990 identified their hospital as the only one among 45 visited throughout the United States that was effectively implementing a customer-focused approach to quality improvement. Chip Caldwell, CEO, describes his hospital's efforts to capture the voices of its customers.

> *We invested a lot of time and effort in measurement because we did not want to guess what our various customer groups felt was quality. One measure we use is our Hospital Quality Trend series. This measures quantitatively, through a regression analysis, all of the processes that go on in the hospital that affect our major customer groups. It also measures how we are performing on those measures. For example, we learned that our physicians measure quality as when their available time is maximized, when their scheduling needs are met, when nurses are skilled, accessible, and informing, and when their reports are timely. In addition, there are several other needs. Now that we know the requirements for physicians, patients, payers, and employees, we have a series of 23 quality indicators hospital-wide that answer the question "How do you measure quality?"*

As Caldwell understands, properly servicing customers starts with collecting information on their needs as they define them and then measuring how well the hospital is doing in their eyes. How can *you* collect information on customer needs and expectations? How can you measure your performance? While there are several methods, some are more useful than others.

## Seek out customer complaints

Many managers assess their performance based on complaints, if and when they occur. To these managers, "no news is good news." The truth is, customers rarely complain. People generally dislike confrontations. It is often easier to allow an insurance policy to lapse, avoid paying a bill, book future reservations on a different airline, or call a competing hospital—anything but complain.

A case in point: Northeastern University recently conducted a survey of Massachusetts households to identify sources of consumer dissatisfaction.[9] Eighty-eight percent of those surveyed expressed dissatisfaction with the large amount of "junk mail" they received each day, yet only 2 percent of those consumers had ever complained to the Massachusetts Executive Office of Consumer Affairs. Despite widespread frustration, few customers complained. Other studies show that only four out of 100 dissatisfied customers complain to appropriate parties.[10] Sometimes this is due to inaccessibility (lack of toll-free telephone numbers or not knowing who to call). Other times it is due to apathy or disgust. When you fail your customer severely, you will usually hear a loud complaint. There is, however, considerable low-grade customer dissatisfaction that many service organizations never hear about.

Although unhappy customers may not be making much noise, seeking them out is good for business. According to the Customer Satisfaction Research Institute, 30–46 percent of customers with complaints switch service vendors if their concerns are not resolved quickly. When their complaints are acknowledged and handled promptly, however, only 5 percent defect.[11] While seeking out unhappy customers may, at first, appear to be an unpleasant chore, it clearly pays to identify your unhappy customers and then take corrective action.

Once you find and pacify your unhappy customers, however, you cannot sit back and rest. Merely locating unhappy customers and fixing their concerns is not total customer focus. Responding to complaints is only part of the story; you must go further. Complaints and defections are lagging indicators of your performance. When responding to customer complaints, you are merely managing after the fact.

Your challenge is to create a blueprint for the future. This requires that you take into consideration your customers' current and future needs. Unearth not only your customers' basic expectations but also their "latent requirements," or unconscious needs and expectations. We all have suppressed needs, needs that we would like to fulfill if only we could pinpoint exactly what is missing. These suppressed needs reflect trends in our thinking and niggling obstacles in our lives that never quite rise to the surface of our consciousness—until someone comes up with a product or service that meets the need. When a "new" need is met, a light goes on in our heads: "Aha! That's just what I've been looking for."

Taking the time to listen actively to your customers, determine their needs and expectations, and get to know them so well that you can sense their latent requirements demands proactive listening skills. If you can slip into your customers' psyches, adopt their mindsets, and wear their shoes, then you will be that much closer to gaining competitive advantage.

## Focus on the total customer experience

When you begin to listen to your customers, you will quickly discover that customers evaluate the *entire* interaction in a service experience. Their perception of quality includes both the "hard" and "soft" aspects of each interaction or experience. Customers evaluate service providers according to their *experience* of the service—getting an annual physical—in addition to the *outcome* of the service rendered—the results of the exam. The diagnosis may say the patient is healthy, but if the physician or an assistant was gruff or otherwise unpleasant or the customer had to wait a long time to be seen, he or she will probably walk away disgruntled. This is true for all services. The ease with which first-time home buyers can manage the mortgage application process will affect their perception of a bank just as strongly as the interest rate charged on the loan. Passengers evaluate how they are treated on an airline flight, not simply whether they arrived at the destination on time. For many customers, the service side of the customer interaction is just as important if not more important than the technical side of the business.

More and more service organizations are beginning to understand the value of managing the service aspects of their business in addition to the "product" side. Whether their "products" are insurance policies, air travel, utilities, management consulting, or information, they realize that in many ways these products are commodities. They must differentiate themselves on some criteria other than interest rate, information, initial purchase price, or transaction. If they do not provide superb service in addition to quality products, their customers will leave. In fact, research shows that only 30 percent of defecting customers leave companies because of the "product" or its cost. The other 70 percent of the customers defect due to poor service quality! Lack of attention or personal contact accounts for 20 percent of the defections. And close to 50 percent of defecting customers leave because of poor quality in the delivery of the service they do receive.[12] The service aspect of every business can be used as a strategic weapon.

What are some key attributes of service? Researchers at Texas A&M University found five generic attributes that affect a customer's perception of quality service. First, customers seek *assurance;* they want to trust the knowledge and courtesy of employees. Second, they want *reliability;* they expect you to deliver the promised service on time every time. Third, they notice the *tangibles,* or the physical surroundings in which you deliver your services. Is the surrounding equipment well-maintained? Do your people look attractive? Fourth, they notice whether your employees are *empathetic.* Do your employees care? Do they give individualized attention? Finally, they judge the quality of your service by how *responsive* your employees are to customer needs.[13]

If you think that these aspects of service are impossible to measure, think again. Some service organizations, such as Fugi Bank in Tokyo, are beginning to use the *total cost* of their products and services to their customer as a competitive weapon. They understand that the initial purchase price of a product or service may only be a fraction of the total cost that a customer ultimately incurs, especially if the service is poor. If the customer has to take time out of his or her day to resolve billing errors over the phone, he or she is unable to proceed with more fruitful activities.

The concept of competing on total cost applies to all services. If you have to wait for several hours to be seen by a physician, that is time that you could be spending doing something more productive. In the case of the insurance company in Sydney, Australia, the time value of money—the $21,000 dollars lost in interest over the weekend—becomes the cost of doing business with that branch bank. Poor service wastes time, and time is money!

## Use innovative knowledge-acquisition techniques

Determining a customer's needs and expectations is not easy. It requires specialized knowledge-acquisition skills. Gone are the days of the old doctor-patient relationship in which the doctor made a diagnosis without consulting the patient and then proceeded to transfer relevant information to the patient. Today, most doctors know that the more they talk with their patients, the higher the level of care they can provide. Whereas our doctors once needed to know how to talk *at* a patient, today they need much stronger interpersonal skills which will enable them to elicit information and *exchange* knowledge with others, remain objective about that information, and then respond appropriately.

Few service organizations systematically collect data on their customers' perceptions. According to the American Marketing Association, service organizations conduct market research less frequently than do goods-producing companies. And in goods-producing companies there remains considerable room for improvement.

Many service organizations that do try to collect customer perceptions do so with structured surveys. Typically, these surveys require customer respondents to rank-order various product and service attributes defined by the service provider, not by the customer. These questionnaires can be frustrating because, while they give the customer preestablished categories and a rating scale (for example, a five-point range from "very poor" to "excellent"), they rarely give them the opportunity to say anything in their own words. They often fail to list service attributes that customers would really like to say something about. Surveys like these only capture a fraction of customers' truths.

Surveys containing some open-ended questions, in contrast, leave respondents room to write down or say exactly what they want. They give respondents a chance to identify for you the key attributes of product and service they desire, and they provide a vehicle for management to continually update its standard list of customer concerns.

While performance indicators are important in tracking progress, in trying to determine the needs of your customers, don't rely too heavily on customer satisfaction indices. Inexperienced service organizations often rely solely on customer satisfaction indices to gauge their customers' feelings. But percentages, if they stay percentages, can obscure the true story. Customer satisfaction measures report averages and can miss small segments of the population that may be valuable to you. When you translate a statistic which doesn't seem too bad into a real number, you may be startled at just how many people you have irritated. That twelve percent of unhappy customers, for example, may translate into 39,000 human bodies. Finally, customer satisfaction indices are not action-oriented—they are numbers and nothing more. A number cannot tell you what is wrong or offer suggestions for improvement.

Too many service organizations ignore their customers' attempts to communicate their "symptoms." Although individual customer requests are handled, no systematic attempt is made to learn and improve. Sandra Arangio, executive director of group special accounts at John Hancock Insurance Company, explains.

> *In the past, we did not record the nature or content of the hundreds of weekly customer contacts we received by telephone. Whether requests for changes on billing addresses, complaints, or suggestions, our customer service reps handled the customer's call on an individual basis, and then that was that. We had no systems in place to capture the nature of these calls, so valuable customer information vaporized daily. We have just begun the process of installing systems that enable us to record the nature and frequency of expressed customer concerns. This information will be used to improve the quality of our management decisions.*

Taking advantage of customer-initiated contacts is one way to collect information about your customer. Another way is for you to meet face to face with your customers. For many managers, meeting face to face with a customer is terrifying. What if the customer is angry or demanding? What if he or she gets a promise out of me that I can't keep? If you can equip people with strong interpersonal skills, they will be able to launch a fruitful dialogue, handle negative feedback, and remain calm enough to promise only what they can deliver. Ridding yourself and your organization of customer phobia can be tremendously rewarding. Market opportunities abound, but you have to talk to your customer to spot them.

While every organization can benefit from increasing its one-on-one customer contacts, there are many other techniques available for capturing the voice of the customer. Among these are open-ended surveys, focus groups of high-revenue, lost, or new customers, "shadowing" the customer, panel discussions, role reversals, and actually testing the service process with a sample customer base. In some progressive hotels and airline companies, executives become "customers" of their own services. They walk through every step of the process that a regular customer experiences. They do this not to check up on their employees but to experience firsthand the loose ends and awkward aspects of their service. Whatever techniques you select, apply them aggressively, consistently, and repeatedly. Here are some other pointers.

• **Make sure you dig deep enough.** When you can get your customers to share their concerns, you are on your way to establishing a promising relationship. The real challenge, however, is to extract information that is not initially obvious. People often have a hard time expressing their beliefs. Why do I really like that organization? What was it about that last experience that angered me? What could be better about this service? Some thoughts are difficult for your customer to articulate, often because they exist in a subliminal soup of feelings and concepts. Good knowledge acquisition skills help your customers realize and then articulate their feelings and perceptions.

• **Don't believe everything you hear.** Surveys often can be inaccurate because people do not always say what they mean. First, customers may feel awkward telling you the truth, especially if they worry that their responses will make them look overly picky, hurt your feelings, get someone in trouble, or negatively influence their future interactions with you. Second, if a customer believes that all banks do a rotten job, he or she still might check off "good" on a survey because his or her expectations of all banks are very low. A well-designed questionnaire will approach sensitive issues from a number of different angles to ensure optimum accuracy in capturing customer perceptions.

• **Look for hidden connections between seemingly unrelated perceptions.** When Don Burr was chairman of People Express, he said, "Coffee stains on the flip-down trays [in the airplane] mean [to the passengers] that we do our engine maintenance wrong."[14] Likewise, a hospitalized patient may infer that the quality of the "hotel" services side of the business indicates the quality of the clinical care. Regardless of the industry, customers form opinions of quality based on many factors unrelated to the technical aspects of the business.

## Communicate the data

You can collect the most consequential data in the world, but if they never make it to the CEO's desk, the product development group's meeting, or the employees on the front line, they are worthless.

I once worked with a bank CEO who showed me some customer data that his subordinates had collected. The survey showed that 87 percent of the bank's customers rated its service as "good to excellent." After some internal investigation, however, my team and I stumbled upon a set of focus group transcripts, stuffed in the bottom drawer of a marketing manager's desk, that told a radically different story. The interviews revealed that customers were disgusted with the service they were receiving. Another buried survey of customer problems revealed numerous areas for improvement. For example, over 50 percent of the surveyed customers reported that the bank had lost critical paperwork. When we showed this additional customer data to the CEO, he was baffled. Never before had he seen such staggering evidence of his bank's failings.

A lot of bad news never makes it to top management. First, many marketing managers do not know how to effectively communicate focus group or open-ended survey results because of the unstructured nature of the data. Second, who wants to be the bearer of bad news? This attitude is more prevalent than you might think, and for good reason. Many executives initially reject unpleasant customer feedback. Consider the bank in the above example. When our team presented to the bank executives the customer feedback revealed in their own focus group transcriptions, they vehemently denied that these problems existed. Instead of being receptive to the viewpoints of their customers, they lashed out at the selection of the focus group participants. Typical comments were "Where did our employees find *those* customers?" and "They were probably customers we wouldn't want anyway." When people can't take "bad" news even from a neutral party, quality consultants they hired, you can bet that their subordinates have a considerably smaller chance of being positively received. Who in their right mind would willingly bear unpleasant news in an environment like this? When management is unwilling to hear bad news, the result can be a devastating decline in its ability to identify areas for quality improvement. Nothing contributes more to organizational gridlock than the outright rejection of customer truth.

If you are a manager, you must obtain honest data, and you must use those data. The only effective way to use data is to distribute them to everyone in the organization who can use them, from the top floor to the shop floor. And you can help others get the most out of the data when you make it clear that the data, if disappointing, are not due to any one person's fault. As you will see in the next two chapters, poor results usually have less to do with front-line employees than with the support or lack of support that they are receiving from existing management systems.

## Take responsibility for the problems and the solutions

Why do so many service organizations ignore their customers' complaints? Too many people believe that the grounds for the complaints are due to events beyond their control. They believe that 60 to 90 percent of their customers' complaints about price, affordability, service quality, and administrative complexity are due to external events and, therefore, are completely beyond their control. They blame their problems on customer ignorance, ever-increasing amounts of litigation, the higher cost of doing business, and the "unfair" actions of regulators. Today, thanks to a tough economy and increasingly intolerant consumers, many service organizations are listening to their customers' concerns; for many managers, responding to customer concerns has become a fundamental responsibility.

You cannot become a customer-focused quality service organization if you fail to feel responsible for *all* of your customers' concerns and take action accordingly. Successful service organizations are proactive. Their managers are so attuned to the customer that they respond immediately—almost intuitively—to their customers' concerns, whether they be in the form of a complaint, an articulated wish, or an undisclosed need.

## THE CONTINUOUS CUSTOMER CAMPAIGN

What do an experienced politician and a customer-focused manager have in common? They both know that the only way to win their particular race is to get out there and shake hands with their constituents. Similar to successful politicians, customer-focused managers work hard to know the people in their districts intimately. They not only understand the issues but also how they are changing over time. Finally, they are acutely aware of where they stand in the polls.

Collecting data on customers does not have to be an overwhelming task. There is a simple approach to organizing customer information in a disciplined and managerially useful way. A specific tool, the customer requirements matrix, is detailed in Appendix A of this book. The essential elements of the process, however, are briefly described here.

### Know your constituents/know your customers

One of the first positive steps toward quality improvement is to identify your customers. No matter where you stand in the hierarchy, quality improvement starts with customer focus.

A customer is anyone who expects something from you. You may initially think that you deal solely with external customers such as hotel guests, airline passengers, hospital patients, or insurance claimants. But you probably have a host of internal partners who are customers as well. The people who depend on you in the billing, phone sales, data processing, engineering, or purchasing departments also have needs and expectations that must be met.

You may also have intermediate customers, people who require your attention because what they do somehow relates to your end users' needs. For example, if you work in the residential mortgage department of a bank, then your intermediate customers include real estate brokers. Health insurers are intermediate customers when a hospital provides health care services to a patient requesting treatment. And corporations can be intermediate customers for airlines when individuals book reservations for business travel. Intermediate customers may not purchase your services directly, but they can refer a substantial amount of business to you. While internal and intermediate customers are critical to success, the external customer remains king.

## Know what your customers want

Once you identify your customers, you can proceed to discover what they want and how they want it delivered. When you know what your customers want, you can design products and services that they will buy and/or support. How can you start? Define your business in terms of the expressed needs of your customers rather than in terms of the specific product or service you provide. For example, a technically focused insurance company might describe its business as selling insurance policies for life, home, health, and property. In contrast, the customer-focused company defines itself in terms of providing security, protection, and relief for families and businesses. Functionally, the company might perform many of the same functions, but the externally focused definition emphasizes issues of immediate concern to its clients.

There are three levels of customer needs and expectations: basic expectations; stated performance requirements; and latent needs/excitement features (see Figure 1.1).

When you want to learn something about your customer's needs and expectations, start by asking your customer directly. The customer's *stated* voice for an insurance policy might sound something like this:

- "I want low monthly payments."
- "I want my bills to be readable and understandable."
- "I want my claims to be paid quickly."
- "I want my phone calls to be returned promptly."

Asking your customers to specify their needs and expectations is an important task. But not all needs and expectations are spoken.

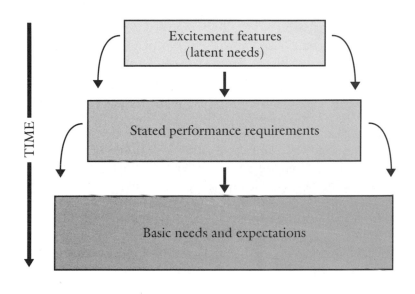

**Figure 1.1:** Three levels of customer needs

Some needs are so *basic* that your customers take them for granted and will not mention them in an interview. If you miss a basic expectation, however, the results can be disastrous. Consider toilet paper. Most customers would never cite having toilet paper as a design feature in a bathroom. But heaven forbid it be forgotten! Some basic needs must be met day in and day out, even if they do not provide your service organization with any means of competitive differentiation.

When you know your customers intimately, you can go beyond basic expectations and stated performance requirements to provide *excitement* features, ones that will delight your customers and cause them to say, "What a great idea! That's so obvious. Why didn't they think of that before?" I'll never forget the time I stayed at the Ritz Carlton in St. Louis before delivering a speech the next morning. As usual, I asked for a morning wake-up call, and, as usual, it came as promised. Unexpectedly, however, the operator asked if I would like a call back in ten minutes, "just in case you fall back to sleep." As someone who worries about this, you can bet that I took him up on his offer. That extra little customer-focused step removed a concern I had not consciously known. The experience raised my expectations for other hotels.

As customers, we often have trouble telling our service providers what we need, let alone envisioning new features that might make us happier. Only persistent, focused questioning can guide us to our truths and help us articulate our many needs. Taking the time to identify and satisfy new needs and changing expectations may require enormous energy. But nothing builds goodwill or increases competitive advantage faster.

## Understand your customers' priorities

In the real world, we have resource constraints. We cannot possibly grant all of our customers' wishes at the beginning of a quality improvement effort. Technology alone often forces us to make tradeoffs. So we must set some priorities.

The good news is that your customers care more about some of their stated needs and desires than others. Their priorities can help you effectively allocate your time and other resources. While it may be tempting to pick your own favorites, your challenge is to remain neutral; your customers are the experts, so let them determine the priorities.

## Know where you stand in the polls and in the marketplace

In the year 500 B.C., a Chinese general named Sun Tzu suggested, "If you know your enemy and know yourself, you need not fear the result of a hundred battles."[15] Knowing where you and your competitors stand in the eyes of your customers is a good way to identify competitive advantage and opportunities for improvement.

When you talk to your customers, be specific. Don't make the common mistake of just asking customers to rate your overall performance vis-à-vis the competition; ask them to compare and rank you and your competitors on an *attribute-by-attribute* basis. Specifically, (1) know how your customers rate your performance on each of the product and service attributes they specify as important to them, and

(2) know how they rate the performance of your competitors on each of these same attributes. Such a comparison will highlight where you have a competitive lead and where you are lagging in performance. It also identifies areas where there is uniformly poor performance throughout the industry. By comparing performance on an attribute-by attribute basis, you can obtain managerially useful information, feedback that contains specifics on how you can act and make changes.

## Know how to stay there: establish long-term partnerships

Getting to know your customers requires more than a single interaction—much more. Many managers say, as they point to various change efforts, that they have "done" the "customer focus thing." You can't "do" customer focus. You can only build it over time. To build customer focus into your organization, you have to create long-term partnerships with your customers, something that can only be accomplished one customer-focused quality interaction at a time. And this requires the participation of every functional area of the organization. Quality is not a one-time event; it extends over the lifetime of the company/customer relationship.

Marketing guru Ted Levitt once said that a contract for professional services is like a marriage contract.[16] Your contract or agreement should signify the beginning of a relationship, not the culmination of your efforts to "bag" a sale. Keeping the romance alive in customer relationships requires maintaining constant vigilance, day in and day out, over the details of communication, the keeping of agreements, and the meeting of expectations. As consultant David Maister warns the architectural design community:

> *The success of the relationship depends on how well the parties live up to the promises made, especially the implicit expectations that each has of the other....Those partnerships with well-managed expectations fare the best.[17]*

Company/customer expectations must be spelled out clearly. How do you go about managing expectations with your customers? Show them that you are genuinely interested in every aspect of their business. Specifically,

- Recognize that you and your customer depend upon each other for success in business. By working to benefit your customer, you will benefit yourself.

- Make realistic commitments to your customer and then follow through on those commitments.

- Inform your customer promptly if you are unable to meet current or future requirements.

- Negotiate in a way that allows you and your customer to meet your respective needs. Design a mutually beneficial solution, one that embodies each party's most important requirements.

- Understand that the contract begins, and not ends, your partnership with your customer.

Expectations change over time. "Delight" factors in your service or product quickly become stated requirements, which in turn usually become basic expectations. Building and maintaining long-term partnerships with your customers means staying on top of their changing expectations. To do this, you must continually update your customer information. Peter Drucker once observed, "Every knowledge eventually loses its value. It becomes obsolete....Knowledge has to progress to remain knowledge." The challenge is to find ways of staying abreast of changing customer needs, values, and expectations—without paying an annuity to a market research firm. Meet with your customers and let them tell you how they feel. Ask them to share their information about themselves with you. Listen to them. As Konsuke Matsushita, founder of the Matsushita Corporation, instructed his staff, "You must take the customer's skin temperature daily."[18] There is no other way of building satisfying, long-term customer relationships.

## SUMMARY

Untangling organizational gridlock begins with a customer focus. Successful organizations not only meet customer expectations regularly but repeatedly exceed them. They scrupulously analyze every step of every process and every penny for its intrinsic value to the customer. They break down internal barriers such as conflicting management priorities, lapsed networks of communication, and inappropriate internal rules and regulations so that the entire organization can focus on the customer. In a customer-focused organization, every department concentrates its energies on one overriding goal—serving the voice of the customer. Every employee, at every level, is responsible for identifying improvement opportunities and for proposing solutions to better fulfill customer needs. As we shall see in the next chapter, we can best translate customer needs and expectations into actions by using task-oriented, logical, and disciplined processes.

| From | To |
| --- | --- |
| internal specifications | customer needs and expectations |
| voice of management | voice of the customer |
| customer as adversary | customer as partner |
| management by guessing | management by fact |
| reactive management | proactive management |
| make a profit | create a customer |

## Notes

1. Frederick F. Reichheld, "Making Sure Customers Come Back for More," *The Wall Street Journal,* 12 March 1990.

2. Jan Carlzon, *Moments of Truth: New Strategies for Today's Customer Driven Economy* (New York: Harper & Row, 1987), 3.

3. Robert D. Buzzell and Bradley T. Gale, *The PIMS Principles* (New York: Free Press, 1987).

4. Reichheld, *Making Sure.*

5. Ibid.

6. Professor Jagdish N. Sheth, University of Southern California.

7. Frederick F. Reichheld and W. Earl Sasser, Jr., "Zero Defections: Quality Comes to Services," *Harvard Business Review*, September/ October 1990, 105–112.

8. Thomas J. Peters and Robert H. Waterman, Jr., *In Search of Excellence* (New York: Warner Books, 1984), 193.

9. *Northeastern University Alumni Magazine*, June 1989.

10. "Consumer Complaint Handling in America: Final Report," Technical Assistance Research Programs, Inc. (TARP) of Washington, D.C., White House Office of Consumer Affairs, NTIS PB-263-082, 1980.

11. Customer Satisfaction Research Institute

12. Richard C. Whitely, *The Customer Driven Company: Moving from Talk to Action* (Reading, Mass.: Addison Wesley, 1991), 9–10.

13. A. Parasuraman, Valarie Zeithaml, and Leonard L. Berry, "Servqual: A Multiple-Item Scale for Measuring Customer Perceptions of Service Quality," working paper of the Marketing Science Institute Research Program, Cambridge, Mass., 1986.

14. Marr, "Letting the Customer Be the Judge of Quality," 47–48.

15. Robert C. Camp, *Benchmarking: The Search for Industry Best Practices that Lead to Superior Performance* (Milwaukee, Wis.: ASQC Quality Press, 1989), 3.

16. Theodore Levitt, "After the Sale," *Harvard Business Review*, September/October 1983, 87–93.

17. David Maister, "Lessons in Client Loving: How to Live Together in Marital Bliss," *Architectural Technology*, Fall 1985, 47–49.

18. Bhote, *Next Operation*, 70.

*Reacting to random variation increases variation.*

—W. Edwards Deming

# The Secret Is in the Wiring:

## The Need for Process Improvement

W hile flying to Chicago last year, I started talking with a fellow passenger. When I told him that I specialized in helping organizations improve the quality of their products and services, Joe said he had a great war story for me, one that proved how desperately some organizations need such help.

He had had a bad experience with his local hospital. While working as the production manager in a small manufacturing firm, he sprained his ankle. "Wow, did that hurt," he told me. "But compared to what I went through at that hospital, the physical pain was nothing." After Joe was brought to the hospital, the nurses and doctors forgot about him. "I must have sat there for at least an hour before anybody came to see me. Now I know they see a lot worse than me, but someone could have had the decency at least to tell me what was going on." Eventually, Joe was sent for x-rays, only to have them repeated several hours later for another doctor. By the time his brother came to take him home, Joe was apoplectic.

"Actually, the worst part was yet to come," Joe said. "It must have taken five months to resolve the paperwork. There were errors in the hospital bills. People did not return my calls. Then no one could find my records. The final straw came when I received a letter from a local collections agency saying that I hadn't paid my bill!"

## TRADITIONAL MANAGEMENT PRACTICES ARE INEFFECTIVE

Unfortunately for Joe, the local hospital did not know how to deliver quality service. The administrative and medical staff, although well-intentioned and highly trained, were unable to do their jobs. Why? As with dedicated personnel in so many service organizations, their best efforts were stymied by a traditional operating and management system that hampered their attempts to work together as an efficient, effective team.

How is it that some organizations seem to work more effectively than others on behalf of the customer? Is it lack of resources? Is it the skill level of the employees? No. The answer is that they are using a management system based on the vertical organizational chart.

Many people, when asked to draw a picture of their business, sketch an organizational chart. It shows the various functions within their organization, such as finance, operations, public relations, and human resources, and it specifies how these functions relate to one another in a vertical fashion. You can look at a typical organizational chart and immediately see where all of the key people sit in the hierarchy.

When an organization manages primarily by the organizational chart, there is heavy emphasis on the vertical reporting relationship. Goals and objectives frequently are set independently at the top of the organization for each function. And performance is evaluated by whether or not you achieve your local objectives. Who evaluates your performance? Those "above" you in the hierarchy. As a result, individuals and subgroups focus on solving problems at the level of local improvement. And they have minimal contact with others outside their own department.

The problem with this traditional method of management is that information in an organizational chart is limited. The chart does not show what business you are in, nor who your customers are. Most important, it does not show how everyone needs to work together to achieve customer satisfaction.

In the real world, products, processes, and customer issues flow *across* functions in a horizontal direction, not a vertical one (see Figure 2.1). Departments and functions are inextricably linked in a set of interdependent activities and processes that interact to determine customer satisfaction or the lack thereof. And guess what? The coordination of this activity typically takes place not in the boxes on the organizational chart but in the "white space" of the chart, the space *between* the boxes. [1]

Traditional business practices based solely on vertical management hamper the smooth functioning of these horizontal processes. When people focus only on their vertical reporting relationship, they ignore the link between what they do and the next function in line. Employees worry more about "looking good" than about doing good. They become enmeshed with local issues and turf battles. Coworkers, the organization as a whole, the customer—all are left out of the self absorbed employee's circle of care. Rather than focus on what's really important, which is to work together to deliver reliable, high-quality service to the customer on time, every time, individuals engage in adversarial relationships with others in the same organization. As a result, important customer issues fall through the cracks.

Because critical business processes typically cross functions, the causes and effects of problems are frequently not close in time and space. A rigid vertical management frequently obscures the root cause of the problem. Consider the situation in which members of a sales department strive to meet the goals and objectives set by others for their department: maximize sales. To increase bookings, members of the sales department may accept orders for customized

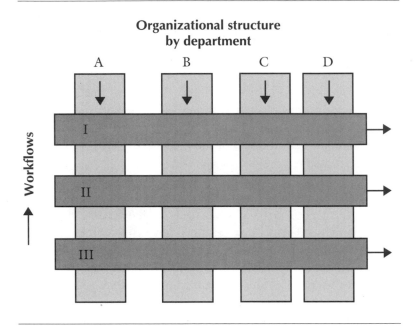

**Figure 2.1:** Business processes run across functions

services that are difficult or impossible to design and deliver at the cost promised and within the required level of quality and time frame. The salesperson may be thrilled to have booked a new order, but at what expense! Because cause and effect are not necessarily close in time or space, a rigid vertical management system creates an atmosphere of "learned helplessness." It makes sense: when you live in a hermetically sealed functional area, oblivious to the needs or nature of the whole, it is easy to assume that the source of all your problems lies elsewhere. The consequence? Overall organizational performance suffers.

In summary, traditional management systems excel at getting people and departments to optimize at the function level, but usually at the expense of others in the organization. The local focus associated with a vertical-only management style subverts total organizational performance. No matter how hard everyone works in the traditional organization, the sum of what everyone does by maximizing local performance will always be less than what it could have been had they worked together.

## THE SECRET IS IN THE WIRING

The solution to myopic management is to change from functional management to process management. In process thinking organizations, employees engage in "behind-the-scenes" cross-functional planning to guarantee that whatever happens on the outside, to the customer, is nothing short of perfect. Starting with the voice of the customer, they translate market needs into operational terms that connect departments in a horizontal way. In short, they wire quality into the organization by streamlining their cross-functional business processes (see Figure 2.2).

Why is process management such a secret in successfully run service organizations? Because in many ways it is invisible. When you have good processes, your customer only knows that he or she is getting good service. Processes are the "wiring" behind the scenes that make the lights go on when the switch is flicked. Just think about the last time you received quality service from an organization. You probably didn't say, "Wow, they sure have great processes in place." Instead, you probably commented on the specific item, feeling, or event. We had a comfortable airplane trip, our hospital stay was pleasant, the delivery was on time, the claim was paid promptly and accurately. Truth is, when you have a good experience with a service provider, you enjoy doing business with an organization that not only focuses on its customers but also rigorously manages its processes. When you pay for service, you are actually buying the outcome of a whole series of reliable sequences that guarantee that you will experience excellent service.

There are several benefits to process control, the most obvious of which is that reliable processes make happy customers. Organizations which manage and continuously improve their internal processes not only meet or exceed their customers' expectations once, they do it time and time again. If you are like many managers, you may be thinking, "But we cannot afford to improve our processes. We do not have the time or money to devote to process

Before                                    After

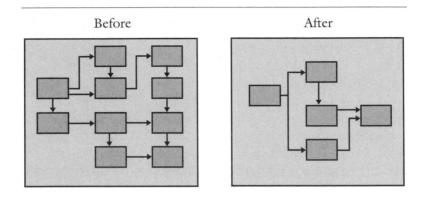

**Figure 2.2:** Reduce waste through process improvement

improvement." The good news is that process control saves you money, time, and energy. Those of you who are numbers conscious will become fans of process control.

## Process improvement saves money

When most people think of improving the quality of their internal processes, they initially think of a whole range of discretionary costs: for example, the cost of inspecting (and rejecting) to ensure quality outcomes, or of buying new materials and training their people. But the overwhelming benefits of process improvement become evident when you consider the *consequential* costs of poor quality: errors do not come free. One senior manager of an insurance company observes,

> *Our efforts were immediately rewarded. We had decided to launch some projects, if only to get some early success stories. One team effort resulted in a 9 percent increase in systems storage capacity. That should result in an annual savings of at least $40,000. Another team identified certain transaction errors which were routinely being put into the system— and routinely rejected. On an ongoing basis, about 26 percent of those transactions had to be reworked. On just their first pass, they got the error rate down to 11 percent for an annual savings of about $200,000. These were small first steps, but*

*they showed us that taking a look at our internal processes
made a lot of sense. We also learned that team problem solving was a great opportunity for us.*

In taking the time to solve recurring problems, employees at
this firm actually found money, money that already belonged to
them. This company didn't have to make additional sales to add
money to its bottom line; instead, employees identified and eliminated waste. Finding and resolving process problems was like finding hidden treasure. Does it take a genius to find errors like these in
your organization? No errors are easy to spot.

*External failures* take place within view of the customer. These
failures are highly visible, as they can lead to unhappy customers,
lost referrals, unpaid bills, account cancellations, and extensive
rework. External failures can be quite expensive to fix. Perhaps an
account representative must visit the customer to address a problem and assure that "it will never happen again." Maybe someone
in billing has to devote an entire afternoon to correcting a billing
error or explaining an unreadable bill. Some organizations have
whole departments devoted to fixing what they call "customer-
related problems."

*Internal failures,* while the customer may never see them, are
also expensive. Consider the hidden costs associated with project
overruns, multiple people handling the same account, or the time
and materials wasted on projects or prospects that never come to
fruition. One financial services organization spent over $36,000
designing and printing a handsome marketing brochure that never
made it to the mailbox. Why? Because the product manager was
moved to a new account. Her replacement never completed the
project due to new priorities.

Whether errors are internal or external, they translate into
unhappy customers and excessive costs. When people begin to track
the amount of time they spend on rework, they are often shocked,
because rework so often masquerades as real work. While corrective
action is certainly necessary when errors occur, it is an unnecessary
expense. This is what we mean by "quality is free." Finding and
eliminating the process bottlenecks in your own practices and procedures produces money that goes straight to the bottom line. Getting

it right the first time means fixing the faulty management systems and processes that "engineered in" the errors right from the start.

## Process improvement saves time

Process-minded people know that in today's rapidly changing competitive environment, taking the time to do something twice is lethal. Gone are the days of lengthy response times and after-the-fact quality control. Taking the time to do something right the second time could kill you. Streamlining processes, beyond saving money otherwise wasted in rework and lost accounts, can save an enormous amount of time. And time, as successful service organizations know, can be used as a strategic weapon.[2]

How is time a strategic weapon? Increased responsiveness gives you a competitive edge. By improving processes, organizations can reduce what is often called "cycle time," the delay between the start of a process and its completion. The shorter the cycle time, the quicker the response. While cycle time has been a household word in the manufacturing industry, it is little known in services. Less than one percent of U.S. companies practice cycle time management in their white collar areas.[3]

What is cycle time in the context of service organizations? An example of cycle time in a hospital setting is the time it takes for a physician's order for medication to be delivered to the hospital pharmacy, prepared, and brought to the floor nurse. An example in the hotel business is the delay between receiving a customer complaint about inadequate accommodations and resolving the problem to the customer's satisfaction. And in most businesses, every day we observe the cycle time between leaving a message by phone and having our call returned.

Poor responsiveness can be costly in the short term as well as the long term. When the speed with which you deliver your service is dramatically curtailed, customers may get frustrated and seek satisfaction elsewhere. But the consequences of constricted processes go beyond the immediacy of customer transactions. Lengthy cycle times can distort true market conditions. In most organizations, for example, there is a lengthy delay between the event that creates a new product or service demand and the time the organization receives that information. Then there are more delays between the

## Estimate your cost of poor quality

You can estimate how much poor quality costs you in money and lost customers by doing the following exercise. First, select a particularly troublesome project, product, or process. Next, briefly list the estimated work hours and/or material costs that your company is wasting on unnecessary activities, such as complaint handling and rework. Remember, time is money. (For a list of typical waste activities, see Appendix B.)

Second, estimate the total cost of quality for your organization as a whole. Experts in the United States and Canada estimate the total cost of quality (for prevention, appraisal, and internal and external failures) to be in the range of 15–40 percent of sales. For a conservative estimate for your own organization, estimate this cost as 15 percent of sales. Now, assume that you could change the way you do business just enough to save 5 percent of this amount. In other words, assume that you could reduce the costs of quality by just 5 percent. For many service organizations, the amount that can be saved exceeds their operating margin.

time the organization receives this information and when it can respond to that information. George Stalk, Jr., vice president of the Boston Consulting Group, points out the danger when delays in cycle times compound.[4] "The longer the delays," he observes, "the more distorted is the view of the market. Those distortions reverberate throughout the system, producing disruption, waste, and inefficiency." Reducing cycle time in all processes at every level creates an organization that is much more responsive to the needs and desires of the marketplace.

Some companies attempt to improve overall performance with cost-reduction strategies, such as switching suppliers or decreasing the size of the workforce. But such strategies are often short-sighted. While traditional cost-cutting strategies may reduce cost in the short term, they often do so at the expense of responsiveness. Today, more and more organizations eliminate delays in all processes to reduce cost and at the same time increase market responsiveness. When you untangle process gridlock, you not only save money but gain opportunity. You are free to devote your energies to more creative work.

## Process management reduces hassles

People who spend their days reworking, putting out fires, and reacting are not stress-free people. Nothing can be more discouraging than to work for an organization in process gridlock, to come to work each day only to face problems that just won't go away. Yet errors are an insidious phenomenon. Have you ever noticed how output errors become input errors, or how errors interact, multiply, and create activities which in turn produce more errors? Some have commented on the pervasiveness of rework by referring to the hidden organization lurking below the surface, the invisible organization that does nothing but produce and correct errors.

Process control, beyond reducing cost and increasing responsiveness, can eliminate the hassles that generate distress. Untangling process gridlock frees you and others to move on to a happier, more productive work experience, one characterized by positive energy. As one middle manager observed in the early stages of participation on a process improvement team,

> *When we visually displayed and studied the process, we could see how we would mutate the process every time. The chart began to reflect the pain and suffering, where we were personally miserable for a day or a month in our lives. We began to see how we could get control over this.*

As this middle manager observed, getting control of the process can reduce unnecessary stress. Improving processes improves employee morale. And lest you think that employee morale cannot be measured, just consider the use of sick time and personal days, a last recourse when the hassles of the job are seemingly never-ending.

In summary, successful service organizations know that the secret to success lies in the wiring. They understand that all of their internal activities, as well as those of customers and suppliers, are connected by complex and invisible threads of interrelated processes. They design their processes with excruciating exactness to yield a predictably positive outcome. They also know that the benefits of process improvement go straight to their bottom line. When you improve your processes, you reduce your costs and increase your revenues. You also improve relationships. Untangling process gridlock helps you to keep your customers happy, regain control over your work life, and eliminate the paralysis that leads to feeling victimized.

## THE CORNERSTONES OF PROCESS IMPROVEMENT

Process-minded organizations design in quality from the start. It takes time, but as we have seen, it is worth it. If you believe that you do not have the time to evaluate and control your processes, Sgt. David Couper from the Department of Police in Madison, Wisconsin, has some advice for you:

> *During the summer, I put on a uniform and go out in a marked patrol car. I spend a month checking the systems. I take drunks to the detoxification tank, make drunk driving arrests, write reports, and see how the system operates. I question and listen to people from my officers to the citizens, our customers. In our organization, we have 400 employees. Some people say they can't do what I do because their organization is too big. I think the point is that if your organization is too big to check your systems, that gives you a strong message that it must be done.*

Getting control over your processes is an important key to companywide quality improvement and a never-ending management responsibility. To this end, every employee must take a problem-solving approach to continuous improvement. How do you ensure that all of your people understand what process management is about? A good way to start is by building an organization-wide understanding of five key principles of process management.

1. Everything is a process.
2. Customer satisfaction is determined by the effectiveness of these processes.
3. Fix the process; do not blame the person.

4. Process improvement is the job of management.

5. Process improvement itself is a process.

Let's take a look at each of these principles in more detail.

## All work gets done through "job processes"

A process is any series of steps or activities that adds value by converting inputs into outputs for a customer. Inputs can include such things as supplies, information, and energy. Outputs can be anything from information in reports or data to service or products. Many people initially think of manufacturing companies when they think of processes. But service organizations have processes too: operational, business, and administrative. Operational processes include filling a pharmaceutical order, processing a passenger for an airplane boarding, making a sales call on a prospective life insurance customer, or resolving a claim. Business processes include processing accounts payable, processing data, and preparing promotional campaigns. Administrative processes include annual planning, budgeting, hiring personnel, training, and so on. When you recognize that everything is a process, then you have made a giant step forward in untangling organizational gridlock.

In the service industry, the process is often more visible and more memorable than the outcome. While customers certainly care about the outcome of a business interaction (Did I get the reservation? Does my haircut look good? Did I receive the correct medication?), many times a satisfactory outcome is taken for granted. Service customers are equally if not more sensitive to the manner in which a service is performed (Was the paperwork done quickly? Did I have to wait long for my appointment? Was my call returned promptly?). Think about the last time you paid for professional services. Do you remember the outcome of your last physical exam? Probably not. Rather, it was probably the service delivery process, with all its "moments of truth," that significantly influenced your evaluation of the quality of service rendered. Excellent service, in the eyes of your customer, happens only when people manage and continually improve all processes behind the scenes.

No service is devoid of opportunity for process improvement. Service professionals such as surgeons, consultants, and trial lawyers may initially resist evaluation; they frequently attribute their success to a personalized style rather than to a method that can be standardized. But everything is an art form if it is not in control. What is important is to recognize that gaining control of a process does not mean that a process cannot be adaptive. The challenge is to balance process control with the capability to continuously and reliably adapt your processes to changing internal and external circumstances.

When you begin to understand that everything is a process, it becomes clear that most processes are not only cross-functional by nature but are also part of even larger processes involving other stakeholders outside the traditional boundaries of the organization. Suppliers, regulatory agencies, and the education system all influence our ability to function effectively. When one organization tries to improve its own part of the mega process with little attention to how its actions affect other groups, it is likely that the outcome of the larger process may be sub-optimized.

## Connect the process to your external customer

Dick Whitely, vice chairman of the Forum Corporation, says, "You process data; you process cheese; you process meat. The job is not just to process someone, it is to create a happy customer."[5] Process improvement efforts are only successful when the process specifications are defined and controlled by the voice of the customer. The adage "garbage in, garbage out" couldn't be more apt. No matter how reliable, accurate, and fast your processes, if you fail to focus on your customer when designing your processes, your quality improvement efforts can backfire.

• **Focus on the external customer.** As Chip Caldwell of West Paces Ferry Hospital discovered, there are two levels of sophistication in process management. One is focused at the level of the existing boxes on the chart, which can bring some improvement. The other, more advantageous, is focused on the external customer. Caldwell notes,

*In the beginning of our effort, we divided responsibility for process improvement according to our traditional organizational boundaries. For example, in striving to improve our medication administration process, we identified several subprocesses. Our first level of business was to study and measure these subprocesses. The first subprocess is the order entry process, which starts when the doctor writes the order and ends when the pharmacy receives the order. The second subprocess involves the actual preparation of the prescription at the pharmacy. The third subprocess begins when the nursing unit receives the medication and ends when the unit administers or delivers the medication to the patient.*

*In approaching our process improvement in this way, we unwittingly invited finger pointing. The team immediately fell back on its individual priorities, forgetting the process and the patient.*

*Today, we view the patient care process radically different than we did three years ago when we began total quality leadership. Today, we look at the patient care process as the reason for us to be. That is why we are here. That is our mission. And that process begins with a patient in the physician's office needing services. Today, the first entry point in our series of processes is the admitting process. That is followed by the nursing process and then, leading to nursing in many different ways, are the diagnostic and therapeutic processes that we bring to bear on the doctor's orders, followed by the discharge process. So the boundary is from the time the patient needs services to the time that those needs are met.*

What happens if you experience inter-departmental conflict? The voice of the customer must be the deciding vote, the ultimate authority. In process management, each functional unit defines its responsibilities in terms of its impact on the customer, as opposed to its function. This shift in focus helps to minimize "turf" problems and other barriers that might undermine the cross-functional processes at work within the organization.

• **Support your internal customers.** An organization's ability to deliver quality products and services depends to a great extent on the effectiveness with which its people work together. Your internal customer, or the next person or process in line who receives the results of your work, needs your input to do his or her job effectively, and so on down the line. People interact very differently with one another with process management than they do with traditional management models. They learn to respect and support the people with whom they work, they pool their resources to solve common problems and they work together to eliminate waste.

In a traditional management system, primary emphasis on the vertical relationship can lead to a "heliotropic sunflower syndrome." That's where top management sees nothing but glowing results from an individual who, although looking great from the top, lords over a demoralized and disenfranchised organization below and is insensitive to internal customers' needs. To rid themselves of this vertical distortion and promote process thinking, some organizations like the First National Bank of Chicago directly connect an individual's performance evaluation with the input of his or her external and internal customers.

## Do not blame the person; fix the process

When we focus only on our local operations, it is easy to blame people or events for the cause of our displeasure. However, you will get a much more realistic and complete picture of the nature of the problem if you take a step back and view your immediate situation as part of a bigger story. Learning to see processes , rather than the "offenders" or "events," is the starting point for performance improvement.

Process-minded people know that when errors occur, it is time to attack their processes, not their people. In fact, quality improvement experts believe that 85–95 percent of errors are caused by faulty management systems, not by the individual employee. Like a high-performance sports car stuck in traffic, even the most talented individual cannot demonstrate his or her abilities until the highways, or processes, are clear and the traffic is flowing. There is nothing worse than putting a talented performer into a flawed performance system.

So how do you turn process gridlock into process advantage? You engineer in quality from the start. Many managers focus on *results:* fourth quarter earnings, month-end shipments, new orders, and so on. Yet managing by result leads to management after the fact. And management after the fact reduces strategic flexibility. In contrast, process-oriented managers are prevention-oriented managers. They believe in the old adage "An ounce of prevention is worth a pound of cure." So they focus on the *means* to achieve their desired results; they create a disciplined process to guarantee their desired outcome. To this end, process-minded people constantly seek to simplify their activities and rid their processes of variability and other waste. Their goal is to build reliability into each step and add value to the whole. In other words, they work smarter, not harder.

"That's all fine and good," you might say, "but I need something to *manage*. I need numbers. I need to be able to track performance." Whether you know it or not, you practice process management every morning. For example, when you decide that you must get to the office by 8:30 A.M. tomorrow, you design a reliable process to ensure that it happens. You set the alarm clock to allow enough time for you to shower, eat breakfast, and make the commute. Prior to setting your alarm, you made sure that you ended your evening by a certain hour. And that decision may have been made after you listened to the weather report to identify any potential delays. Getting to work by 8:30 is your desired result. But guaranteeing that you will achieve that outcome depends on how well you manage all of the steps along the way, namely the process. Is getting to work the only process that you manage every day? Definitely not. Almost everything that you do can be described in terms of a process.

• **Make the process visible.** While the process of getting to work in the morning is easy to envision, many organizational processes are more complex. As the saying goes, what you cannot see, you cannot manage. An important step in getting control over your processes is to draw a picture of how things really happen—not how they are supposed to happen, or what people think should happen, but what actually happens. Once you make the headaches visible, you will understand anew why it is so important to have the people who touch the process be members of its improvement team; one person cannot see or control the whole process. By making your processes visible, you can achieve consensus on the shortcomings and strengths of those processes.

How do you draw a picture of a process? There are several valuable yet simple techniques for understanding and improving processes. "Process mapping," a core technology for improving quality, can help you locate waste within your organization.[6] In process mapping, a team draws a diagram of the flow of information, activities, and materials that connects customers and suppliers. When you examine the wiring behind the scenes you may be surprised at what you see. Most people find that their working process looks more like a bowl of spaghetti than a business process. "The power of the picture" couldn't be more clear.

• **Locate and fix disconnections.** As a result of process mapping, you may unearth previously unrecognized delays in other departments that affect your process. For instance, you may find that it takes an excessive length of time for a customer service request to reach the field service function. You may discover multiple loops and wastelands that not only do not add value to the customer but probably increase the chance for errors.

Process mapping can reveal dozens of "disconnections." Some of these include:

- Flaws in outputs
  —missing outputs
  —late outputs
  —substandard outputs

- Flaws in inputs
  —missing inputs
  —late inputs
  —substandard inputs

- Flaws in the logic of the process
  —missing steps
  —redundant steps
  —unnecessary steps
  —bottlenecks
  —illogical steps

- Execution failures (human failure to carry out a well-designed process)
  —lack of training
  —rewarding wrong behaviors
  —inadequate tools or resources[7]

In summary, your process can only go as fast as your slowest administrative link. So draw a picture of the process, locate your bottlenecks, analyze the problems behind the difficulties, and take action. What you want instead of process gridlock is a seamless set of steps in the workflow with appropriate process performance measures.

## Use a cross-functional team approach

A key step in launching a process improvement effort is to acknowledge openly that no one person can really understand how a process works from beginning to end. Nor, in the same vein, can individual employees possibly understand all of the implications of their actions on others in the organization. Due to the limitations of individual perspective, examining and improving a process requires a team approach.

It is important to select team members from the various functions that "touch" the process. Your team must represent every viewpoint that affects the process as it winds it way from start to finish. Chip Caldwell of West Paces Ferry Hospital tells how his executive team members learned about the strength of cross-functional teams when they set out to improve some of their processes:

> At first, we denied the importance of building a cross-functional team. We made assumptions about our processes, believing that we (the executive team) knew how things worked, and started flow-charting the process. We didn't get anywhere.
>
> Later, once we had people represented on the team from every step of the process, we realized that no one person can ever really know how a process works, particularly one that goes cross-functionally through multiple departments. For example, we organized an operating room turnover team to reduce the length of time it takes to get patients into the operating room and out again.
>
> When the team finished flow-charting the process, they found that we inspected for lab x-rays and EKG work eight times. Worse yet, we saw that there were three people who performed those same inspections, and that none of them knew that there were two other people doing exactly the same thing.

*Being a member of a process team also helped all of us under-stand the implications of our actions on other people and their jobs within the organization.*

Once you have formed your process improvement team, give it every chance to be effective. Remember that this is the time to put politics and pride aside; the only way you can build an effective team is if you select knowledge over rank when choosing specific team members. One inappropriate "political pick" can dampen the team's enthusiasm and ruin its prospects for success.

In summary, when you take responsibility for your processes, you no longer blame others for any problems that arise. Instead, you analyze and perfect your processes and systems. Gone are the days of finger pointing, complaining, and managing by reaction When you place the spotlight on interrelationships and interdependencies, it becomes difficult to ignore problems that come your way. Instead, individuals become genuinely concerned about their upstream and downstream processes and peers. They work harder to ensure the integrity of every process they touch and, over time, build quality into the fabric of the organization.

## Start today: wire quality into your processes

"Use your head, not your money," says Taiichi Ohno of Toyota when he speaks of quality and process improvement.[8] Carefully and systematically studying and improving the work flow is a time-intensive approach to improving quality and customer satisfaction, not a capital-intensive one. Your objective is to wire quality into all of your processes.

Slowing down to take the time to analyze all of your processes may at first seem counter-intuitive, or at least unproductive. It's no wonder: many service organizations in the United States today are short-term oriented, reflecting a national culture that focuses on the quick fix and the "here-and-now." When an organization is so eager to "get there," however, it often neglects to examine the processes by which its results are achieved. Too many people complain that they never have the time to do things right the first time, but they always seem to find the time to do it over.

Process improvement itself is a process. Reaping the benefits of process improvement requires discipline. How can you start? The following nine steps can help.

1. Focus on the customer.

2. Select a critical process.

3. Recruit the right people.

4. Make the current process visible.

5. Study your process scientifically.

6. Improve process design.

7. Implement improvements.

8. Track performance.

9. Celebrate and repeat: continuously improve the process.

Let's see how each of these steps works.

**Focus on the customer.** When first getting into process management, start with your customer. It is important to identify your customer, obtain customer requirements, and convert your customer expectations into measures. To begin with, each person within your organization might ask, "Who is my immediate customer?" Your first customer may be another department or division within your organization. Next, ask, "Who is my second customer?" Continue to identify your intermediate customers in the chain until you get to the final customer who buys your product or service. To be truly customer-focused, everyone in the organization must understand how their daily activites connect to the end customer. Then they can take responsibility for making customer desires primary managerial responsibilities by translating vague, non-measurable customer requirements such as "accuracy," "consistency," "uniformity," and "timeliness" into concrete, measurable system or process design goals, actions, and features.

**Select a critical process.** Any internal or external failure represents an opportunity for process improvement. However, the following questions may help you identify a good prospect for a pilot test.

• Which processes are most visible to and/or directly affect your external customer? Examples include application processes, complaint handling processes, and processes associated with the delivery of products or services. Processes which may not be directly visible to the customer but which directly affect important product and service attributes such as reliability, timeliness, and accuracy are also good candidates for immediate attention.

• Which processes have poor reputations within the organization? Examples include processes which are associated with long delays, high cost, high employee turnover, high number of complaints, and low productivity.

• Which processes are within the control of your process team? You are more likely to succeed if you pick an area that you know well and that is manageable in size for a first application.

• Which processes are linked with critical business issues where there is a sense of urgency? An example might be the new product development process.

**Recruit the right people.** Once you select a particular process to work on, determine exactly who should be a member of that process improvement team. Gather the people who touch the process, rather than having a few people get together to decide what others "should" do. Assign one person the responsibility of ensuring that the team does its job as effectively as possible. A team leader is invaluable in spotting gaps in logic or organization that naturally occur in a new team and can help team members learn to take responsibility for the entire process and coordinate their activity as they move forward.

**Make the current process visible.** When you set out to improve a process, identify the boundaries of the process. Then document and analyze it. Many people want to jump from the definition of the problem to the solution. But taking the time to map the current process provides a richness of detail and forced learning that is unequalled in business experience. Although you may be excited about the improvement process and want to get going, hold back. Until you have mapped the entire process as it exists now, studied it carefully, and then reached agreement on what it should look like, any improvement is premature.

**Study your process scientifically.** When you take the time to dissect your processes, you will discover a myriad of previously misunderstood mysteries that make your life miserable day in and day out. Bringing the ghosts of the process out into daylight makes them disappear. Aleta Holub, vice president of quality at First National Bank of Chicago, notes, "You start off and encounter many kinds of 'corporate folklore' things that you have been doing forever but that shouldn't be done—systemic errors you are making. You immediately see that if you fix the process, then you are going to be out of the error-prone environment with easy hits." How do you identify these opportunities for improvement? First you test the reliability of your process as a whole. Then you select priority problems for corrective action, collect data to better understand these problems, and finally, search for and eliminate the root cause of the problems.

**Build in quality through reliable process design.** Once you identify a high-outcome process, you must carefully identify, diagnose, and subsequently resolve all of the "disconnections" that you discover. Design a "should" process map with control points and standards that embodies the wisdom of all the members on the process improvement team. Having the members who know the process create the new design not only ensures that their "streetwise" experience is incorporated into the new process map but also builds group commitment to the new way. Your goal is to enhance the process continuously so that the people who use it can get it right the first time and know how it was that they got it right. Some people additionally design a "could" map, a design which, given additional resources, could yield significant improvements. Teams are generally encouraged, however, to get on with the "should," leaving the "could" to be determined over time.

**Implement changes.** Once you have designed the new process, you can go ahead and implement specific changes. This is an exciting time, because even more learning can take place during implementation. Communication is needed so that anyone even remotely connected with the process will understand the nature of the efforts underway.

**Track performance.** Your last step is to implement your changes, right? The answer is no. When you improve a process, you must also take specific steps to ensure that the process is monitored and improved continuously. Drive out variability through process measures as well as results measures. While most of us are familiar with results measures, such as the number of widgets per hour or spelling errors per page, we are less familiar with process measures the behind-the-scenes measures that, when managed properly, will guarantee that your results come in on target. Remember the example earlier in this chapter about getting to work on time? While morning arrival time is the result measure (you either got there on time or you didn't), everything you did to get there, such as going to bed on time, is a process measure. By controlling your process measures, you can monitor and control your results.

**Celebrate and repeat: continuously improve the process.** Making improvements once is not good enough. It is important to constantly review your latest version of the process, making it the operational map of the absolutely best method that you and your peers can invent. Once you can demonstrate improvement, establish standards to hold the gains and then look for additional ways to improve the process. William Eggleston, vice president of quality at IBM, notes,

> *Processes tend to adapt for comfort with their environment over time rather than stay lean and competitive. This is one reason why declining productivity sets in. People build buffers seeking to minimize the effect of external change on their day-to-day activities. It is management's job to keep resources productive. We go one step further and say it is management's job to adapt to and improve the process on an ongoing basis.*

Process improvement is only successful if it is continually practiced. If you cut cycle time in half the first time, try to shave off 10 percent more the next time around. If you reduced rework by 50 percent, repeat the improvement process and try for a 75 percent reduction. Process improvement is a never-ending process.

## SUMMARY

Many service organizations are tripping over their own feet when it comes to delivering quality service to their customers. How? They are tangled up in their own unreliable malfunctioning internal processes. For years, many service organizations believed that 70–80 percent of their price, affordability, and service complexity problems were beyond their control. They blamed their problems on regulators, uninformed consumers, or the high cost of their suppliers. But today, more and more organizations are looking inward to discover that many of their problems arise from lack of internal coordination.

The key to untangling organizational gridlock is to recognize that the solutions to customer concerns cannot be found by focusing solely on one box on an organizational chart. Instead, solutions are found in processes that run horizontally across functions. In a relay race, winning the race has as much to do with improving the handoff—passing the baton from one team member to the next— as it does with the individual performance of the team players. When managers begin to gain control of these horizontal handoffs and processes, only then can significant improvements in reduced costs, improved responsiveness, and reduced stress be achieved.

How will you know when you have improved your processes? You will know that life is improving once people start reporting tangible improvements in the way they do work, when you find yourself spending less time fighting fires, when the people you work with seem friendlier, when your customers, both internal and external, seem happier, and when your costs decrease.

### Notes

1. Geary A. Rummler and Alan Brache, *Improving Performance: How to Manage the Whitespace on the Organization Chart* (San Francisco: Jossey-Bass Publishers, 1990), 5–9.

2. George Stalk, Jr., "Time—The Next Source of Competitive Advantage," *Harvard Business Review,* July/August 1988, 41–51.

3. Bhote, *Next Operation*

4. Stalk, "Time," 47.

5. Richard C. Whitley, *Fortune* conference, 1991.

6. They are several technologies available to assist with process mapping. The Rummler-Brache Group in Warren, New Jersey, and High Performance Systems, Inc., in Hanover, New Hampshire, represent two popular schools of thought.

7. Process management workshop, 1990, the Rummler-Brache Group, Warren, New Jersey, 37.

8. Masaaki Imai, *Kaizen: The Key to Japan's Competitive Success* (New York: Random House, 1986), 84.

*Business, we know, is now so complex and difficult, the survival of firms so hazardous, in an environment increasingly unpredictable, competitive, and fraught with danger, that their continued existence depends on the day-to-day mobilization of every ounce of intelligence.*
—Konsuke Matsushita

# Management Anorexia:

## The Need for Universal Participation

How many times have you heard, "I don't make the rules, I just follow them," "It's not my job," or "Sorry, the manager is not in. Can you come back later?" As a customer, how do you react when someone speaks to you in this way? I feel frustrated. I wonder why an organization is paying wages for a human body without giving that person the power to make decisions on my behalf.

People helping people—that's what total quality is all about. Whether it is the waitress who bends over backward to help a young couple with children or a ticket counter agent who responds quickly to a passenger's crisis, these people not only seem to know the right thing to do but also want to do it right.

How can you get caring and intelligent people like these to work for you? Think of the competitive advantage your organization would have if its people were so dedicated and "take-charge." Open your eyes—they are already working for you.

## Management anorexia: an organizational disease

From your customer's viewpoint, employees don't just provide the service—very often, they *are* the service. Some organizations know this. Amica Mutual Insurance Company, for example, sells its employees as much, if not more, than the insurance that it sells. As Charles E. Horne III, vice president, says, without employees, an organization is nothing.

> *If you talk with a lot of people in the insurance industry, they would say that automobile insurance is a commodity. We get very upset about that—Amica insurance is not a commodity. You are not just buying a piece of paper—you're buying assets, which are very considerable; but what you are really buying is the Amica team, the Amica people. Our Amica people are our most important product, really. We sell insurance, but the employees that we put together and stay with us work for our customer's advantage. If you take away our people, we are nothing. We are really seeking career employees. As it turns out, we have been fortunate enough to get career clients.*

As Horne understands, the assets of most service organizations walk out the door at the end of each day. In the banking industry, Rodney Baker-Bates, group planning director of Midland Bank in London, similarly values this "intellectual property." He observes that when his customers complain, they usually associate their bad experience with "the bank." When they have praise to give, however, they almost always name an individual. The customer's experience with the employee, not with the anonymous institution, is the determining factor in customer satisfaction. Customers automatically associate excellence with the individual employee and, in the event of poor service, associate problems with the inability of the institution to get it right.

If employee intelligence is so readily available, why are so many service organizations not taking advantage of this valuable resource? Today, many managers operate much like the anorexic. Anorexia nervosa, characterized by self-inflicted starvation, is a serious disease which can lead to death. Although food is readily available, anorexics refuse to eat. Why? Because they are obsessed with control and equate safety with thinness. The disease eventually can progress to the point where the individual must be force fed to survive. Many managers suffer from a similar disease. These managers believe that control is equal to knowing all the answers themselves.

While organizations have tasks and processes that can be significantly improved with employee input, people who suffer from management anorexia reject such contributions. Soliciting opinion is too risky—it would mean exposing their ignorance. Inviting others to join them in the decision-making process means giving up some control. The problem is that others possess valuable knowledge about the realities of the business. No manager can possibly be everywhere at once to discover, understand, and respond immediately to all the problems within the organization. Still, people suffering from management anorexia are unwilling to take advantage of the intelligence of others. They starve their organizations by refusing to ingest the valuable knowledge their employees and peers offer. Managerial anorexia is not something that others outside the organization inflict. Sadly, it is something organizations and managers bring upon themselves.

## The answer is universal participation

How do humans stay healthy? Current medical research indicates that a varied diet, one which includes foods from several food groups, is key. Similarly, organizations can stay vital by drawing upon the varied intelligences of their employees. As human bodies have functions and processes supported by ingesting varied foods, so do organizations have tasks and processes that can be maintained and improved with employee contributions.

Does this mean that only a few people in the organization, perhaps those in the quality department, should have responsibility for the continual improvement of all products, services, and processes? No. It means universal participation by all in the organization to seek and act upon opportunities for improvement. From the CEO to the front-line personnel, every level of the organization must be involved with customer-focused quality improvement. Every employee at every level of the organization must be invited and supported by the organization to seek and act upon opportunities for improvement. Rather than isolate people from the rest of the organization, involve them in every decision that affects their area of expertise and responsibility.

This is a challenge for most service organizations. In product work, where suggestions are elicited more frequently than in support services, the average rate in Japan for employee suggestions for improvement is eight suggestions per employee per year. In the United States, it is less than 0.1 per employee per year. Even more striking, the rate of implementation of these suggestions in the United States is less than 30 percent, compared to 75 percent for Japan.[1] A manager's challenge is to make added value out of existing knowledge; remember that your employees are "intellectual property." Don't work harder than you have to. Instead, work smarter. Every employee comes with a brain, so use it!

## Universal participation pays

But isn't it easier, and faster, just to do it yourself? Beyond collecting valuable information, there are additional advantages to universal participation in the early stages of decision-making. Once you understand the far-reaching benefits of universal participation, you will gladly take the time to involve others. It might take some getting used to, but the benefits far outweigh the hassle.

• **Early detection of errors.** Big failures do not emerge out of nowhere; there are often a lot of little failures that occur along the way which snowball. When you are accessible to the people who work for and around you, you are more likely to hear about small failures before they become big problems.

• **Higher quality decisions.** Taking the time to involve others in the early stages of the decision-making process provides a richer experience base. A decision made in a vacuum cannot compare with a creative decision made in a melting pot of experience and input.

Participative decision-making eliminates many of the I-could-have-told-you-so's.

• **Increased commitment.** When people who are affected by a decision have the opportunity to participate in the decision-making process and be heard, they are more committed to the outcome. It may appear to take more time up front to inquire about and explore employee concerns, but in the long run you will save enormous time and energy battling resistance. Early involvement in the design process often prevents painful and costly backtracking later.

• **Added value.** When you recognize the capabilities of others and let them handle issues that directly affect their jobs, you can get on to managing the white space on the organizational chart. Rather than devote countless hours re-managing and supervising the efforts of your direct subordinates, you can move on to more creative things. You were not hired to do your subordinates' work for them, you were hired to add value to the organization.

• **Improved employee morale.** People like to be involved. They want to be involved. Most often, they are just waiting to be given permission to jump on the bandwagon.

The benefits of total employee involvement are tremendous. Better decisions, increased commitment, and early detection of potential areas of concern give participative organizational cultures a competitive advantage over others.

## KEYS TO UNIVERSAL PARTICIPATION

Universal participation is critical to achieving continuous quality improvement. Before you can engage others in quality improvement activities, however, you must make sure that the underlying organizational culture supports their efforts. Employees may already understand what excellence means, which is to meet or exceed customer expectations, and that it will be measured via customer requirements. But if you want their participation in identifying opportunities for improvement and taking immediate corrective action, then it is their right to work in an organizational climate that fosters innovation. You need an organizational climate in which people feel safe not only to take risks but to work unencumbered on their customers' behalf. What is the mark of a totally supportive culture? There are four specific practices that can leverage the creative intelligence of others.

• **Value your people.** The wise person knows that intelligent people are not defined as workers or as managers but as individuals, specialists, professionals, and leaders. Thank goodness, the older definitions of *manager* and *worker* are slowly becoming obsolete in our generation. Everyone, no matter their background, level of education, or intellectual capability, has something to contribute. Employee input is critical when key decisions are being made because only the people closest to the job know the realistic capabilities of the business.

• **Trust your people.** Believe in the capability of your subordinates to interpret the needs of a given situation and decide what to do. No manager or supervisor can be everywhere at once, nor can any one person possibly discover, understand, and respond quickly to all improvement opportunities in the organization. So create an environment in which individuals feel comfortable sharing difficult information. Understand that having your views challenged does not indicate a lack of commitment on the part of others.

• **Involve others, and stay involved.** The best way to work with intelligent individuals is by doing just that: working *with* them. The days of telling people what to do are over. Intelligent individuals are managed not by command but by consent. Obedience cannot be demanded. Instead, creating a collaborative culture and a shared understanding among colleagues is the only way to make things happen.

• **Improve your interpersonal skills.** Effective problem solvers are skilled communicators. They know how to listen—a major challenge for many of us—and they know how to communicate difficult feedback in a developmental and nonthreatening way.

They adapt their listening, speaking, and managing styles to each person and situation.

If you can master these four practices, you are well on your way to building a culture that can support universal participation. Let's look at each practice in more detail, after which we'll move on to how you can incorporate these practices into your work life.

## Value your employees

To build customer focus, you must first build employee focus into the organization. Companies that embrace a total quality management philosophy believe that employees are customers too, albeit internal ones, and have their own values, needs, and expectations. Frederick W. Smith, chairman and chief executive officer of Federal Express Corporation, puts it nicely:

> We learned a long time ago that employee satisfaction is a prerequisite to customer satisfaction. That belief is articulated in three words within our corporate philosophy statement: people, service, and profit....The bottom line is that to satisfy our customers, we must first treat our employees as customers.

As Smith understands, paying attention to employee needs and expectations is good for business. An overworked bank teller, a frustrated administrative assistant, or an unsupported and isolated customer service representative cannot be expected to add value to your organization cheerfully and diligently, let alone meet or exceed customer expectations. How people feel within and about your organization directly influences their ability to continuously improve the way they serve their customers and do their jobs. How can you best support them? First, no matter where they stand in the hierarchy and no matter what their job, they have a customer to serve. That customer might be someone in the next department or the traditional external customer. Second, know that they will attempt to do things right the first time on behalf of their customer; create an environment where no one will pass along a defect to their customer, internal or external.

Take a hard, honest look at your employees. Do you see a bunch of ne'er-do-wells or a group of talented people who want to lead productive and fulfilling lives? What prejudices do you carry about the people with whom you work, either within your own functional area or elsewhere?

In my consulting work, I often meet managers who indulge in an underlying arrogance toward their subordinates. You, too, may know a few people like this. With a "holier than thou" attitude, however tacit, they are the ones whose every action seems to say, "I am smarter, better educated, more experienced, ambitious, and successful than this crew. I am where I am, and I have the power that I have, because I know more than they do." Ironically, it is these very same managers who get raked over the coals during confidential interviews by those who report directly to them. I can't tell you the number of times I have heard comments along these lines: "The man is profoundly stupid about the realities of the business," "She is out of touch in her thinking; she never reads, let alone keeps up with the latest techniques," "He could be a good manager if only...," or "When the economy improves, I hope to move on. My skills are not being used in this job."

Despite the perception of many managers that they are somehow superior in intelligence or achievement, those who report to them can see significant gaps in their knowledge base. These knowledge deficiencies, if closed, would create significant improvements in performance for the organization as a whole. The very existence of management arrogance and lack of respect for the intelligence of others creates and feeds a vicious cycle of bad feeling and limited knowledge exchange.

What is the way out of this trap if you believe you may be one of these managers? Start by freely admitting that you may not have all the answers and that there are others who do. If you have an even mildly disdainful attitude toward your peers, managers, or subordinates, you will never get good results. High performance requires an underlying culture that respects and values all of its partners, whether they be customers, suppliers, neighbors, or employees.

Changing a well-established mindset can be hard. One way to change your innate attitude toward your subordinates is by putting yourself in their shoes. Get curious. What makes them tick? What has to happen to make them say, "Wow, did I have a great time at work today?" If you do not know what motivates them, you need to spend more time listening and looking. Take a genuine interest in their attitudes and concerns. Ask them questions, and then listen to their answers. If you can view the people with whom you work with non-judgmental eyes, or at least with the basic judgment that they are good, then you will be well on your way to wanting to help them realize their full potential.

How are people motivated or, at the very least, satisfied? At the basic level, everyone needs interactions which invite them to

- feel important
- engage in learning and growth
- participate in the solution of problems
- feel part of something bigger than themselves

Once these basic needs are satisfied, different people are motivated by different things. For example, the desire for autonomy may inspire one person, whereas the need for security may drive another. Everyone wants and needs to be involved in activities that they can accomplish and for which they can be recognized. The challenge is to be sensitive and creative enough to provide others with ongoing and diverse opportunities to excel.

What are *your* regulators? What motivates you to work on a weekend? What accomplishment makes you especially proud? Which recognitions do you "let slip" to your close friends? Asking yourself these questions is a useful exercise, if only because it may increase your sensitivity to those around you. Often, what motivates you may very well be what also motivates others. But sometimes the opposite is true. Seeing the company go public, holding large, formal recognition dinners, or hitting aggressive sales targets may be motivating to you yet totally irrelevant to others in the organization. You must work to know and understand what motivates others so that you can establish mutually beneficial outcomes.

The bottom line is that you cannot achieve continuous improvement by delegating the responsibility for customer satisfaction to yourself or a few key employees. Everyone, including yourself, must act on behalf of continuous improvement and total customer satisfaction. This means that you must respect the needs and expectations of others. If you respect your subordinates, your subordinates will respect you. If you respect your employees' needs, expectations, and knowledge base, then they in turn will respect the customers' needs and expectations. Value your employees and the contributions they make, for satisfied employees make for good business.

## Trust others

Universal participation in quality improvement suggests two things. First, everyone is invited to participate, no matter what their area of expertise or level in the hierarchy. Second, in participating, everyone will be trying to make changes to improve the system. It is this second element of employee involvement that can shake people's confidence in their own abilities and those of others. For changing the system means challenging established policies, practices, and procedures, and that can feel destabilizing, if not outright frightening, at any level of the organization.

In making changes to the system, you are asking people to take many risks. People must be willing to challenge the status quo. This means going up against established policies, practices, and power figures, the very things that, adhered to in the past, virtually guaranteed job security. People must also be willing to acquire new competencies. They may initially experience failure when they try to acquire new skills—that is part of learning. Whether it is challenging the system or acquiring new skills, in asking people to improve the performance of the system, you are asking them to expose themselves to being vulnerable.

Most people will not take risks until they have job security. If you want people to change dysfunctional policies, practices, procedures, and processes, then you must first create an environment where it is safe to try new behaviors and challenge other individuals. This includes being able to confront senior managers on those practices which, in the eyes of others, are contradictory to customer-focused quality improvement. Individuals need to be able to trust management not to retaliate. Senior management must demonstrate that it trusts the wisdom of its employees.

In so many organizations, lack of trust is the factor most limiting employee involvement in quality improvement. Having grown up in New England, I am aware that lost travelers in Maine who ask for directions often hear the response, "You can't get there from here." In a state that has much wilderness and few roads, confused travelers often must retrace their steps to a prior location and begin again. Building trust is similar to traversing the wilderness of Maine. If the destination is universal participation in quality improvement and you are in an environment where there is no trust, then no matter how much energy and effort you put into attempting to advance the organizational change process, you will end up having to go back to square one.

What is this elusive thing called trust? Trust is the knowledge that I can tell you what I am thinking without fear of reprisal. It means I can express a controversial opinion without my commitment to the organization being questioned. It means that I can experiment with new ways of approaching my job on behalf of the organization because I know that my job is secure.

If this sounds like common sense, that's because it is. The problem is that too many individuals and organizations behave in ways that create an environment of fear rather than trust. How do people and organizations lose this precious thing called trust? Perhaps your organization has recently reduced its workforce, or perhaps the layoffs were handled in an especially insensitive way. A poor economy, rude behavior on the part of senior managers, threats made to peers or subordinates, and inappropriate actions of prior management teams can have long-lasting effects on employee willingness to take risks. Whatever the source, lack of trust is a debilitating factor in making significant progress toward getting employee commitment to change.

Are you building trust into all of your key relationships? Most people are not aware of how fragile is this thing called trust. When was the last time a subordinate out-and-out disagreed with you or told you that something couldn't be done? Did you tell this person to do it your way anyway? Did you say it's a tough job market out there and those who don't like it can start looking elsewhere? Each time you fail to listen, get defensive, or belittle an associate, you are shutting the door on quality improvement and on your own learning process.

Too many people in authority avoid confrontation, yet confrontation is an important part of the learning process. If there is no confrontation, you cannot uncover the underlying conflicts that operate in your organization, the very norms and assumptions that inhibit you and others from doing the best possible job for the organization.

Some people wonder who should make the first move toward building more trusting relationships. The answer is to "just do it." If you are trying to cross a mountain stream, you cannot get from one side to the other by straddling it. At some point you have to jump— you have to go for it. Taking that jump requires an enormous leap of faith. The journey of continuous improvement is a long and sometimes painful one. You have to trust your people. Start today.

## Involve others, and stay involved

What, exactly, does the phrase "employee involvement" mean? Frequently, managers view involvement as passive. For example, I often hear people say, "We need employee involvement" or "They just are not involved." These comments imply that "involvement" is limited to the execution of strategy, not the planning of that strategy. They also suggest that these managers see the lack of involvement as something outside the domain of their influence.

*Involve* is intended to mean total active participation in all aspects of a decision that touches a person's area of expertise and responsibility. Do you involve your subordinates in the decision-making process? Do you involve them in the design phase of plans and projects? Or do you simply tell them what to do, shout them down if they disagree with you, attempt to make them feel inept, and then say, "Our people just are not involved enough."

To truly involve others in a decision-making process, you must be willing to share your power. This is difficult for many managers who have been used to a more autocratic management culture. Often there is a powerful refusal to transfer real power from a minority of managers to a majority of employees, due to a belief in the power of elites. But organizations can be crippled when management is unable to relinquish any real power. Sgt. Couper of Madison, Wisconsin, describes the benefit of getting over this awkwardness.

> *We had to buy some new squad cars. I used to be the one who decided what type of cars to buy. Now it no longer made sense to me. Why should I tell the employees what kind of car they*

*could drive? They are the ones who use the cars, not me. As it turns out, the employees were wondering the same thing. So I told them that they could form a team and make the decision themselves. I only gave them two conditions. One, they had to stay within budget, and two, they had to canvass all of the employees. I told them that if they did those two things, I would rubber stamp their decision. And I did. Well, they did a better job than we ever did. They went out and got more data and did more testing and came to a higher quality decision than the managers. Why? Because they had their hearts in it. It was very important to them.*

Getting employees involved in decisions that affect them is what universal participation is about. When you value your employees, it is a natural next step to seek their opinions.

While it is easy to practice employee involvement when you get the answers that you expected, it is more challenging when you do not get the answer that you initially had in mind. This is the litmus test for whether you are practicing authentic participative management. You can tell your people that you are practicing employee involvement, but until the philosophy finds its roots in you, it is just a fantasy. And people can see through the illusion. As others have noted, too many leaders approach employee involvement in a way that is reminiscent of the man in the joke who wanted to catch a clever mouse. Lacking cheese, he placed a picture of a piece of cheese in his mousetrap. What did he catch? A picture of a mouse. Many managers substitute speeches, slogans, or memoranda for behavior. You may fool yourself, and you may think that you fooled your employees. But they can see through the glitz when it comes to sharing power in the decision-making process. In successful organizations universal participation is more than a management fantasy. It is an emotional commitment. In the end, employees judge the commitment of their leaders not by what they say, but face to face in the heat of the moment.

When was the last time an employee out-and-out disagreed with you? What did you do? What did you do the last time an employee confronted you with your own behavior? Did you listen and revise your approach or did you belittle him or her? What did

---

### Listen and talk

Too many managers are unaware of how frequently they interrupt their employees. Often at the end of group meetings I recommend a listen and talk exchange. People pair off, and for the first five minutes one individual talks about his or her impressions of the accomplishments of the meeting. The other individual listens without interrupting, not as a passive listener, but actively listening by encouraging the other silently. Some people find it hard to keep talking for the full five minutes, but those are the ground rules. Others find that the five minutes go by quickly. At the end of the five minutes they switch. The individual who listened the first time now speaks, and vice versa. Many managers need a lot of practice on the listening part.

---

you do the last time an employee told you that something couldn't be done? Did you say that may be what they think, but they are just going to have to do it anyway? If you did, you have slammed the door on quality improvement. You have slammed the door on your own learning process.

Many managers, when confronted with feedback they don't want, understand, or expect, automatically go on the offensive. They didn't hear what they wanted to hear—"Oh, sure, we can deliver that service in two days, boss"—and somehow decide that these people are not committed. If these people were truly committed, they would meet my deadline; they would do it the way I asked for it. The result? They dismiss the employee's concerns and go ahead and make the decision as they had originally envisioned. When problems arise later, a careful investigation frequently reveals that someone, whether it be a technical person or another manager, understood the issue months before, but because of the underlying culture and situational dynamics, was powerless to intercede.

When you seek others' opinions you will get just that: other opinions. Your technical people may see the problem in terms of technological issues. Your management people may view the problem in terms of relationships between people and departments. A division manager may see the problem as related to the organization's ability to remain flexible and adaptive. Depending on the nature of the problem, the opinions that you solicit may be wildly different and, you can bet, controversial to someone. But they are all valuable and must be accommodated.

How do you know when you have it right? You know that you have authentic employee participation when you are able to accept challenge and not believe that challenge reflects lack of commitment. You bring others into the decision-making process not only when it suits you (usually because they are agreeing with you) but even when their answers don't suit you. Intelligent people need an environment in which they can express doubts and concerns about the leader's decisions. This should not be interpreted as lack of commitment to the business or the method selected. Rather, it should be understood as valuable expertise offered on decisions. A questioning mind is an alive mind. You cannot keep valuable, intelligent people at arm's length.

Some people, frustrated upon finding it difficult to give up control and yet wanting to support their people, extricate themselves from the group decision-making process. I recently worked with a senior vice president of marketing who was so thoroughly incapable of listening and sharing power that he dominated every meeting with his subordinates. His people were demoralized. In attempting to foster employee participation, he and his subordinates decided that he shouldn't come to any of their meetings. While his people immediately started to hold effective meetings, unfortunately for all, the gap between manager and subordinates widened. The tragedy of this decision was that he and they lost the opportunity to learn how to work together.

This is an example of "either I make the decision or I give up control and leave it to others" thinking. It says that I must control the process or abdicate; there can be no sharing of responsibility. But the opposite of dominating a meeting is not being silent or being absent. Involving others does not preclude involving yourself. Universal participation means, instead, learning how to interact and stay involved in a way that helps everyone learn and feel valued. After all, new knowledge does not emanate from the manager or the subordinate but from the "between" in the relationship between manager and subordinate.[2] People cannot build new knowledge all by themselves. The productivity of employee involvement correlates positively with each one's level of active participation, mutual trust, openness, and authenticity in the encounter.

In summary, employee involvement means that you actively involve others in the decision-making process and stay involved on an as-needed basis. It means that you are open to changing your point of view as a result of information exchange. You become an active, listening, adaptive, contributing participant.

## Improve your interpersonal skills

Involving others will require a host of new interpersonal skills. When you involve others in a decision, it means that you work closely with them. Your interpersonal skills have a profound effect on the quality of the interaction.

At the individual level, the hallmark of strong interpersonal skills is the ability to

- be an active listener, ask clarifying questions, and try not to defend a position you have already taken
- accept confrontation without questioning the commitment of the confronting individual
- deliver unpleasant news in a non-threatening way
- differentiate between inquiry—exploring an issue while reserving judgment on the outcome—and advocacy—pushing or selling of one's own position
- stay engaged in dialogue even when you do not get the answer you had hoped for, sticking it out until there is an outcome that both parties can take credit for designing, and change your position as a result of the information you receive

Whether it is listening skills, delivery skills, or inquiry skills, the need for effective communication has never been more important. Getting it right the first time saves you the possibility of future confusion, wasted energy, and needless offense.

A work team characterized by strong interpersonal skills will not get dragged down by turf wars or petty differences. Because the

## Exercise to develop rapport with others: awareness

Dialogue is the last thing that happens between two people. Much communication takes place before a single word is spoken. Trust, respect, receptivity, and enthusiasm are communicated in many ways, including body language. Here is an exercise called "mirroring" which helps build awareness of others and improves nonverbal communication between individuals in work groups as well as in interaction with the customer. By concentrating on the other individual, you become more attentive to his or her behaviors and feelings as expressed in the most simple way: body language.

This exercise works best in groups of three. One member, "Subject," goes out of the room. This person is told to think up a brief story to tell the other two when he or she returns. While Subject is away, the remaining two are assigned roles: "Mirror" and "Mismatch." They can also be called "sympathetic" and "oppositional." Mirror is going to mirror the physical motions of Subject when he or she returns to tell the story. If Subject crosses his or her legs, so does Mirror. If Subject sits on his or her hands, so does Mirror, and so on. In addition, Mirror will maintain eye contact when Subject initiates it.

In contrast, Mismatch will do everything opposite. If Subject crosses his or her arms, then Mismatch will not do so. If Subject leans forward, then Mismatch will lean another direction. Mismatch will casually avoid eye contact when Subject initiates it.

Subject is now asked to reenter the room, sit down with the other two members of their group, and tell the story. When he or she has completed the story, they are asked to say with which person they felt more comfortable. Nine out of ten times, Subject picks the person who was mirroring them.

Paying attention to others is important in building rapport. But keep your intentions honest. The purpose is not to manipulate others but to increase your attentiveness to their comfort level in an authentic and caring way.

team is able to clarify key issues and consider everyone's input, it will reach decisions faster, and its meetings will be shorter. Everyone's ideas are given a hearing, not just those with the most rank, seniority, or volume. Persons are not rejected or accepted. Instead, *ideas* are rejected or accepted. Most decisions are reached by consensus. This means that everyone who will be affected by the outcome has a chance to express individual views. And lastly, people refrain from judging a situation until they have all the data. People use facts about business results and customer satisfaction, not personal dominance, as the criteria for judging decisions.

Today, many managers lack adequate interpersonal skills. In particular, many of them consciously or unconsciously dominate meetings. One exercise I do with executive teams as well as shop floor work groups is to have one member of the group monitor how much time each person speaks during a meeting. At the end of the session, we display a "talk time" bar chart for all to see. In dysfunctional groups, there are usually one or two very high bars on the chart and a lot of bars down near the zero line. In a well-functioning group, there is a greater uniformity in the height of all the bars. A picture is worth a thousand words!

Most people intuitively understand the value of strong interpersonal skills and are increasingly aware of the need for effective group management skills for team problem solving. But many senior managers forget that there are also important communication skills needed at the *organizational* level. People have a need to know. Bad feelings can build if employees have been told that there are "quality" meetings taking place among top managers but are not told exactly what is happening and in what time frame they can expect to see some changes, as well as the nature of those changes. Managing expectations is just as important in organizations as it is in personal relationships. Manage the grapevine before it conjures up its own interpretation of events.

In soliciting quality information, it is critical to continually acquire new and improved communication skills. If you offend an individual while delivering information or requesting justification for actions taken, then you run the risk that that individual will never again come forward with valuable information. The information may never come, it may come too late, or it may come in a distorted fashion. And that is not the fault of the individual withholding the information. It is the responsibility of the manager to create an environment where it is safe to communicate authentic feelings, information, and concerns. When faced with information gaps, start by examining your own management methods.

## PARTNERSHIP FOR CUSTOMER FOCUS: TAPPING EMPLOYEE INTELLIGENCE

Getting the most out of employees is critical to the success of your organization. But does getting the most out of your employees mean working them harder? No. Instead, it means working smarter you and they together.

Unfortunately, many managers coming from the traditional school of boss/subordinate relations are ill-equipped to access this valuable resource. Learning how to tap this knowledge requires new skills on the part of managers. What are these skills? They revolve around three important employee involvement channels.

- one-on-one encounters
- group decision-making
- suggestion systems

### Abolish "colonial" management

Unfortunately, many service organizations do not respect their employees, at least those employees who have the most customer contact and are closest to the source of the problems. Why? Employees with the most customer contact, like service representatives, bank tellers, administrative assistants, and attendants, tend to be at the bottom of the organization, "too low-level to bother with." Top management rarely asks these boundary agents for their opinions and consistently "forgets" to solicit their input in job design, the development of service standards, or the identification of improvement opportunities.

Organizations like these practice a "colonial" model of management.[3] Much like a colonizing nation that believes its culture is so superior that it should be exported to those needing "civilizing," organizations with colonial management styles feature top managers who likewise view themselves as superior to their "low-level" employees. These managers believe employees are unwilling or unable to improve knowledge, skills, and quality of performance. The employees, in turn, are programmed to expect to be directed by a management "expert" and to know that should they attempt the "difficult" task of acquiring management decision-making skills, they probably will fail. Should an employee ever make it to the management level, he or she is expected to maintain the traditions and attitudes of other top managers, especially in regard to restrictions imposed on other employees.

Managers who practice colonial-style management are easy to spot. They are the ones who, failing to hear the voice of their employees, devote countless hours to developing elegant strategies, complex policies, and a host of procedures and protocols. Many like to be the center of attention and work hard to minimize communication among the others in the system. Ready to use coercion at the slightest intimation of divergence from their view of the situation, they manage by fear. They assume that employees are expendable. Parasitical in nature, these individuals suck nutrients from employees and other parts of the organization to further their own parochial objectives. At best, such managers get compliance. At worst, they get resistance. They never get commitment.

In the case of the colonial style of management, the management system becomes a powerful and secret tool of top managers, incomprehensible to the average employee. But for whom is the management system designed? If the management system is to contribute to the democraticization of knowledge and decision-making capability, then we must ensure that the management system is transparent to all stakeholders.

## Develop and support your employees

There is an alternative to the colonial style of management. It provides for extended participation of others, with policies more often emerging out of interaction between the manager and the employees. It provides for the care and feeding of the self-esteem of employees in an authentic way. (Remember G. K. Chesterton's

## Effective information exchange

Some managers need assistance in learning how to manage in a consensual way, not an authoritarian way. They need guidance on how to achieve a mutually agreeable outcome. If you are one of these managers, the following steps may help you. Too often, managers want to jump to the "doing" stage (step 5) without first establishing a mutual understanding about the outcome. These are the managers who must rework their plan later because they failed to take steps to determine feasibility and ensure commitment.

1. Start with a blank slate. In other words, assume that no shared information exists.

2. Next, exchange information on your needs as well as those of the other party. Ask questions. Be as specific as possible. How much? What do you mean by that? When?

3. After sharing information, establish a mutual understanding. Ask questions to confirm your understanding. You must wait until everyone can agree. Agreement usually comes about through disclosure and consideration of everyone's internal regulators.

4. When you achieve mutual understanding, determine the next steps and make commitments for action.

5. Following commitments for action, concentrate on the follow-through.

6. Obtain feedback on progress, and celebrate.

warning: "Sentiment is jam on your bread. Sentimentality is jam all over your face.") Rather, it provides self-esteem in a substantive way that results in higher quality decisions, more creative solutions, and higher commitment to the chosen path.

How can managers involve their employees in a way that taps the creative potential of the collective whole? By employing a "partnering" management model. This way of managing operates on the assumption that, since employees are capable of acquiring and mastering many complex rule systems like multiple languages, or banking and finance in their personal affairs, they are capable of acquiring an organizational knowledge base far greater than traditionally assumed or utilized.

In contrast to the colonial model of management, where the boss is the customer, in the partnering management culture the employees are treated like customers. Managers exist to serve and be partners with their subordinates, encouraging teamwork and promoting group effectiveness. They teach, coach, remove obstacles, and help individuals develop. If they define work processes and boundaries, they do so as guides, leaving small employee teams free to figure out the best way to get the job done within the defined boundaries.

The colonial style and the partnering style illustrate the contrast between knowledge exchange and knowledge transfer. In the colonial style of management, the manager suffers from the illusion that he or she already knows what is good for others. The emphasis is on making decisions and telling people how these decisions will be implemented. In the partnering style of management, manager and employees together add value to their collective knowledge bases.

"Partnering" managers assume that others are willing to improve their own performance. They not only expect them to initiate the improvement process, but they also expect them to challenge the processes and the management system itself to support continuous improvement. They ask questions like "What do you need from me that you are not getting now that will help you do your job better?" and "What are you getting from me now that you do not want?"

The employees, in turn, expect to learn from their managers, people who, while expert in their domain, know that they themselves have a lot to learn. Everyone, no matter what their level, expects that working together will be pleasant, albeit demanding. And employees in high-performing service organizations also know that, once they become expert themselves, they must, in turn, teach and coach the next round of employees.

What are the benefits of the partnering model? In contrast to the negative consequences of the colonial management style, they include better information, higher-quality decisions, increased responsiveness to customer concerns, higher commitment, and improved employee morale. Remember, morale *can* be measured; employee retention and customer satisfaction go up when employees are enthusiastically engaged in making a shared vision a reality.

Moving from the colonial method to the partnering style is not easy. Chip Caldwell of West Paces Ferry Hospital describes the difficult role reversal process in his own organization early in its transition to a total quality management culture.

> *We spent months at my level with the people who report to me struggling with the question, "What do you expect of us?" One of my key managers was assigned the role of continually and publicly asking that question in our senior management meetings. And I spent months in answering, "Jim, what I expect of the management team is to tell me what you need." This was a visible sign of the old way/new way kind of thinking. For months, we went back and forth in sort of a taffy pull. I kept saying, "What do you need to advance quality improvement? What do you need as a division manager? What do your department managers need to make these quality indicators better? What resources need to be assigned?" And they said to me, "What do you expect from us in quality improvement?" I am the boss, and they were not used to me saying "tell me what you need." It is difficult to describe how that feels. To me this was and still is one of the most critical factors in the cultural transformation to a total quality improvement environment.*

## Group decision-making teams: your invisible resource

Wise leaders know that they cannot accomplish companywide quality improvement on their own. Instead, they involve people at all levels of the organization in the never-ending effort to continuously meet and exceed their customers' needs and expectations. Not surprisingly, high-performing service organizations know that one of the best ways to mobilize collective intelligence is teamwork. They know that a properly established team can reap enormous benefits, not the least of which is the strong sense of partnership which comes when people are given the opportunity to work with others on issues of common concern. Some other benefits of group decision making include the following.

• **Increased intelligence.** Each of us has imperfect awareness. We are like windows in old buildings with bubbles, dirty spots, and wavy areas. There are areas of organizational experience in which we see clearly, and others in which we are unclear or confused. Coming together as a group provides a rich collection of perspectives and experiences with which to solve complex problems. A team has access to diverse people and information, so its members can make higher quality decisions.

• **Unity of purpose.** Teams can help people better understand and focus on the issues at hand. Most important, teamwork helps people with different backgrounds and perspectives focus on the common goal of pleasing the customer.

• **Skill building.** Participating on a problem-solving team can help build a range of skills, such as a person's ability to communicate, coordinate, cooperate, and solve problems.

• **Ownership.** Teams also provide the stimulus for people to take responsibility for their own actions. Group activities are the informal structures that represent an alternative to the formal organizational structure. Informal activities are typically linked to a compelling vision of the future.

Although there are various types of teams, such as standing committees, ad hoc cross-functional committees, process teams, and task teams, what counts is that the committee divide the work into manageable tasks, appoint members to teams, provide each team with a clear mission statement, and monitor its progress. Whether or not an employee is selected to be on a team is determined by the extent to which he or she "touches" the problem. The most effective teams contain all of the viewpoints that affect the service or product from cradle to grave. Because they are interfunctional, they bring all of the resources of the organization to bear. Effective teams also have a common vision in which each team member has a specific role. Team members share power. So focused are they on the team's vision that no one team member tries to outdo or overpower another. "We are in this together" is their motto.

Of course, where there are teams, there are meetings. One of the scariest aspects of employee involvement for managers inexperienced in participative management is wondering how to control employee behavior during group meetings. No one wants to experiment with truly participative meetings if there is a high risk of failure and the subsequent possibility of losing face, particularly in a culture which has traditionally embraced control.

If you take the teamwork approach, you have to learn how to run an effective meeting. Too many meetings are characterized by a fuzzy focus, rambling discussions, poor time management, unequal participation, conflicts, and an absence of closure. Some managers, in the interest of time and focus, try to control employee behavior only to unwittingly squelch true involvement.

Team problem solving does not need to get out of control. There are techniques to help people run effective meetings, brainstorm, and solve problems. One that is particularly useful is called the nominal group technique. Originally developed in the health care industry in the 1960s, this brainstorming technique capitalizes on the strengths of group thinking while minimizing its difficulties. This disciplined management tool can help transform "garbage can decision making" into a clean decision-making process in which participants focus on the issues, not on the people proposing them, and reach consensus on important choices. The technique is highly structured and easy to use, and provides documentation of ideas with assigned priorities for action (see Appendix C).

Group efforts are essential for effective problem solving. Since most problems are cross-functional and affect multiple levels in the hierarchy, it is essential to get the right people with access to the data affecting the situation. They are the ones who, in concert, can get at the root cause of the problem, generate creative solutions, and affect the implementation of any future changes.

## Suggestion systems

Little things can sometimes get in the way of doing a good job. Some things directly affect the ability of people to deliver superior products and services to their customers. Others have an indirect impact. A broken vending machine, an outdated copy machine, or an excessively loud paging system, can affect the quality of your product or service. Who knows what silent resentments and opportunities for improvement are fleeing the minds of individuals as they hurdle yet another "minor" inconvenience? Remember, the way you treat your employees affects how they treat your customers.

When the opportunity for improvement is local, people can fix the problem or enhance the product or service on their own. The problem is that, in many cases, the observation of the opportunity for improvement occurs outside the functional domain of the problem's source. While an individual may recognize an opportunity for improvement, he or she may be unable to accomplish change given his or her location in the hierarchy.

A suggestion system can provide people with the opportunity to make known their ideas for improvement. It is only as good, however, as the effectiveness of the action on the part of the organization. Kenjiro Yamada, the managing director of the Japan Human Relations Association, recommends that you initially encourage as many individuals as possible to submit suggestions for improvement.[4] Then, over time, emphasize employee education so that the quality of suggestions improves, and, eventually, build in a means to assess the economic impact of the suggestions.

In striving to make as much quality progress as quickly as possible, many people rush to implement a suggestion system, only to find that they are quickly buried in suggestions. As soon as you ask for suggestions, they will come, and in great numbers. You cannot possibly overestimate the number of pent up frustrations and ideas for improvement that individuals hoard privately.

If you wish to implement a suggestion system, take the time to do it right. Be sure to have a system in place for handling the suggestions. People will stop giving their opinions and ideas if you fail to respond, take too long to respond, or exhibit any behavior that indicates a lack of real interest in what they have to say. While you work out the details of managing an organizationwide suggestion system, you can begin locally. Ask people to make suggestions that fall within the control of their own work group. Let your organization practice managing suggestions at the local level and then move up to a companywide system.

## SUMMARY

In summary, your success is only as good as the knowledge you have. Collective intelligence is better than individual intelligence. No one knows every aspect of every process, not even you. In today's competitive environment, human resources has moved from being a discrete set of issues to a core competency for the organization. Support your people and they will support your customer. Involve them in critical decision-making processes, and the outcomes will be of higher quality and have higher levels of employee commitment.

| From | To |
| --- | --- |
| employees as expense | employees as assets |
| adversarial relations | partnerships |
| control | sharing power |
| individual contribution | team player |
| being managed | managing self |

## Notes

1. Bhote, *Next Operation*, 3.

2. Ludmila W. Hoffman, *Old Scapes, New Maps: A Training Program for Psychotherapy Supervisors* (Cambridge, Mass.: Milusik Press, 1990), 16.

3. J. Hilton, "Skill, Education, and Social Value: Some Thoughts on the Metonomy of Skill and Skill Transfer," *Knowledge, Skill and Artificial Intelligence*, ed. Bo Goranzon and Ingela Josefson, (London: Springer-Verlag, 1988), 98.

4. Imai, *Kaizen*, 113.

— ✧ —

*If there are no problems, there can be no solutions.*

—Masaaki Imai

— ✧ —

*Facts often kill a good argument.*

—Brian L. Joiner

— ✧ —

*Success is never final.*

—J. W. Marriott, Sr.

— ✧ —

# A Physical Workout:
## The Need for Continuous Improvement

**D**o you know what happens when you put a frog in a pot of boiling water? It hops out immediately. What happens when you put a frog in warm water and gradually increase the heat until the water is boiling? The frog boils to death. Like many organizations, frogs are great at crisis management, but they fail miserably when it comes to figuring out that their environment is slowly changing—until it's too late.[1]

Some organizations are impervious to change. Over the years, they have built up elaborate protective systems to shield themselves from external interference and internal challenges. Their top managers are maintenance oriented, have little interest in challenging the status quo, and, like frogs, limit their changes and reactions to obvious life-threatening crises. Impervious organizations are very focused. Unfortunately, they focus their energies mostly inward, which only perpetuates the status quo and impedes growing or changing with the times.

As the property and casualty insurance industry in the United States painfully learned, refusing to change can have dire consequences. All through the 1980s, the insurance industry refused to manage the complex issues behind its rising costs, choosing instead to pass increased costs on to its customers. When consumers complained, the industry launched massive campaigns to "educate the customer" on the complexity of its products and services. Such a strategic stance worked well when the environment was stable and consumers had low expectations. By the late 1980s, however, consumers no longer bought the "pass through" argument and took matters into their own hands. Instead of pacifying its customers, the industry unwittingly provoked them further. In 1989, consumers in California passed a landmark public referendum, Proposition 103, which rolled back auto insurance rates, imposed ceilings on current and future auto insurance rates, and made it illegal for any auto insurance company to leave the state. At the time, the country's insurance industry was outraged. Today, realizing that their cries have fallen on deaf ears, an increasing number of insurers are working to regain customer confidence.

Are the California auto insurers the only ones to be caught by surprise? Certainly not. Many service organizations have merged or vanished in recent years. While the market signals were there, they chose to ignore them.

Changing customer expectations, technological advances, and changing alliances create an external environment with a life of its own. You can adapt to that changing environment at your own will or remain silent—until the environment forces you to change, or kills you. As the California auto insurers discovered, impervious institutions *can* change. Unfortunately, they usually change as a means of last resort, by which time the change process is extremely painful. Those institutions which out and out refuse to change on their own initiative experience nothing short of death by torture; their demise may take a while, but the market eventually will control their destiny.

## Adaptive organizations survive, barely

There is another type of organization trying to make it out there. More adaptive in nature, these organizations are skilled at changing. Unfortunately, they know only one kind of change, and it is reactive, not proactive, in nature. A bank changes its hours to accommodate shifting customer patterns, a hospital reduces its pharmacy cycle time to stay competitive, an insurance company introduces a new customer service training program to improve employee telephone manners, a fast-food chain changes the color of its uniforms to "get with the times." While these one-time events may appear to be responsive to customer concerns, they do not, by themselves, create competitive advantage in the long run.

What happens when you fail to take the lead in innovation? You are doomed to management after the fact, and this limits strategic flexibility. In the late 1970s, Merrill Lynch created a new product, the cash management account, that earned high interest while functioning as a checking account. Consumers nationwide began demanding similar services from their financial institutions, many of whom jumped onto the bandwagon. While these organizations adapted quickly to an immediate competitive threat, their response lacked creativity and was limited to meeting current requirements and expectations.

Most people naturally gravitate toward local or incremental changes, if only because these are the easiest and most comfortable changes to make. We all want to believe that our lives are essentially stable, and that all it takes to improve things is to tweak something here or there and our organization will miraculously change. But add-ons and tweaks do not create lasting change. When you concentrate all of your efforts on blending in with the environment and merely staying alive, you can never hope to gain and sustain a competitive edge. More proactive organizations will always be ahead of you. While managers in adaptive organizations may know how to make changes and always look busy, their actions lack creativity and their hearts lack the courage that their organizations need to beat the market.

## Take action: the continually learning way

So what can you do if you do not want to be at the whim of crises and competitive catch-up? You can take responsibility for making changes in advance of pressure from outsiders. You can take the initiative to change yourself, whereby you end up changing the operating environment to which others must then respond. In action-adaptive organizations, innovation and change are, refreshingly, part of the culture. Action-adaptive organizations are usually exciting places to work—there is little gridlock. Their people see the world in new ways long before circumstances force them to. If they occasionally adapt to local environments, they do so proactively and with a sense of vision.

Action-adaptive organizations excel at predicting and creating change. The result? They consistently beat the market. Their strategy? They strive to improve their products and processes at all times. Organizations with cultures that foster continuous improvement believe that, no matter how successful they are, they can always be better. They strive toward 100 percent perfection with a sense of urgency and a firm belief that lesser expectations are unacceptable. Specifically, the hallmarks of an action-adaptive organizations include the following.

- They are proactive in making changes.

- All employees, from the clean-up crew to top management, work hard to improve every aspect of the business every day. Continuous improvement is a natural extension of how they approach their jobs.

- They believe that errors are not inevitable. Many organizations believe that errors are a part of life so they establish "acceptable quality levels" or go so far as to define acceptable failure rates per project. In contrast, action-adaptive organizations strive for zero defects. "Zero defects," you might say, "that's impossible!" Not so. There are some areas of life in which most people expect zero defects. If certain suppliers or service providers were only 99.9 percent accurate, the following errors would occur.

    —There would be at least 20,000 drug prescriptions incorrectly filled each year.

    —More than 15,000 newborn babies would be accidentally dropped by doctors or nurses each year.

—Your drinking water would be unsafe for almost one hour each month.

—You would lose your electricity, water, and heat for over eight hours each year.

—Surgeons would perform nearly 500 incorrect operations per week.

—The post office would lose nearly 2000 articles of mail per hour. [2]

Action-adaptive organizations aim for zero defects. They change before change finds them. They take the lead—they are agents of change rather than victims of circumstance. They systematically learn from mistakes, continuously reduce costs, and, most importantly, continuously increase customer satisfaction and delight.

---

### A calendar that speaks quality

Review your calendar from the past two weeks. Estimate how much time you spent in the following three categories. (The three combined should total 100 percent.)

- Routine work (answering phone messages, traveling, and so on)
  _____ %

- Firefighting (dealing with unhappy customers, working to resolve internal delivery problems)
  _____ %

- Improving processes (improving a budget forecast system, streamlining a delivery process, taking the initiative to contact customers even though there are no immediate complaints)
  _____ %

What does your distribution of time say about your commitment to proactive, prevention-oriented continuous improvement? Are you just talking about quality, or are you working to achieve it? Let your calendar do the talking.

---

## "WINNING IS A MATTER OF INCHES"

Given today's rapidly changing business environment, you have no choice but to keep improving. Standing still in today's competitive environment means going backward. You cannot just improve things once or even twice. Instead, you must constantly seek new and better ways of doing what you have always been doing. As action-adaptive organizations know, quality improvement means continuous improvement.

When many people aim for quality improvement, they often initially think of breakthroughs. While breakthroughs are exciting, they tend to be few and far between. From the discovery of electricity to the invention of NutraSweet®*, breakthroughs tend to be technologically oriented and often require an intense infusion of capital, time, and effort. Wonderful discoveries are yet to happen, and in chapter 9 we will explore how individuals can collaborate to achieve strategic breakthroughs. But organizations cannot depend solely on strategic breakthroughs to create quality improvement.

How else can you make significant improvements in customer satisfaction, profits, and waste reduction? By making sure everyone in your organization works to uncover and implement improvements in the many little things that define "business as usual." Tom Peters, author of the best-selling *In Search of Excellence*, wisely noted that "winning is a matter of inches." Incremental improvements, in contrast to breakthroughs, come as tiny steps. Each step may seem insignificant, but taken together, they move the organization forward consistently and continuously, and over time can provide you with a significant competitive advantage. Unlike breakthroughs, small improvements typically are not capital-intensive. Instead, they are time-intensive. They demand that every employee within the organization devote full attention to spotting and acting upon opportunities for improvement. As Sgt. Couper of Madison, Wisconsin, says:

> *Quality is not about doing one thing 99 percent better, it is about doing 1000 things 1 percent better. I think there are a lot of people out there looking for the cookbook—just give me the recipe and I will put all the parts together and make it work. It's not a cookbook. There are 1001 things that can be*

---

*NutraSweet® is a registered trademark of The NutraSweet Company.

*improved, and they are different for every organization. As the recipe might say, if you are at a different altitude, the oven needs to be set at a different temperature. Likewise, each organization may have to handle things differently. That's the challenge that is so overwhelming to people that they can't understand it or don't want to spend the time or energy on it.*

As we saw in the previous chapter on universal participation, the collective intelligence of others is just waiting to be tapped and harnessed for sustained improvement. Enhance competitive advantage by focusing on incremental improvements.

## BUILDING A CONTINUOUS IMPROVEMENT CULTURE: THE FIVE BASICS OF CONTINUOUS IMPROVEMENT

Taking the continuous improvement approach may require that you push yourself harder than you ever thought possible. While it is often easy to find early successes, a focus on continuous improvement means that over time challenges become increasingly difficult. Aleta Holub, vice president of quality at First Bank of Chicago, learned that whereas initial improvements can sometimes be a matter of increased efficiency, real "stretching" often doesn't start until you get down to the wire.

*When you first start examining yourself and your organization, you discover all sorts of errors that are systemic. Many of these errors are part of the corporate folklore—things that you have been doing forever—and are relatively easy to fix. We found that we could go from a 500 error frequency rate to a 100 rate rather easily. But to get that 100 down to 50 and that 50 down to 25 and that 25 down to 12—now that was a major challenge.*

If you work for a competitor of an action-adaptive organization, then hearing about managers like Holub emphasizing continuous improvement might be unsettling. How can you possibly compete with an organization that has motivated, focused people like these? People and organizations that strive to continuously improve, and that constantly push themselves to new limits, are indeed a tough act to follow.

How can you create an action-adaptive culture in your organization? You can start by building the concept of continuous improvement into every job function from CEO to front-line employee. Specifically, organizations which live and breathe continuous improvement adhere to the following four principles (see Figure 4.1).

- They hold continuous improvement attitudes and beliefs.
- They agree to manage by data, not emotion.
- They think like detectives, systematically going after the root cause of a problem rather than its symptom.
- They manage the problem-solving *context*.

Let's look at each of these principles in greater depth.

## Build the right attitudes and beliefs into your culture—open inquiry

"Where there are no problems, there is no potential for improvement," says Masaaki Imai, author of the renowned book on Japanese quality practices, *Kaizen*.[3] Organizations which practice continuous improvement have managers who know how to listen, are not threatened by dissenting opinions, and encourage people to identify problems. In many companies, individuals who reveal problems are quietly classified as troublemakers. The challenge is to foster an environment that encourages the revelation of problems and even treats them as treasures.

Many traditional organizational cultures restrict recognition and rewards to the firefighters, heroes who singlehandedly save the organization from itself. In contrast, organizations with continuous improvement cultures reward and recognize people who methodically, quietly, and patiently take the time to do it right the first time. They emphasize personal mastery and believe that the skills of all people can always be strengthened and improved. Every person within the organization accepts his or her contribution to

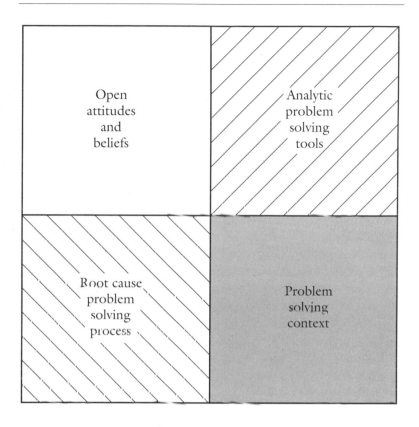

**Figure 4.1:** Problem solving

any problem. And they take the time to systematically identify the root cause of their problems to prevent themselves from getting caught in the trap of solving them over and over again.

Since one of the starting points for continuous improvement involves the speedy identification and acceptance of problems, it is important to create an organizational culture in which admitting failure is okay. In most organizations, it is the workers who spot problems. If the culture discourages the discovery of problems, then management will never learn about mundane problems until they add up to a demoralized workforce, a grumbling customer base, or a knock-down, drag-out problem that demands full management attention. Every time an employee is too frightened to tell his or her boss about a problem, a golden opportunity for increasing your competitive edge disappears. "That doesn't sound like me," you might be thinking. "My people know that they should come forward with problems when they occur." But what about the political problems? What about the "undiscussable" issues? Every organization has them. If you can create a culture in which the identification and exposure of problems is risk-free, psychologically okay, and even encouraged, then you are well on your way to becoming a total quality company.

## Manage by fact, not emotion

The more information you have about your performance, the better decisions you can make about how you need to change that performance. Managers who operate on intuition rather than fact leave themselves wide open to missing the mark. Yet few individuals and organizations take the time to collect and analyze data relevant to the problem at hand. As many Japanese firms understand, taking the time upfront to collect the facts pays off. For many Western managers reared on short-term planning, however, taking the time to thoroughly research an issue may at first seem unnatural. As Michael Pugh of Park View Episcopal Medical Center observes,

> *A major obstacle that I find is the lack of discipline to get all the data first, before making a decision. Some people are too impatient, while others have a mistaken belief that, because of their position, they should have all of the answers. When people are unwilling to take the time up front to get all of the facts and to talk to all of the stakeholders, they end up spending an inordinate amount of time later on retracing their steps, managing by crisis, and being ineffective and inefficient. The failure to use a disciplined analytical process is a great hindrance to quality improvement.*

As Pugh understands, measurement is key to achieving total quality. You can use measurements to show progress, indicate where to focus future improvements, provide specific feedback, generate data for making decisions, reward and recognize the efforts of others, suggest corrective action, and so on.

When managing by facts, there are two rules to follow: use appropriate measurements and practice visual management.

**1. Locate appropriate data.** Organizations which have problems with their customers usually do not have appropriate systems in place to get information relevant to the problem at hand. They may have management information systems and reams of statistics on everything from their sales volume to the percentage of shipments delivered on time. But these measurements, while interesting, are lagging indicators of performance. They are results oriented and lead to management after the fact. They also offer few insights into potential solutions and perpetuate the *gulfs of evaluation and execution*.

The *gulf of evaluation* is the difference between actual performance and our knowledge of results. The gulf is small when the management system provides information about performance in a form that is easy to get and easy to interpret, and which matches the way employees and customers think about the system. The gulf is large when there is little information on the effects of actions taken. When cause and effect are loosely coupled, management by superstition reigns supreme. And steering by trial and error can be disastrous.

The *gulf of execution* is the difference between our intentions and what actually gets implemented. Sometimes we are able to implement exactly what we had planned. Other times what is actually implemented differs substantially from what we had intended. Being able to understand what part of our error is due to poor implementation of otherwise good strategies versus what part is due to poor strategies is critical to unraveling the ultimate mysteries of performance.

Good performance measures can help bridge the difficulty in going from the general to the specific. When measures are adequate, accurate, easily accessible, understandable, and relevant, they are most informative. Who should select the performance measures to be used? Not surprisingly, the very people who know the customer requirements and do the work. Process standards, designed in full or in part by operating personnel, tend to be more appropriate and at the same time "tougher" than those developed by management. Involving employees in the design of measurement, reward, and performance management systems

- puts the responsibility for improvement in the hands of those capable of affecting performance
- leverages more intimate knowledge of the processes involved
- builds group commitment to the desired outcomes
- increases organizational learning
- links results with improvement capabilities

Starting today, be a role model when it comes to using data. Insist that you and the people around you make decisions only after carefully researching the subject at hand, and not just when it's convenient. Be willing to end a meeting, even if the pressure is on for a fast decision, if there are no data to support a position. If people know that you will not tolerate decision-making by instinct, they will gather facts before approaching you on any subject.

When people begin to manage using data, they frequently discover that the data they really need are unavailable. This is an eye-opening experience. While many organizations have plenty of data, there is very little *useful* data. A simple way to start managing with data in all of your decision-making processes is to practice what the Japanese call "the three actuals." If you are having a hard time clarifying a problem,

1. go to the actual place of the problem
2. see the actual problem
3. talk directly to those involved, and get the actual facts

**2. Practice visual management.** Often, "speaking" with data is not enough. People need to see the data.

Because important trends and relationships are frequently hidden in the data, it is important to learn how to effectively display the data that you collect. Some common analytic tools include histograms, ordered bar charts, and line graphs (see Figure 4.2). What

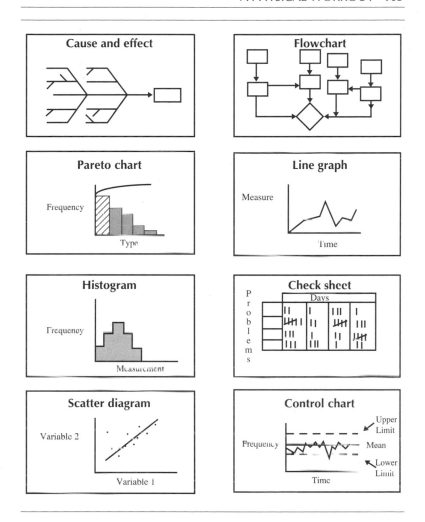

**Figure 4.2:** Eight analytic tools for quality control

is important is that a handful of these display formats be adopted as a form of companywide language.

Beyond displaying the data for personal use in the problem-solving process, important benefits come from publicly displaying performance data. Visual tracking can support your performance and process measures. Chip Caldwell describes the success of story-boards to track progress in his organization.

*Every department has a storyboard that hangs prominently in the department. If you were to come here to visit, if we were to walk down the hall to neurosurgery and the orthopedic floor, hanging there for you to see at the elevator is a storyboard, which is a 4-by-4-foot board. It shows how they are performing on their measures of quality relative to their department. It also shows a PDCA cycle, and you can see where they are in the cycle. In the bottom corner, there is a little road map where the department will be six months from now. So we have carried vision from my level all the way down to the department level.*

The bottom line is to measure, measure, measure. Remember, what you cannot measure, you cannot manage. Taking the mystery out of performance problems starts with data that you can see and share.

## Ferret out the root cause of each problem

In a traditional organization characterized by a rigid vertical management system, people frequently try to solve problems based on what they control locally. They base their judgments on instinct or locally available data. And, because they are typically pressed for time, they tend to try to solve their problems quickly. While a "quick fix" approach to problem solving may make us look successful in the short term, we often end up generating additional problems for others to fix down the road. This causes other departments to spend a great deal of energy protecting themselves from problems that others generate in this way.

Many organizational problems cannot be solved locally. Often, what you view as a problem is merely the symptom of a deeper, more complex problem involving many departments and individuals. Following the trail of a problem may take you on a magical mystery tour through many aspects of the organization until you reach the true source(s) or what we call the root cause(s) of the problem. In most cases, cause and effect are not close in time or space. Isolated attempts at local solutions can never solve complex or cross-functional problems.

Effective problem solving can only take place when you solve your problem at the root cause level. How can you identify the root cause(s) of a problem? One simple method is called the "five whys." Next time you face a problem, simply ask "why?" five times. Your first question, "Why do we have this problem?" usually elicits a "cover your tail" answer. The answer to the next "why" may just begin to get at the true nature of the problem. By the time you get to the fifth "why," you are usually down to the bedrock of the problem. If you use this technique properly, the root cause(s) will lie beyond your local territory or control. You may find yourself dealing with soft issues like reward and recognition systems, communication processes, or safety issues.

Another technique used to identify root causes of problems is a diagram called variously the fishbone diagram, the Ishikawa diagram, or the cause and effect diagram (see Figure 4.2).[4] It is called the Ishikawa diagram because it was developed by Kaoru Ishikawa of Japan; a fishbone diagram because of its appearance; and a cause and effect diagram because of its function. The main purpose of the technique is to identify and map the major contributing factors to the development of a problem. Factors such as inadequate measurements, lack of training, last-minute information, and supplier problems all can be neatly outlined in small groupings. The major advantage? Cause and effect diagrams help to organize thinking, emphasize the presence of multiple contributing factors, and suggest additional individuals to include in the problem solving process.

## Use teamwork to traverse local boundaries

Solving problems at the root cause level, not merely at the symptom level, requires cross-functional problem solving, and that means teamwork! Despite good intentions, most significant organizational problems cannot be solved on a local basis. As such, root cause problem solving strikes right at the heart of management omnipotence.

**Be a team player.** While many managers have spent years learning how to "solve" problems by themselves, few possess the people skills they need to launch joint inquiries and team problem solving. They are genuinely uncomfortable when working with employees from other parts of the organization.

How you handle the *group process* can make or break your organization's ability to solve problems and identify opportunities for improvement. Every problem is different, but usually every problem requires a certain amount of sensitivity to be solved properly. A variety of "hot" issues typically surrounds problems, and the issues are often why problems become problems in the first place. Turf issues, varying experience bases, different levels in the hierarchy, and sometimes different geographical representation can make problem solving a challenge for those involved. How team members give and receive feedback, accept differing opinions, and establish criteria of what is "good" determine a group's effectiveness. The problem solving process demands that everyone be attentive to people issues. This means that you must first and foremost create a safe environment in which people can share sensitive data, express disagreements, and brainstorm creative ideas.

When you manage the group process well, you and others will want to continue the problem solving process. People will feel valued, your meetings will run more effectively, and everyone will have more fun. How can you monitor your team effectiveness? Take time out to check on the group process aspects of teamwork. Never believe that you are so expert on teamwork that you do not have to check on how you all are doing. Don't wait until someone feels uncomfortable.

**Manage the organizational context.** Beyond creating good internal team dynamics, successful problem solving teams understand how teams work within the larger organization. *Boundary management,* the process by which group members manage interactions with other parts of the wider organizational environment, frequently goes unaddressed in many quality team initiatives. Yet this is a critical success factor. Research conducted by Deborah Gladstein Ancona and David Caldwell at the Massachusetts Institute of Technology on 45 product development teams shows that high-performing product development teams generally carry out more external activity than do low-performing teams. Specifically, Ancona and Caldwell found that members of high-performing teams assume at least four distinct roles: ambassador, task coordinator, scout, and scanner.[5]

Ambassadors buffer and protect the team, help build organizational support and enthusiasm, and work to fit the team's efforts into the overall corporate strategy. Task coordinators initiate communication laterally, rather than vertically, into the organization. Their main objective is to coordinate team efforts with other initiatives underway in the organization. Scouts collect information and resources critical to the completion of the project and, scanners look to the future informing group members about events that might occur which could have relevance to the group.

Upon completing their study, Ancona and Caldwell reported their findings to the product development teams that had participated. There were mixed reactions:

> *When we interviewed members of top performing teams, they frequently reported that communication with top management was necessary in order to obtain resources, to prepare their proposals in line with corporate thinking, and to build a reputation for excellent work that could be spread throughout the firm. Yet, when the pivotal role of ambassadorial activity was reported, members were often surprised and disappointed in the role that "politics" played in successful products. Team members also found it somewhat paradoxical that large amounts of time spent working outside the group can facilitate the group's efforts. Leaders were not at all surprised by this finding and saw their ambassadorial activity as a critical mechanism to move the product across functional lines and through the organization.*

The more you can understand about how teams work, the more efficient and effective a team you can build. Focusing on the concerns of those outside the boundaries of the team who are affected by the team's progress is just as important as internal team dynamics if the team is to successfully implement its recommendations.

## HOW TO CREATE A CONTINUOUS IMPROVEMENT CULTURE

As action-adaptive organizations know, the quest for total quality never ends. Rather, it becomes a business fundamental. The concept of total quality is synonymous with the concept of continuous improvement. So how do you build an environment of collaborative inquiry? How can you ensure that this time next year you will be working to solve new problems and not the same ones that challenge you today? There are two ways:

- Build a continuous improvement process using W. Edwards Deming's Plan-Do-Study-Act cycle.[6]

- Rigorously manage the problem solving process using the SUPERSOLVER technique.

## The PDSA cycle: management means Plan-Do-Study-Act

When left to your own devices, how do you usually go about solving problems? Many people just jump into the "doing" without ever taking the time to plan. They see one and only one right solution. They believe that exploring the vagaries of a problem is a waste of precious time. Other people spend a lot of time planning for change, but they never get around to the doing. Still others proceed with a plan but fail to check their results. They "mandate and move on"; they have no idea whether their plans were implemented as intended or if their initiatives brought them their desired results. Lastly, others take the time to monitor progress, but when they experience disappointing results, they fail to analyze what went wrong. They move straight to designing a new plan without understanding which of their many operating assumptions were faulty.

Whether appropriate solutions never get implemented, faulty operating assumptions are never discovered, or the outcomes of actions are never known, much energy and time are spent on efforts to solve problems with little progress to show for it. Is problem solving such a "fuzzy" process that one cannot hope for better results? No. There is a discipline for solving problems which, when used properly, can build and sustain continuous quality improvement in everything you do. It is called the Plan-Do-Study-Act (PDSA) cycle for continuous improvement (see Figure 4.3). (Some people use a similar cycle, called the PDCA cycle, which refers to Plan-Do-Check-Act.) It can be used to solve problems at the macro level of an organization, such as in implementing a corporate strategy, or at the micro level in daily functions.

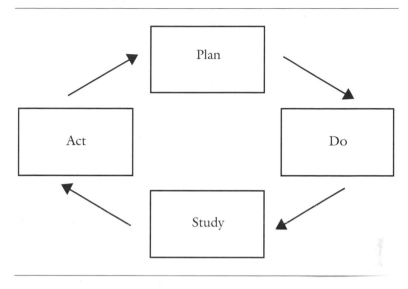

**Figure 4.3:** The PDSA improvement cycle

Developed by W. Edwards Deming, the PDSA cycle, like a conditioning drill, builds capability, the organizational muscle that provides strength through continuous quality improvement. The PDSA cycle contains four distinct problem solving stages.

- **Plan.** Start with an idea for an improvement. Then create a plan to test the idea.

- **Do.** Implement your plan. Carry out your test on a small scale according to the layout specified in the plan.

- **Study.** Check the improvement process to see if it accomplished the desired outcome. Analyze results to uncover incorrect operating assumptions.

- **Act.** Adopt the change. Adjust the approach or abandon it. Should an obvious defect surface, fix it immediately. If the outcome successfully matches your expectations, then standardize the improvement so that it becomes institutionalized.

The PDSA cycle is just that, a cycle. Similar to a diet or a workout regimen, it is a *continuous* practice. Through continuous practice it becomes a way of life. As soon as a process or problem is analyzed and new standards have been established, the PDSA cycle begins again with the planning phase. Plan-Do-Study-Act, Plan-Do-Study-Act, Plan-Do-Study-Act, Plan-Do....

When used properly, the PDSA cycle shows that your job is never over. If you focus on problem solving just once, then you are practicing nothing other than reactive management; you are merely firefighting. And when people remain event-oriented, they miss out on the opportunity to see and control the underlying structural process that caused the event. In contrast, PDSA practitioners constantly look for new ways and new data to support new and improved standards for all products, services and processes. They take the initiative to seek out potential sources of problems and fix them before they become serious concerns. In this way, the PDSA cycle *is* continuous improvement.

*The PDSA cycle is one of the single most powerful tools for continuous improvement.* If this is so, why isn't it being used everywhere? One of the most prevalent reasons is that too many people fail to take the initiative when it comes to learning new techniques. They fall victim to the "they" syndrome, whereby everyone waits for someone else to act first.

Many top managers, when they first discover the PDSA cycle, immediately recognize the value of such an approach to doing business. Unfortunately, they view it as applicable only to people lower in the hierarchy who work on routine tasks. They themselves never get fully trained in the PDSA cycle and never apply it to their own tasks.

Subordinates will not be motivated to apply the cycle if top managers are not using PDSA as the management method of choice. Why should they? If top managers really believed in PDSA, they would be using it, right? Even if individuals were to attempt to use the PDSA cycle regularly, how successful can they be if top managers are using a different management method for running the business? As their solutions to organizational problems percolate up to senior levels, top managers may inadvertently, or perhaps even conspicuously, subvert their successes. Why? Because top managers are not skilled in the use of PDSA themselves. They are still practicing reactive management rather than prevention-oriented management. They will still be looking for the quick fix.

The PDSA cycle can be, and should be, applied by everyone in every function. Any individual who is not using PDSA on every critical function or process is not practicing quality management and cannot expect others to take seriously their commitment to the quality improvement cause. This goes for the CEO as well as each individual on the front line. If you are not using the PDSA cycle, you can blame no one but yourself for a lack of quality improvement in your organization. The PDSA improvement cycle applies to virtually every area, challenge, and problem within your firm. The strategic planning process, hiring and training processes, employee communication process, design and adminis- tration of customer surveys, resolution of customer complaints, and, as we will see in Part II of this book, the process of making your corporate vision and values a living policy, can all benefit from the discipline of the PDSA cycle.

As the old maxim says, "If at first you don't succeed, try, try again." Don't be afraid of the learning process. The problem solving process can easily take six months due to the complexity of the prob- lem and the lack of initially available data. This requires patience. In cultures where heroics have traditionally been rewarded and recog- nized, asking people to spend time improving their processes up front to prevent problems from occurring can be counter-cultural at first. However, moving from a reactive management to a preven- tion-oriented culture is essential for continuous improvement. The PDSA cycle is a tool to guide you through this process.

## Use discipline and innovation

What can "oil" the Deming wheel? Discipline, discipline, disci- pline. Deciding to use the Deming wheel the first time may be easy. But it takes real discipline and commitment to use it repeatedly until it becomes second nature. Michael Pugh, CEO of Parkview Episcopal Medical Center, can attest to that.

> *It is harder to run an organization practicing continuous quality improvement than it is in the traditional manage- ment convention. Initially, it is hard work. It takes a lot of dis- cipline to say "no," to say "I don't know enough about that to make the decision," and to give others authority to make that decision. It is hard work to sit down and plot information over time when you are not used to doing that. I find it takes a tremendous amount of discipline. The disappointments are*

*great because the change comes slowly. We can see our successes. But we also see our failures in a much more clear light than we ever saw before. And that becomes discouraging at times. But when somebody from the outside comes to say "You are really doing some great things," then we realize that we are making remarkable progress after all.*

Having the discipline to systematically plan improvements and follow through with implementation can bring dramatic improvements to every organization. Taking the time to see things as recurring processes rather than as events and using the PDSA cycle together to create a quality improvement engine drives continuous improvement into the very fabric of the business.

A second challenge in using the PDSA cycle for continuous improvement is our discomfort with innovation. While we often wish we could "change things around here," when it comes to the real task of innovation, it is easy to become wedded to the status quo. It is difficult to challenge our own fundamental mindsets. Chip Caldwell of West Paces Ferry Hospital describes the challenge for his organization.

*Innovation is missing in many organizations, including my own. We have become quite good with the left brain/analytical aspects of the problem solving process. We come up with wonderful Pareto charts on major sources of variation. When we get to the next phase of the improvement cycle requiring innovation to reduce that major source of variation, however, we often lock up. We freeze, and there is very little innovation. I believe that people rush through that part of the cycle because it feels uncomfortable. I see people making improvements that they thought of before the team ever started to work together because they are uncomfortable wrestling with "How can I break down my paradigms?"*

As Pugh and Caldwell understand, discipline and innovation are essential to the continuous improvement process. When we apply our creativity to problems that we have taken the time to thoroughly understand up front, we create new possibilities for ourselves and our customers.

## SUPERSOLVER

While the PDSA cycle is critical to continuous quality improvement, some people find it a little vague in application. To assist in the application process, some people have found the following elaboration of the continuous improvement cycle helpful. Called the SUPERSOLVER™, this technique integrates the PDSA cycle with the need to solve problems at the root cause level, manage using facts, and leverage teamwork.[7] While there are other problem solving models out there, most emphasize data analysis and standardization in the problem solving process. Many people, especially in the early stages of learning about how to improve quality, need to be reminded that there are important people issues and organizational structures to be dealt with before they can get on with solving the problem.

| | | |
|---|---|---|
| S | = | Select the issue |
| U | = | Unite as a team |
| P | = | Pick a sponsor |
| E | = | Enlist your supervisor's support |
| R | = | Record the ground rules |
| | | |
| S | = | Search for data |
| O | = | Obtain root cause |
| L | = | List alternate solutions |
| V | = | Venture pilot test |
| E | = | Evaluate results |
| R | = | Reinforce with standards and repeat |

## S = Select the issue

When possible, start with the voice of the customer. Tying your improvement activities to customer needs and expectations is critical to improving market performance. Even if your local work group does not have direct contact with the external customer, take the time to identify how your daily activities affect the customer.

How you state a problem can radically affect which issues you choose to go after first. There are two styles of stating a problem. One is to increase an advantage (like "increase sales"). A drawback of this style is that it can lead prematurely into consideration of what to do (that is, profits are low, so we must increase sales—which is not really doing anything differently). Another is to eliminate weaknesses (reduce number of customer complaints, reduce cycle time in our delivery process). This is often a more useful approach to solving problems. Stating the problem in "negative" terms reinforces the management philosophy that it is okay to be honest about the fact that the organization has problems.

Sometimes problems are clearly defined in our minds and we can describe them easily. Reducing express shipment cost or reducing the waiting time in an emergency room in a hospital are problems that can be quantified easily because we already have a clear idea of what we would consider an improvement. At other times, however, we are not so fortunate in having such a clearly defined problem. The problem we face may initially appear to be more qualitative. These "fuzzy" problems do not lend themselves to easily quantifiable results so that we know whether or not we have made an improvement. Converting the problem statement into something that is actionable and therefore measurable can help in this regard. How can you accomplish this? Usually by asking for specificity. Ultimately, any qualitative issue can be converted into a measurable problem statement.

## U = Unite as a team

Don't try to solve your problems alone. Chances are, your problem is someone else's, too. The best approach is to work as a team. And beware the pitfall of surrounding yourself with only friendly supporters. Many people, when they first begin to problem solve, exclude "difficult" people or the "constant complainers." Yet these are the very people who are critical to your success, if only to provide differing opinions and perspectives. Involving them also means that they share ownership of the outcome, reducing the likelihood that they will overtly or inadvertently sabotage your efforts. In any case, all relevant stakeholders should be represented on your team. After you select your team, appoint a leader, someone to coordinate your team efforts and keep the problem solving process going.

## P = Pick a sponsor

Select an individual higher in the hierarchy who can be useful to you and your team should you need assistance with data collection, getting access to resources, or facilitating internal politics. It is often best to select someone who is not directly above you in the hierarchy. Instead, look for an internal customer who has a vested interest in helping you and your team solve the problem. Select someone in whom you have confidence and keep them informed of your progress. Remember, it helps if you select someone who will directly benefit from your improvement efforts.

## E = Enlist your supervisor's support

Be sure to enlist your immediate supervisor's approval and support before committing to work on a problem solving team. The problem solving process can be time consuming, so be sure that your supervisor understands why you are addressing this particular problem and how the outcome will positively affect his or her function. If you have difficulties reaching agreement with your supervisor, ask your sponsor for assistance.

## R = Record the ground rules

How often will your problem solving team meet? For how long? Will individuals commit to being prompt? How will you handle differences of opinion during meetings? Be sure to establish ground rules for the group right from the start. Issues to consider are when, where, and how often you should meet, and what to expect in terms of meeting attendance, interpersonal behavior, and listening skills. Everyone comes to a meeting or task with different expectations. You can avoid major problems down the road if you take the time today to ask everybody to verbalize their expectations and talk them out until everyone's expectations are in alignment. Getting group issues out on the table up front is one of the most supportive actions you can take toward a good team process. You should also schedule regular "process checks" throughout your meetings to see how you are doing as a group and to improve on your group process skills as time goes on.

## S = Search for data

As we saw earlier in this chapter, individuals often make decisions by gut instinct. It's an easy trap to fall prey to. But to solve a problem effectively, we must first understand it. This means gathering all the relevant facts. And the data that you collect must be organized to be easily understood. In the early stages of any problem solving process, data are often scarce, and it's tempting to want to accelerate the problem solving process by moving right into the action stages. This is where real discipline comes in. The team must discipline itself to take the time to search for data describing the current situation. You may have to look outside the boundaries of your group, asking others to contribute data or to take the time to track a detail in their own workflow. And be sure to use analytic quality tools to collect and analyze the data. Once you have collected your data, use the eight quality tools (fishbone diagram, Pareto chart, histogram, line chart, scatter diagram, control chart, flow chart, and check sheet) to analyze them (see Appendix D). New ways of thinking will emerge when the data have a chance to speak. This step will take more time than you expect but, once you complete it, you will be informed on the complexities of the problem.

## O = Obtain root cause

We spoke earlier in this chapter about the need to go after the root cause rather than merely the symptom of a problem. Most problems are more complex that we initially believe. Taking the time to search for the root cause(s) often leads to some surprising insights. Conducting this part of the problem solving process may feel like going on a magical mystery tour, visiting places, processes, and issues in the organization that you never expected. The five why's and the fishbone diagram can be especially helpful at this step of the problem solving process. You might also want to use some of the systems tools that we will visit in chapter 5. Above all, make sure that you involve others in the problem solving process; the success of this step depends upon your ability to get outside your box on the organizational chart. Work with others to identify any and all root cause(s) of the problem at hand.

## L = List alternate solutions

Don't jump to the conclusion that one particular solution is the only solution. Take the time to identify and consider alternative solutions and counter measures. This is perhaps the most innovative and creative part of the problem solving process. Unlike mathematical problems which often allow for only one answer, problems related to quality improvement have many possible solutions. When overall improvement is the goal, it is important initially to formulate as many ideas as possible. The sheer quantity of ideas inevitably leads to a quality solution. Brainstorm with people both inside and outside of your group. Do not judge the quality of your solutions, even the crazy ones, until you exhaust the brainstorming process. Many ideas will be "rough drafts" that need to be polished. To help you in the brainstorming activity, review the nominal group technique described in chapter 3. Select an approach that is financially feasible, has the best chance of being implemented, and has a high impact on solving the problem. You may have more than one solution, particularly if you identified more than one root cause in the preceding step.

## V = Venture pilot test

Your ideas may be exciting, but don't rush out and implement them full scale today. Running "hog wild" usually courts disappointment and truncates the learning process. Instead, take the time to test-pilot solutions on a small scale before rolling them out organizationwide. As we saw in chapter 2, select key measures of both process and results to track your success. Prepare carefully. Obtain the approval of your supervisors and the cooperation of technical staff and colleagues. Make individual responsibilities clear and establish a daily schedule for the improvement plan. Notify anybody who might be affected by your changes before you begin implementation. Remember, this is a trial period, so take the time to understand and deal with any problems that occur during this time.

## E = Evaluate results

This is where you get to see how well you have done. Is the problem subsiding? Do you see any improvement? What have you learned during the pilot test that may cause you to modify your approach? Are there any assumptions that need to be modified? Check whether your "solution" produced the desired effect. If the results are not satisfactory, it may be necessary to revisit some earlier steps in the process. Do you need to rework the improvement plan?

## R = Reinforce with standards and repeat

Once you have caught hold of a "winner," it is important to retain your gain. By establishing standards, you can prevent rolling backward later on. Gather data until the benefits stabilize. After you can confirm that you achieved your desired effect, communicate the improvement. Unless changes in processes, tools, or procedures are publicized and made familiar to all involved, the very improvements that you worked so hard to accomplish can easily be neglected or replaced with past practices. An improvement is never an improvement until every step, including follow-up, is implemented. This can include revising procedure sheets and training others on the new procedure. Then look for new ways to improve. Remember, your job is not over. Continuous improvement is just that—continuous.


## SUMMARY

Should you find that your problem solving efforts are not moving you toward continuous improvement, step back and make sure that you are treating problem solving as the process it should be, not as a one-time event. Continuous improvement is a management philosophy and a discipline. It is hard work, but when done properly, it creates meaningful learning. Your curiosity will be stretched and your creativity unleashed, and best of all, you get to see your solutions implemented as intended.

Where can you start? You can start today, right in your own office. Continuous improvement can start anywhere. Once you play the continuous improvement game wholeheartedly, you will find yourself in it for keeps. There are two reasons for this. The first is that you need to be in it forever—continually improving is critical to your organization's survival. The second reason is that, once you have fully adapted continuous improvement as a way of life, you will have raised your own and everyone else's expectations and standards. Once you incorporate continuous improvement into your organization's culture, it takes on a life of its own. This moves the organization well beyond survival to becoming a tough and challenging competitor.

| **From** | **To** |
|---|---|
| Solving problems is separate from my job | My job is to solve problems |
| Problem solving is an event | Problem solving is a process |
| Firefighting | Prevention |
| This is my job | My job is to figure out how to do my job better |

## Notes

1. This is a favorite analogy of professionals in the field of systems dynamics.

2. Information supplied by the American Society for Quality Control.

3. Imai, *Kaizen,* 163.

4. Kaoru Ishikawa, *What Is Total Quality Control? The Japanese Way* (Englewood Cliffs, N.J.: Prentice Hall, 1985), 63–64.

5. Deborah Gladstein Ancona and David Caldwell, "Improving the Performance of New Product Teams," *Research Technology Management,* March/April 1990, 25–29.

6. The Deming cycle is described by Imai in *Kaizen,* 60–62.

7. Instructional materials for SUPERSOLVER™ can be obtained by calling 617-721-4235.

*There is nothing more difficult to take in hand, more perilous to conduct, or more uncertain in its success than to take the lead in the introduction of a new order of things. Because the innovator has for enemies all those who have done well under the old conditions and lukewarm defenders in those who may do well under the new.*
—Niccolo Machiavelli

# PART II

# The Process of Becoming

What would happen if you stopped reading this book now—if you finished Part I and never considered Part II? You would not be alone. Like many managers, you may believe that, once you accept customer focus, process improvement, employee involvement, and continuous improvement as critical to the survival of your business, you can stop learning and get on with it. A lot of managers get so excited by what they learn in the initial stages of a consultation or training effort that they stop listening, stop learning, cut things short, and move on to "change things around here." But for all their good intentions, three out of four managers fail; they do not stick around long enough to learn that how you manage the change process is as important as what it is you are trying to change.

Moving from a traditional operating system to one focused on continuous quality improvement cannot be accomplished via trivial change. We need to learn to play a new game with new rules, new skills, new boundaries, new ways of scoring, and new competitors. This means that some things must come apart before new things can come together. You saw many of these changes in Part I: Decisions which used to be made by the voice of the hierarchy are now being directed from the voice of the customer. The traditional "colonial" style of management is being replaced with a more participative one. Organizations are no longer managing quality and cost as tradeoffs. Making the transition to total quality management requires skill in shifting many organizational norms to create a whole new management culture.

The hitch is that you still have a business to run. We have customers to serve and competitors to fend off. In our enthusiasm for change, we cannot afford to wreak havoc on our organization and jeopardize our current successes.

This requires skill in effecting large-scale organizational change. Organizational change is the process by which you transform the existing culture of an organization—that is, its social, motivational, and resource configuration—to another. The challenge is to responsibly transform the organization in a timely fashion with as little disruption as possible.

So how can you become an effective change agent? How can you guarantee that you will create a total quality management organization, rather than merely a partial quality management one? Part II of this book addresses these questions, starting with a look at how organizations and the people in them learn new behaviors and make positive change.

*The art of progress is to preserve order amid change and to preserve change amid order.*

—Alfred North Whitehead

## CHAPTER 5

# Making the Transition:

## Battling the Immune System

Take a moment to write one thing that you would change about yourself or a situation if you could.

Now take three minutes to write how you might start to solve this problem in the next three weeks.

Take a look at your paper. Did you create a list of "action items" or one-time events? Whether it is losing weight, improving an intimate relationship, or reducing work-related stress, we often approach our most perplexing personal problems by creating a list of most important things to do. We assume that, by accomplishing each item on our list, we will eliminate our problem. Unfortunately, this approach to change rarely solves our personal problems. While we are often delighted with our initial results and believe that more of the same will bring continuous improvement, we do not achieve lasting change. We gain weight after our initial losses. We find certain unpleasant dynamics repeating themselves in our relationships. Our levels of stress are actually higher rather than lower.

We failed. So what do most of us do? We start over. We alter the items on our list, deleting some and adding others, to reflect our newly expanded understanding of the nature of our problem as well as to include corrective actions for unforeseen and unintended consequences of our initial actions. (When we decided to work fewer hours to reduce our work-related stress, we didn't anticipate that the work we didn't finish on Tuesday night would still be there on Wednesday morning, and that our boss might be a little upset, so we add "reassuring the boss" to our list, as well as working through our lunch hour so that we can make sure that Wednesday's issues are finished by the end of the day on Wednesday, and…) Then we start all over again with the first item on our list.

## "To do" lists do not work

Even though "to do" lists don't eliminate recurring problems in our personal lives, we still insist on using this approach in business. We just love those lists! Let one CEO describe his experience.

*Once my executive team and I got educated on the basics of total quality management, we sat down and made a list of all the things that we felt we needed to change. Our priorities included basic training on statistical methods and the problem solving process for all employees companywide, more customer contact through focus groups and customer surveys, and getting some cross-functional problem solving teams going in our organization. We also initiated an employee suggestion system.*

*After we got going, we discovered a lot of things that we didn't know when we started. So we had to add a number of things to our original list of action items. We discovered that our performance management system had to be revised. We are still working on that. And we had a near disaster with our employee suggestion system. We never expected the number of suggestions that our employees submitted—so many that we had to discontinue the program for a while; we had a difficult time responding to them all in a timely fashion. We are still dealing with some employee morale issues concerning that. And of course, like a number of other companies that I know, we have the classic problem of middle management resistance to change. We call it our "thermal layer of resistance."*

*Even though we are spending an increasing amount of management time and money on quality related issues—we have spent over a half-million dollars so far on various training programs, and my team and I spend about half of our time on quality related issues—we don't seem to be making any significant progress. Our successes are short-lived, the quality tools and root cause problem solving processes are unevenly practiced throughout our organization, and we are not always satisfying our customers. This "quality thing" has become so complicated that we can't seem to sort out our priorities; it seems like everything is important. I feel like we, at the executive level, are running the "Red Queen's race," putting more and more time, money, and energy into this whole quality thing at a faster and faster rate, yet we are still essentially in the same place.*

If continuous customer-focused quality improvement is the competitive strategy of choice (after all, it is just common sense), how is it that this CEO and others like him are experiencing so much difficulty in transforming their organizations? How is it that management teams like this one experience so many unpleasant surprises in the course of their journey? Is there a better approach to transformation that allows people to feel they are more in control of the change process? The answer is a resounding yes. Learning to see interrelationships, not just one-time events, is a starting point.

Lists can beget lists. At the beginning of a change process, many people feel in control; they limit their focus to a few issues "just to get things rolling." Once the changes begin to *interact* with other aspects of our life, however, the change process has a way of becoming more complicated. The action items on our list, intended to promote change, call into play other dynamic forces in our life that affect our ability to implement fundamental change. The result? Our list of action items grows and our problem remains systemic.

You can avoid the list trap by taking the time to understand that your organization is a dynamically interdependent *system* of interacting people, activities, ideas, resources, emotions, and time. Success comes to those who understand the various elements that define their organization, the interrelationships among these elements, and the way the organization is linked with the larger system of relationships that constitutes its environment. When you approach the change process as a systems thinker rather than as a "tinkerer," you have a far greater chance of making your change efforts stick. Let's examine some key characteristics of organizational systems and see if you are already a systems thinker.

## YOUR ORGANIZATION IS A COMPLEX, DYNAMICALLY EVOLVING SYSTEM

When you take action, do you consider the impact of your choices on others upstream and downstream of your activity? Many people tend to focus only on what is right in front of them in time and space. As we saw in chapter 3, however, at a minimum level of complexity, every service organization is a giant network of interconnected processes and tasks. Making local changes in a vacuum can have disastrous consequences down the road on other parts of the organization and on overall performance.

You will increase your probability of success when you view your organization as a complex system of vertical and horizontal processes. Systems thinkers see *beyond the immediate*. They have peripheral vision. They focus not only on their local performance within the system but also on the overall performance of the system. Taking the time to work with others in the organization to design and coordinate change efforts, they aim to prevent their solution from becoming someone else's problem down the road.

### The "hard" stuff is easy, it's the "soft" stuff that's hard: treat the human issues

If systems thinking was only about analyzing and understanding complex, fairly tangible business processes, then we could have stopped with the process mapping tools in chapter 2. But business

### Change management myths

What happens when people fail to see the relationships between key behavioral variables? They fall victim to certain change management myths. These include the following.

- **"I can make isolated changes."** They fail to appreciate that their actions have far-reaching consequences on the rest of the business.

- **"I can ignore the 'fuzzy' issues; they will care of themselves."** They fail to see the psychological and social consequences of their actions.

- **"The problem begins and ends with others."** They fail to see their own contribution to the problem.

- **"The harder I push, the better results I will see."** They fail to recognize natural limiting factors to growth.

- **"I can solve the problem by fixing all the parts."** They fail to see the interconnections among all parts of the management system.

- **"I will see the results of my changes in the near term. Things that happened a long time ago (like layoffs or rude management behavior) have been forgotten."** They fail to understand that there is often a delay between cause and effect.

- **"When faced with contradiction, I must choose one side and defend my position."** They fail to understand that reality is made up of and's, not or's.

processes alone do not define our organization. Management systems are corrections of many interacting processes fraught with many intangibles and other important dynamics.[1]

While the structural and operational issues, or the "hard stuff," are important to the change process, logic alone does not explain living things or organizational behavior. Numerous psychological and social issues—the "soft stuff"—such as employee morale, trust, workplace conditions, and the need for recognition can make or break overall performance. Unfortunately, too many people ignore these "fuzzy" issues when they design their change strategies. For them, only the rational aspects of the business such as performance metrics, task assignments, or reporting structures link cause and effect. These same people later bemoan employee resistance to change and complain that their elegant strategies for change are not being implemented as intended.

In contrast to a purely mechanistic approach, systems thinkers plan interventions that affect structural systems as well as *human* processes. They give the human factors equal weight with the numbers, and they consider the psychological and social implications of their actions before they proceed with implementation. What is the prevailing mood of those who work in your organization? What are their concerns, however irrational they may at first appear to you? Do you address the human issues in your strategy for change? Systems thinkers understand that, while more difficult to map, understand, and manage than the hard aspects of the business, the soft issues often make the difference between mediocre performance and outstanding accomplishment.

## Actions invite reactions: manage the loop

When you made your notes in the earlier exercise on personal change, did you consider how the effects of your actions might *feed back* to influence the factors driving your change process? A key implicit assumption behind a list of action items is that causality runs one way, from cause to effect. Each of the factors we list is assumed to cause whatever overall effect we are trying to achieve (see Figure 5.1). Laundry list thinking assumes that there is a clear distinction between cause and effect. The basic assumption is that "this set of causes produces this particular effect." But this is not how the real world works.

Nothing is ever influenced in only one direction. In the real world, it is difficult to distinguish cause and effect because every action is both cause *and* effect. When customers scream loudly enough, we respond to their complaints. When we respond positively to their concerns, they experience the benefit of our attention. In this way, our organization and the customer are linked in a *circle of causality*. The organization influences the customer, and

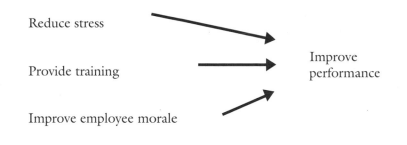

Reduce stress

Provide training

Improve employee morale

Improve
performance

**Figure 5.1:** A list of action items assumes one-way causality

the customer, likewise, influences the organization. The same is true for relationships between subordinates and supervisors, regulatory agencies and industry groups, husbands and wives, parents and children, owners and pets. We experience circles of causality every day.

In addition to important relationships between people who touch and are touched by the change process, circular relationships also exist between key behavioral variables (see Figure 5.2). For example, an employee suggestion system may influence the number of new ideas being implemented, and the number of new ideas being implemented may feed back to influence the degree to which the suggestion system is used. (As new ideas are implemented, more employees are likely to take advantage of the suggestion system. On the other hand, if few ideas are implemented, they may withhold additional suggestions.) In this way, the suggestion system and the number of new ideas being implemented are linked in a circular causal relationship.

But why choose to view things this way? How can seeing circular phenomena help you be more successful in implementing your change strategy? The answer is simple. Seeing circular relationships is key to anticipating the negative and positive consequences of your change tactics. Non-systems thinkers have a static view of the world. They believe that "A causes B, and that's that!" They design their change strategies based on "hit and run" tactics, and then they move on to new challenges. While they may believe they solved their problems in the short term, these people often create conditions for

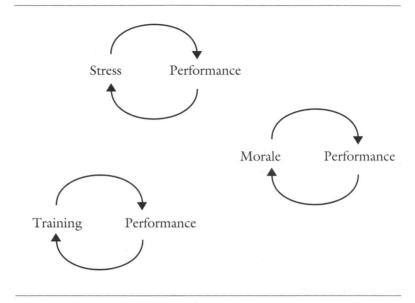

**Figure 5.2:** Cause and effect are often circular

unpleasant surprises later on. They are ignorant of how the effects of their changes may feed back to them over time.

In contrast, systems thinkers take the time to anticipate how the positive and negative effects of their changes may feed back to them in aggregation and over time. They understand that causal relationships are circular, that "A causes B, and then B feeds back to cause A" in an ongoing dynamic process of change. So they design their change strategies to reflect their understanding of these relationships, anticipate obstacles, and identify opportunities to accelerate the change process.

## Manage the relationship, not just the event

When we fail to see the loop or the circle of causality, we often see things as events, or in the case of change management, unpleasant surprises. A supervisor says, "I reprimanded my employees because they didn't use the problem solving skills and quality tools that we trained them in." The employee team says, "We didn't have time to use the tools because our supervisor wanted results *now!*"

The supervisor sees the resistance of employees to use quality tools as an "event." He or she may react with anger and negative feedback. The subordinates see their supervisor's demand for instant results as an "event." They may react with anger and negative feelings. Is the failure to use the problem solving tools an action or a reaction? Is the event a cause or an effect? The problem is often one of semantics.

The events that a supervisor or employee team experience are only part of a much bigger picture. The supervisor and employee team are linked in a relationship with certain structural properties that, if not attended to, will cause these unpleasant events to recur again and again. Unless the fundamental dynamics behind the events are addressed, the problem—in this case, people not using the quality tools—can become systemic.

What are some other examples of event thinking? "The boss's secretary went ballistic." "The customer threw a fit." "The employee up and quit." Event thinking also shows up in strategies for change. "Let's put everyone through a three-day training course; that ought to do it," or "Issue a memo, that ought to make it clear to everyone," or "Let's run a customer survey; that ought to tell us how we are doing." These are all examples of how people design their change strategies around one-time events.

Are your strategies designed around one-time events? Non-systems thinkers approach the change process by creating a series of stand-alone events and reacting to unpleasant surprises. They spend their time providing event explanations—who did what to whom—rather than examining the structural aspects of the relationships over time that created the event and others like it. What happens when non-systems thinkers focus only on one-time events? At best, they can make the most of a bad situation; they can only react. They become victims of circumstances, not creators of their own future.

In contrast, systems thinkers manage interrelationships, not just events, and they manage these relationships in a proactive way. They know that it is a waste of time to blame each other, their customers, various special interest groups, or their suppliers. Instead of seeing behavior as arising from a series of shocks delivered by outside forces beyond their control, systems thinkers take the time to stand back and observe in a neutral way the structural dynamics that produced the situation. They elicit feedback from their customers and employees to learn what issues to address *before* they become big problems. They also examine their own role in perpetuating any undesirable situations. Systems thinkers take responsibility for aspects of circular relationships that they can control and, in this way, they create their future.

## Loops are connected to loops: manage the interrelationships

Look back, again, at your notes on personal change. Are there any arrows connecting individual contributing factors to one another? Many people assume that the causal factors that they put on their laundry list exert influence on the problem independent of one another. But consider the diagram in Figure 5.3 of what really is going on behind the scenes when you tinker with performance variables in your organization.

Figure 5.3 shows a collection of *interdependent* rather than independent factors. When looking at such a picture, it's easy to see why isolating "a most important factor" or selecting a "top priority" from our list of action items is simply not possible. It's impossible because it is not so much the factors but the relationships among the factors that are so important.[2] What is the benefit of seeing the interrelationships operating in your organization? The answer is simple. We can better understand how making changes in one factor can set in motion a specific dynamic over time. And increased understanding improves the quality of our change strategies.

Casual loops describe human behavior and change in human systems. As words combine into sentences, sentences into paragraphs, and paragraphs into stories, causal loops are linked in a unique way that defines the dynamics of our living organization. In the grand scheme of things, everything is connected to everything else. One rude comment by a senior manager to lower level employees may reverberate around the system for years. Likewise, one positive experience—a moment of appreciation in a single customer encounter—may last for years.

When you design your change strategies, do you consider the interrelationships among key performance variables or do you simply

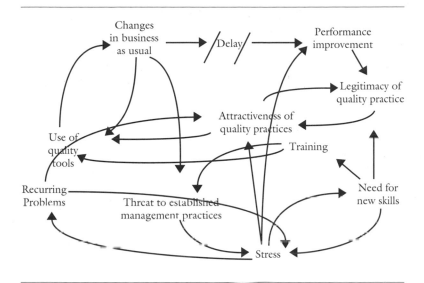

**Figure 5.3:** Success factors are interrelated

press a handful of independent change buttons? Do you focus on problem symptoms or do you address the structural dynamics of the situation? Non-systems thinkers design their change strategies around a set of "independent" tactical approaches. They assume that the causes of their problems are related in obvious ways to problem symptoms. So they end up solving problems at the *symptom* level. The result? They generally experience short-term relief. Performance over time declines, however, as the structural dynamics that created the problem in the first place remain unaltered.

Solving problems the systems thinking way forces us to examine the dynamics at work behind the scenes. Systems thinkers know that they and others are linked in circular relationships where events are frequently the symptoms of far more insidious circular phenomena operating behind the scenes, ones that they contribute to, however inadvertently. So they work to change the system—the collection of loops that tells the story. By paying attention to the system dynamics, they better anticipate the consequences of their actions over time. They move from feeling like victims to feeling in control of the change process.

## Human systems are inherently paradoxical

Some aspects of organizational behavior are not only interrelated, they can appear to be outright contradictory. For example, we often want to be both "a part" of the group and at the same time "apart" from the group. We like to feel that we can have unilateral control, but at the same time we want others to like our decisions, which implies consensus. We seek to maximize our private interests, but at the same time understand that, in aggregation and over time, everyone doing the same thing might bring collective ruin. While we may want our organizations to change with the times, we may resist any new expectations of us that threaten our sense of stability. In these ways, and many others, organizations and the people in them are inherently paradoxical.

Non-systems thinkers see the paradoxical nature of the management process as a limitation. They see the management challenge as the burden of choosing one thing or the other, and then they work hard to defend their position. We have all heard "You can only have it one way. Which way do you want it?" This attitude is often coupled with an "I'm right, you're wrong" mentality. Such a win/lose orientation allows little room for innovation and creativity.

In contrast, systems thinkers are "dilemma busters."[3] They see mere dualities as "being" and the management of paradox as "becoming."[4] They know that the real world is made up of and's, not just or's, so they address the multiple conflicting yet valid goals and objectives operating in their organization. Systems thinkers understand that the inevitable rubbing of behavioral contradictions against each other generates and energizes organizational change,[5] so they creatively approach their problems with a win/win attitude. They create flexibility through structure, centralize power through decentralization, make innovation part of regular day-to-day operations, and provide individual incentives for collective efforts. They improve quality and reduce cost simultaneously, integrate disparate individual motives with inspiring shared visions, and know when to break the rules to preserve the rules. The ingenuity of systems thinking goes beyond the contradictions to create new convictions.

Systems thinking is "general management" in the true sense of the word.[6] It focuses on the structure of interrelationships—

relationships among marketing, manufacturing, R&D, and finance—as well as relationships among employee morale, new ideas, performance appraisal systems, and turnover, all the relationships that determine organizational success. Individuals who are successful at creating positive change recognize that a commitment to continuous improvement is a commitment to thinking both systemically and dynamically.

## THE BENEFITS OF BEING A SYSTEMS THINKER

Working with systems thinkers is fun. They have the ability to view their organizations as a buzzing, interacting, paradoxical whole. They can see the interconnectedness of all things, they can see the many subsystems that work to resist change, and they understand that the consequences of today's actions, while essential to the change process, may not be visible or felt for a long time. Much like those in a helicopter during an ocean rescue mission, systems thinkers can see the whole operation. Their perspective on change enables them to better anticipate and control the change process. In this way they possess certain advantages over their sea-level coast guard partners.

- An aerial view helps to understand the magnitude and nature of the problem
- An extended horizon helps to minimize unpleasant surprises and identify opportunities from afar.
- The panoramic view enhances design and coordination of local efforts to reduce redundant and/or conflicting activities.
- A vertical view helps to track overall performance.

Systems thinkers add value by providing the big picture perspective. Rather than having their whole management team on a rubber life raft bobbing about in the rough seas and unable to see beyond the next wave, making survival a matter of skillful reaction, systems thinkers provide leadership and progressive direction from above.

## TRADITIONAL MANAGEMENT TOOLS DO NOT HELP

When you look back at the bowl of spaghetti in Figure 5.3, is there any hope for creating meaningful change? Can we ever hope to get our hands around this whole mess? Replacing dysfunctional management practices with more competitive ones is not easy. Some people have likened the process of understanding organizational behavior to trying to solve a differential equation with 1700 variables. Others have said it is like nailing gelatin to the wall or trying to fix a commercial passenger plane in midflight. As Russell Ackoff suggests in "The Second Industrial Revolution," the answer lies in thinking about a good old-fashioned mess.

> *I am going to call this thing a mess. Then we say that what reality consists of are messes, not problems.*
>
> *Now what is a problem? Let's take a mess for a moment, which is what you're confronted with in the morning when you come to work, and let's analyze it. Remember what analysis is—to take something apart. So if we take a mess and start to break it up into its components, what do we find that those parts are? The parts are problems. Therefore, a problem is an abstraction obtained by analyzing a mess.*
>
> *Then what is a mess? That's the significant thing—a mess is a system of problems. Now, the significance of this is that the traditional way of managing is to take a mess and break it up into problems and solve each problem separately, with the assumption that the mess is solved if we solve each part of it.*
>
> *But remember...if you break a system into parts and make every part behave as effectively as possible, the whole will not behave as effectively as possible. Therefore, the solution to a mess does not consist of the sum of the solutions to the problems that make it up. And that is absolutely fundamental.[7]*

As Ackoff understands, we must approach the change process in a holistic way, a synthesis of the diverse aspects of our organizational experience. To fix a mess, we must focus on each of the parts as well as how all the parts are related to each other.

The problem is that we have been raised in a society (and have therefore created a corresponding management culture) which thrives on management reductionism and analysis. This is not to say that problem solving based on analysis is not useful. Quite the reverse—problem solving through analysis is essential if an organization is to make operational improvements. Reduction in number of billing errors, shortening of cycle time between receiving orders and delivery of products or services, and increasing customer satisfaction all can be accomplished steadily and with remarkable efficiency by using analytic tools such as Pareto charts, scatter diagrams, line charts, histograms, and process flow diagrams, as we saw in chapter 4. While great at solving local problems, however, these analytic tools tend to leave us high and dry when we try to strategically manage a complex environment.[8]

• **Most existing management tools are linear.** As we have seen, the organization and its stakeholders are inextricably linked in circular relationships. Yet most analytic tools, such as process maps, line graphs, and even fishbone diagrams, show one way causality; they are typically characterized by straight lines running from left to right. They do not give you a handle on important circular feedback relationships.

• **Most existing management tools are static.** While fishbone diagrams, traditional process mapping tools, and the "five whys" initially can help us penetrate the bedrock of organizational interconnectedness, these tools are static in nature; they treat the structural relationships as if they were snapshots in time. They are unable to link the structural aspects of the system to the dynamic patterns of behavior that operate over time.

• **Most existing management tools are designed to analyze events that occur close to one another in time and space.** Tools such as statistical process control charts and check sheets enable one to monitor the performance of a process by capturing data over short intervals. They are not helpful when events have consequences in the distant future.

• **Most existing management tools emphasize analysis of the parts.** Most problem solving methods and analytic tools can help you examine the procedural or mechanical aspects of a system, but they cannot help you see how all the parts of the system, both hard and soft, fit and work together.

• **Most existing management tools focus on quantifiable variables.** With the exception of the fishbone diagram and the "five whys" that we saw in chapter 4, most quality tools do not accomodate non-quantifiable information about important behavioral and cultural elements that affect the change process. To truly understand our organization as a system, we need to view it as the synthesis of disparate variables, including the many intangibles that have traditionally been considered too "soft" to measure.

An analytical approach to problem solving is essential to the continuous improvement of many individual aspects of our organization. However, it is not sufficient for inquiring into problems of a systemic nature. Analytic tools, especially those that are statistically based, are great when we need to see how things are working up close. But when we are talking about a shift in frame of mind and total management configuration, we need a *different* approach. It's like the figure/foreground effect. We cannot afford to get lost in the detail. We need tools that help us see big-picture interactions. To implement large-scale organizational change, we must acquire additional skills.

## THE LANGUAGE OF COMPLEX SYSTEMS: THREE BUILDING BLOCKS OF DYNAMIC BEHAVIOR

While behavioral problems do not lend themselves to the neatness and apparent accuracy of analytic tools, there are some fundamental concepts for understanding the big-picture interactions behind organizational change. These include

- reinforcing feedback loops
- balancing feedback loops
- delays

Understanding these three building blocks of dynamic behavior brings increased clarity and foresight when designing strategies for change.

## Reinforcing feedback loops drive change

Two kinds of circular feedback processes affect the ability of humans and organizations to make significant changes in their behavior. One amplifies change in the direction that it was started. The other controls change. Understanding the difference between these circular feedback processes can improve your probability of success at implementing change.

Some feedback processes are self-reinforcing. They compound; in other words each change adds to the next. A supervisor's sincere thanks for a subordinate's suggestion on how the work team might improve quality can motivate the subordinate to try to come up with an even better suggestion the next time. More recognition leads to more suggestions, and we have the basics of positive reinforcement. In the absence of any limiting factors, over time, a reinforcing feedback process creates exponential growth (see Figure 5.4a).

Why are reinforcing loops so important to the change process? Reinforcing processes generate growth and *change the status quo*. When changes in external conditions threaten our survival, a conventional approach to business becomes too risky; it takes too much time and energy to do it the traditional way. So we must change to survive. Reinforcing feedback processes can accelerate the change process.[9]

Before you applaud reinforcing processes, remember that not all reinforcing feedback processes are desirable. We may like the fact that enthusiasm is contagious and positive recognition inspires more employee suggestions, but the deleterious effects of unhappy customers and the spread of unpleasant rumors are examples of exponential growth that are anything but attractive. The fact that a phenomenon is a reinforcing process is neither good nor bad. It just is.

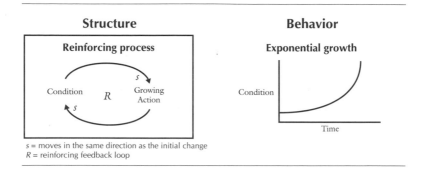

s = moves in the same direction as the initial change
R = reinforcing feedback loop

**Figure 5.4a:** A reinforcing process leads to exponential growth

## Balancing feedback loops limit change

Change sometimes creates secondary side effects that can limit the growth of success. Innovation doesn't fit well with all the other management systems already in place. Reward and recognition systems, annual planning processes, and a hierarchical structure are designed to work together the old way. When you introduce change into a network of systems designed to keep the organization in balance, you contradict implicit operating goals, habits, and norms that others strive to maintain. This can cause someone elsewhere in the organization to put their foot to the brake.

Just as individuals and organizations must change and grow to survive, there is a second and equally important law of survival. To survive, we must be able to *maintain stability* amidst disturbances in our environment. We must be able to balance vital conditions. How do we do this? First, we set *goals*. By setting a goal or a target for every vital condition, we create an operational definition about what it takes to survive. Once a norm is established for each vital condition, we can monitor and maintain the vital conditions. Survival is enhanced when we know where we stand in relation to our goals so that we can respond to deviations and take corrective action.[10] (See Figure 5.4b.)

We call these control mechanisms self-regulating or *balancing* feedback processes. Whether it is stress level, workload, prices, costs, or supplies, certain factors drive and control our ability to change; they determine when "enough is enough." When change

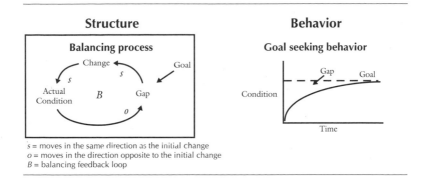

| Structure | Behavior |
| --- | --- |
| **Balancing process** | **Goal seeking behavior** |

s = moves in the same direction as the initial change
o = moves in the direction opposite to the initial change
B = balancing feedback loop

**Figure 5.4b:** A balancing process controls change

is too much, they cause us to push back or feed back in the opposite direction. While many goals and limiting factors are explicit, when it comes to cultural change, the most powerful controlling factors are often the *implicit* norms—for example, the real number of hours people work in contrast to the stated work week.

Before you complain about controlling factors, remember that balancing processes seek to maintain certain conditions. Depending on the situation, they can work for or against you. In the case of unhappy customers, balancing feedback is provided by regulatory agencies and special interest groups. The greater the number of unhappy customers, the more pressure is exerted on industry to satisfy them. The more action that is brought to bear, the fewer unhappy customers. Customers benefit from the balancing processes provided by regulatory agencies and special interest groups.

Balancing feedback is invisible to the non-systems thinker. It is more difficult to see than reinforcing feedback because it often looks like nothing is happening. There is no dramatic growth in sales, employee suggestions, or enthusiasm. As a result, to the non-systems thinker, resistance to change seems to come out of nowhere.

In contrast, systems thinkers are sensitive to the presence of balancing processes. They know that the greatest challenges in the change process are often the limiting factors, especially those implicit or hidden goals that operate beneath the surface awareness of others.[11] They know that balancing processes often work to maintain the status quo and can resist change even when all the participants want change. So they take the time to anticipate and address the limiting factors.

## There are significant time lags: drive out delays

Time adds another dimension to managing change. There is often a delay between what appears to be an immediate benefit and what later proves to be a negative consequence. Likewise, some actions, when diligently pursued, pay off in the long run even though they appear to have little benefit up front. Ex-Congressman T. V. Smith once described the consequence of the "lag between our way of thought and our way of life" by referring to an anonymous poem:

> There was a dachshund once, so long
>
> He hadn't any notion
>
> How long it took to notify
>
> His tail of his emotion;
>
> And so it happened, while his eyes
>
> Were filled with woe and sadness,
>
> His little tail went wagging on
>
> Because of previous gladness.[12]

People often make poor decisions when they are ignorant of the delay between cause and effect; the longer the delay between cause and effect, the harder it is to recognize and identify systemic problems and take appropriate action.

Non-systems thinkers evaluate progress over a relatively short time frame. They assume that they will see the benefits of today's actions in the near future. Likewise, they assume that events that took place several months or years ago, such as layoffs, rude management behavior, or repeated changes in top management, have been forgotten. The results? Non-systems thinkers often take corrective action prematurely only to create "overkill" later on. In other situations, they take too little action too late and lose significant opportunity to make progress.

Systems thinkers understand that there is often a delay between cause and effect. They know that the most critical decisions have systemwide consequences that can stretch over many years or decades. So they design their change strategies to anticipate the negative and positive consequences of their actions over time.

First, they are patient. They do not expect to see results immediately. They typically take a multi-year view. Systems thinkers understand that events such as rude management behavior, layoffs, and failing to respond to employee suggestions, even if they happened several years ago, can limit their ability to get others to take risks today and in the future. They also manage others' expectations to help them realize that it will take time to see the payoff of today's change strategies.

Second, they are sensitive to the amount of pressure that they apply. They know that pushing too fast will only create an unstable system. As with a sluggish shower system, the more aggressive your behavior in turning the faucet, the greater the swings in temperature; the greater the swings, the longer it will take to reach the temperature that you desire. That's one of the "counter-intuitive" lessons of delayed feedback: the more aggressive your behavior, the less likely you are to reach your goal.[13]

Third, they eliminate delays from the system. Systems thinkers know that the appropriateness of their strategies is highly dependent on the delay between cause and effect and their knowledge of these effects. The longer the delay, the more distorted is their view of their market, their work environment, and their internal challenges. Such distortions wreak havoc on their organization, creating disruption, waste, and inefficiency. So systems thinkers take control. They eliminate lengthy feedback processes from their management system to improve the quality and speed with which they receive information critical to their operations.[14]

Do you ever overcompensate for a lag in the system? Do you try to rush the change process? A common management trap that can sabotage your efforts to change is a balancing feedback loop with a delay. Resistance is at work, but there is a delay before it becomes visible. How can you diagnose whether a balancing feedback loop with a delay is at work in your organization? Look for oscillation, a fluctuating behavior. The longer the lag in the system, the greater the amplitude of the oscillations (see Figure 5.4c).

| Structure | Behavior |
|---|---|

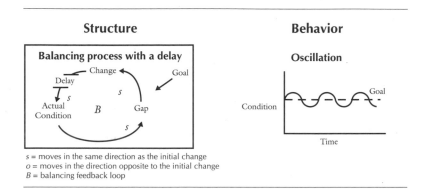

s = moves in the same direction as the initial change
o = moves in the direction opposite to the initial change
B = balancing feedback loop

**Figure 5.4c:** The effects of a delay in feedback

## AVOID COMMON MANAGEMENT TRAPS

Reinforcing feedback processes generate change. Balancing feedback processes can limit change. And time lags distort our knowledge of cause and effect. What do you get when you hook the three phenomena together? A wide variety of behaviors. While all organizations manage similar success factors, such as training, balanced workload, and communication, the success of any particular strategy is determined by the combination of driving forces, limiting factors, and delays unique to that organization.

Although every organization follows a singular path, certain operating principles distinguish organizations which succeed at change from those which fail. These include

1. Start from the top.

2. Go slower rather than faster.

3. Manage the process, not the program.

4. Manage the dynamic structure, not the event.

5. Remove the limiting factors.

6. Stop shifting the burden.

7. Be an agent of change.

Let's examine each of these in more detail.

## Start from the top

Learning new behaviors at the top of the organization is essential if the organization as a whole is to make the transition to a new operating culture. Joe Posk, director of quality at Narragansett Electric Company in Rhode Island, describes the difference between attacking the change process from the trenches and approaching it from the top of the organization.

> *I spent three years working in a large division of our company. We made tremendous progress in a relatively short period. The employees at the lowest level were not only enthusiastic but took on problems that had been systemic, and they actually solved them. The problem was that I was viewed as the "quality leader." Because I was there at the chairman's request, I was sacred ground. But the local leadership, the management in the division, began to contradict the results and recommendations of the employee teams. I believe that they were embarrassed because these employees were solving problems that they had been unable to solve themselves over many years. They felt threatened.*
>
> *Despite their objections, we continued to make outstanding improvements. I later left that division to come to corporate, and within a few years most of the quality improvement efforts we had started had disappeared; there was no senior management support to keep the efforts going. Today, we are concentrating our efforts on the top 100 senior managers of our organization. While our progress seems to be slower than the quick hits we got in the earlier years, our progress is sticking; we are not sliding backward. We have the leadership attention and support.*

You cannot create sustained quality improvement without the support of top management. Getting that support requires patience, if only because people need time to find ways to "reposition" without invalidating themselves.

Changing behavior at the top is not easy. Michael Pugh of Park View Episcopal Medical Center describes the important yet difficult position in which senior managers are placed when making the transition.

*"Walking the talk" is important. It is very hard to do because we are continuously placed in situations where an old way of thinking or an old approach is what somebody wants you to do—whether it be the board, the medical staff, or a department manager. They just want somebody to make the decision. You have to be careful and always be aware of how your actions are playing out in the organization. That is why our senior managers are responsible for championing improvement. I think that the push from the top helps to accelerate the process.*

Implementing customer-focused quality improvement from the top of the organization distinguishes organizations that succeed in managing the transition from those that fail. As Joe Posk, Michael Pugh, and others observe, the commitment of top managers is essential not only to create a continuously improving organization but also to sustain the gains. First, top managers are part of the problem. Rather than blame others, only they can remove the obstacles blocking the progress of others. Second, senior managers need to learn how difficult it is to acquire new skills before they can ask others to do so. Taking the time to absorb and apply new skills at their own level helps to manage their expectations about what is really achievable over time.

As you will see in the next several chapters, the ability of top managers to learn, clarify mission, vision, and values, and demonstrate effective leadership is essential to the change process. While you may get some quick hits by focusing on the "others" in the organization at lower levels in the hierarchy, in the long run, total quality management is only "partial quality management" if it is not implemented and supported from the top.

## Manage the process, not the program

I am always dismayed when I hear top management talk about "our quality program." Why? Because it reveals an event mentality. "Programs" have beginnings and ends; there are program managers or directors; teams and staff may become responsible for outcomes without ever owning the processes in which the problems occur. Sgt. David Couper describes the danger of this.

*When we started to implement continuous quality improvement, we had a t-shirt made up that had the last fifteen programs on it. A lot of them had been good ideas. But why didn't they work? When I asked the employees about this, they said that I had lost interest after three to six months. They said, "We will know that you are serious about quality when you can maintain your focus and attention over six months." Today we have been going four years. There may be a lot of things they don't like about their boss, but there is one thing for certain, he really is focused on quality. He has not backed off this, and we are moving forward. As slow as it may be, imperfectly at times, we are still moving forward.*

Implementing organizational change is not an event or a series of events. Rather, it is a shift to a new kind of management. Unlike event mania, managing the change process from a systems thinking approach does not yield an immediate high or provide instant gratification. The belief that you can create a continuously improving organization with new programs, exciting speeches, and heavy training alone is only an illusion. Changing old habits is neither easy nor a quick fix.

## Slower is faster: manage change within the context of a longer time frame

Taking the time to build the proper foundation to support long-term improvement often requires doing some things that do not yield immediate results but which, if done properly at the beginning, more than make up for a slow start. Going slow does not mean that you must be lethargic. It does mean that you must prepare the soil (things like unity of purpose in the way of shared mission, vision, and values) before you plant the seeds (new directions) and provide water (in the way of training, coaching, and system support). Michael Pugh observes

*We jumped into total quality management pretty quickly. I began working on it in February/March. By September, we were having on-site three-day sessions for all department*

*managers. By the end of September, we had 100 people who were theoretically trained in quality improvement. I look back now and realize that we made people aware of quality improvement, but by no means had we trained people in quality improvement. Looking back, I would spend more time up front to bring the senior management team together and gain a common understanding of the whole quality improvement philosophy before I started rolling this out hospital-wide. I would go slower initially before I rolled out beyond my own senior management group.*

Michael Pugh learned the benefit of laying a proper foundation before proceeding with significant change efforts. While it may be tempting to "get on with it" as quickly as possible, learning new behaviors and creating the necessary commitment to change takes time. Chip Caldwell of West Paces Ferry Hospital describes the feeling of impatience.

*Making the transition to total quality management requires incredible patience on the part of the CEO. CEOs, I think, by nature are very impatient. I expect results of myself and all those people around me. One of the most important things to me was that my mentor continued to drive in to me: "Back off!", "Be cool," "These things will be okay. Look how far you have come. You can see where you are going. Don't expect it to happen this minute." That advice was invaluable.*

Individuals who violate the principle of "slower is faster" tend to focus on the quick fix. They view the continuous improvement process as a way to fix problems rather than as a way to prevent them. And they readily abandon the process if it takes too long. But human systems are complex. You can never fully understand complex human systems. If there is anything that you ever fully understand, almost by definition, it's something relatively simple or almost trivial.

That there is no single "This is how to do it, so now go do it" answer to organizational change is disconcerting to many people. Many people believe, "If it isn't something that I can learn in a three-hour seminar or one week of practice, then it is useless." But think about this for a minute. What if you can't learn how to change your organization in one day? What if the nature of organizational change is that you've got to devote a lot of time to the process—a lot of time inquiring, studying, practicing, and failing? Is it worth giving up on you and your organization just because you would rather take a shortcut?

The very length of time that it takes to successfully make the transition from old ways to new ones is why some service organizations fail to make it at all. Organizational change is something that you have to be serious about. It is hard work. Whereas organizational charts are relatively easy to change, changing established mindsets about how a job should be done is a different matter.

How can you increase your probability of success? Organizations which have successfully made the transition to a total quality management culture take a long-term view. Making the move from traditional management practices to new ones requires patience and time to endure a multi-year transformation. Multiyear? You bet. Even when done properly, it can take from three to five years of sustained hard work before management can begin to see improvements in the bottom line. In many cases, it can take much longer. Old habits die hard.

## Recognize behavior/structure pairs

As we have seen, focusing solely on events can keep us trapped in the here and now. A short-term orientation leads to a reactive stance. And management after the fact provides fewer options and less strategic flexibility. We must get beyond the event if we are ever to create.

How can you get beyond the events in a meaningful way? There are two paths. One is identifying a pattern of behavior over time. The other is recognizing a familiar causal loop structure, a particular combination of reinforcing processes, balancing processes and delays. Paying attention to behavior/structure pairs can help us avoid the perceptual traps that confound others with a short-term orientation.[15]

Events are often linked to a pattern of behavior over time. When you take a step back and reflect on the past, today's problem is often only the most recent event in a larger pattern of behavior.

The pattern may describe oscillating behavior, an S-shaped growth curve, or a downward or upward trend. Whatever the pattern, a focus on the local event can obscure a bigger story (see Figure 5.5).

In and of itself, a pattern of behavior merely shows us how we are trapped. It does not show us how we can change. To make lasting change, we need to get behind the pattern to diagnose the underlying dynamic structure creating the pattern, a structure we can control.

The good news is that particular behavior patterns are associated with specific combinations of self-reinforcing and balancing feedback relationships. These blueprints describe the social engineering that trap us in certain behavior patterns. Making change in these structural dynamics creates more far-reaching change than does tinkering with the events. As we move from the event level to the behavior-over-time level to the structural level, we increase our understanding of what is really happening in our complex system (see Figure 5.6). And better understanding increases our ability to influence the situation.

How can you diagnose which dynamic structure(s) keep your organization in a bind? How can you extricate yourself from repetitive dysfunctional behavior? As there are only a finite number of plots used over and over again in mystery novels, certain behavior/structure pairs are common themes in the change process. Learning how to recognize the storyline can help us diagnose a phenomenon that—if we do not take certain action— will sabotage our efforts to change. Like a car fanatic who can say "That is a Porsche 911," "That is a Triumph Spider," and "That is a Ford Escort," we can learn to recognize common behavioral scenarios. Whether the phenomemon is escalation, shifting the burden, limits to growth, or eroding goals, a skilled systems thinker can identify the unique dynamic structure that creates the behavioral or perceptual trap.[16] (Some common structure/behavior pairs are presented in Appendix E.)

By learning to recognize casual loop archetypes, we can turbocharge our intuition. As in the case of all good stories, the punchline is often counter-intuitive. Seeing the archetype is a discipline of telling ourselves the truth. When we see the structure behind our behavior, we are forced to squarely answer the question

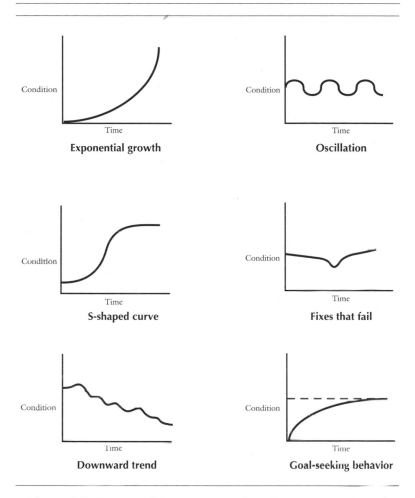

**Figure 5.5:** Do any of these patterns describe your experience?

"What do I really want to do?" Let's look at two common structural traps: limits to growth and shifting the burden.

## Remove the limiting factors

How is it that you may get some early wins by pushing hard in one direction, only to find that more of the same does not yield additional growth? Many people believe that their change efforts meet resistance simply because others do not want to change. Truth

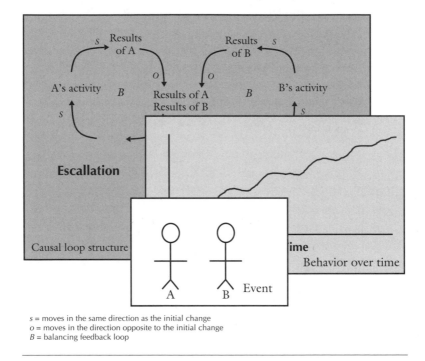

s = moves in the same direction as the initial change
o = moves in the direction opposite to the initial change
B = balancing feedback loop

**Figure 5.6:** Three levels of understanding

is, resistance to change occurs less as a result of individuals not wanting to change than from various elements and subsystems interacting within the organization to prevent change.

As we have seen, reinforcing and balancing feedback processes influence the change process. The degree to which we manage them ultimately determines the direction and rate of change.

Non-systems thinkers design change strategies that primarily push the driving forces behind change. Their implementation plans emphasize activities that will help drive the growth of total quality management activities—more training, advertising early successes, making speeches, writing memos, or starting process improvement teams. An implicit assumption behind this strategy is that if one does all those things to direct the reinforcing loops, the implementation process will grow and be self-sustaining. While this often works in the initial stages of implementation, the "push" approach alone is less than optimal.

Despite a number of early wins, there comes a point where more of the same does not bring additional success. When the initial growth in a total quality management effort begins to slow down, what do non-systems thinkers do? They often push harder on the original growing actions that promoted growth in the first place, rather than try to understand the limiting factors. Yet, this only leads to diminishing returns from the reinforcing processes and increasing resistance from the balancing forces. When their total quality management "program" begins to fail, non-systems thinkers tend to abandon the effort or to blame the failure on the consultant, the company that provided the training, the director of quality, the CEO, or the board of directors. But the problem is not with the quality management principles or other people, it is with the approach to implementation itself.

The solution is not to push harder. Pushing only makes the situation worse. For example, asking employees to submit more suggestions for improvement to a supervisor who already feels overwhelmed or threatened only aggravates an already bad situation. It only makes such a supervisor work even harder to keep the number and quality of suggestions submitted by employees at an "acceptable" level.

It is often more expedient to *remove the barriers* than to push harder on traditional levers of change. Working to increase the feeling of well-being and sense of competency among the middle managers provides more leverage than the traditional approach to change that emphasizes pushing. While reinforcing processes are important in promoting change, it is equally important to identify and remove any limiting factors.

What are some of the limiting factors operating in your environment? What structural aspects of your organization are inhibiting your change efforts? Perhaps you are asking your employees to do something in an organizational context that provides reward and recognition for contradictory behavior. Or perhaps cross-functional process team members are caught between the "quality improvement stuff" and their regular vertical functional management responsibilities. Perhaps you are asking your employees to take time away from their regular duties to engage in training activities within a management system that rewards employees for "productive" time only. Look for opportunities for significant progress that are not the same old push. Identify and remove barriers.

How can you diagnose whether a "limits to growth" archetype is at work in your implementation? Look for an S-shaped growth curve (see Figure 5.7a). Rapid progress in early stages is followed by slower growth. High growth in the early stages of implementation signifies the presence of driving factors. The slowing of progress is a signal that a balancing or limiting factor is at work. The basic structural dynamic is one reinforcing feedback loop (R) linked with one or more balancing loops (B).

Can you ever eliminate all of the limiting factors to growth? Never. No matter how hard you work at making change, you will always find more limiting factors around the corner. Just as you weaken or remove one source of limitation, another is bound to pop up. The challenge in sustaining growth is to continually anticipate your next limiting factors to growth. If you do not find them first, the system will provide them for you.

The lesson of the limits to growth archetype is: *do not ignore the limiting factors.* To do so means an aborted change process. As Colleen Lannon-Kim, executive director of The Systems Thinker, says, "The lesson is clear: even if you gun your engine, you won't get very far if you don't take your foot off the brake."[17] Don't get caught spinning your wheels—remove your obstacles to growth.

## Break your addiction to the quick fix: stop shifting the burden

Another management trap that can sabotage change is our addiction to the quick fix or the symptomatic solution. When faced with a pressing problem, we often ignore addressing the root cause(s) of our problems—a process which can be painful and time-consuming—in favor of a solution which appears to be more expedient and/or easier to handle.

Like the alcoholic who takes a drink to reduce stress rather than address the underlying cause of the stress, so are many managers similarly addicted. Some managers are firefighting addicts. They regularly shift the burden of quality management from prevention to heroism

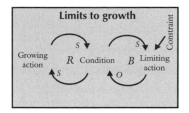

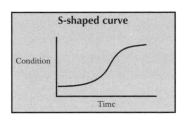

*s* = moves in the same direction as the initial change
*o* = moves in the direction opposite to the initial change
*R* = reinforcing feedback loop
*B* = balancing feedback loop

**Figure 5.7a:** A common management trap: limits to growth

and correction after the fact. Other managers regularly spend money on training courses rather than open safe and effective communication pathways with subordinates; these "communication avoidance" addicts shift the burden of employee communication from line management to the human resources department. Carrying high levels of inventory is easier than fixing the problems that generate defects and missing materials; inventory addicts shift the burden of poor quality from operations to the stock room. Whether your addiction is to firefighting, communication avoidance, or inventory, it is merely a fantasy that you are in control of your business.

What is the long-term consequence of shifting the burden? Today's copout becomes tomorrow's addiction. Over time, not only does the fundamental problem remain systemic but overall performance begins to decline. When this happens, we become increasingly reactive. We react to urgent matters with more and more of the quick fix. Firefighting leads to more firefighting. Low levels of trust breed more distrust. Hiding a few operational problems with inventory leads to hiding more problems with inventory. *The quick fix, over time, destroys the overall health of the organization.* We are so concentrated on the here and now that we lose sight of our long-term performance and our desired outcomes.

How can you diagnose whether you are shifting the burden? Look for an increased need for the quick fix coupled with an overall decline in performance (see Figure 5.7b). The basic structural dynamic behind the behavior is two balancing processes. Each is trying to

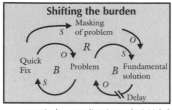 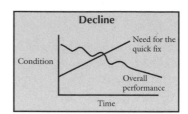

s = moves in the same direction as the initial change
o = moves in the direction opposite to the initial change
R = reinforcing feedback loop
B = balancing feedback loop

**Figure 5.7b:** Another common management trap:
shifting the burden

correct the same problem symptom but in different ways. The fundamental solution is marked by delay; it generally takes time to see the results. The other, the quick fix, is more temporary in nature.

The copout or symptomatic fix is merely our refusal to deal with what we already know to be the truth. In opting for the quick fix, we collude with others so that we don't have to deal with the truth.

How do you break the cycle? As in the first step in recovery from alcoholism, admit the truth. Admit that you are addicted to the quick fix. Second, ask for the support of those around you. Then ask yourself what you truly want. Over the long term, what do you want your organization to be like? When faced with a choice, ask yourself, "Am I shifting the burden here?" "If not, what symptomatic solution am I about to make? Is this going to give me what I really want in the long run?" Finally, be patient. With a fundamental solution there is often a delay between corrective action and the future benefit. Don't let this delay lure you back to the "comfort" of your disease.

While you may be committed to change, beware of those around you. As in alcoholism, there are co-dependents—those who are part of the problem. While they may initially support your attempts to make fundamental change, at times they may secretly want you to "change back." After all, they have built certain competencies and coping behaviors around your weakness. If your addiction is to firefighting, look for those who may have created

## How to get out of a vicious circle

To get out of a vicious circle, ask yourself the following questions. Be truthful.

- Is there a structural process at work here? If so, which one? (See Appendix C.)

- Am I shifting the burden? If I am not shifting the burden, what's the underlying fundamental action that I am not willing to do or do not perceive myself able to do? Why am I not doing it? Am I afraid? Do I think it will take too long? Did I try it once before and it didn't work, so I assume it won't work at all?

- What is the symptomatic fix I am about to follow? What are the long-term consequences of these actions?

- What is my time horizon—a week, a month, a year, a decade? Two, three, or six months down the road, am I going to be right back in the same pickle? Will I be doing more of the same? Am I examining behavior over time?

- If I really tell myself the truth, what's the long-term cost? What is it I really want to do?

- Am I pushing traditional levers of change, or am I attempting to remove the limiting factors?

- Am I eliminating delays from the system?

- Am I reacting to events? Am I creating events?

- What are the physical or other boundaries of the system that I am studying? What variables will be included? What variables will be excluded? What level, micro or macro, am I concerned with?

- Have I analyzed the situation from event, behavior-over-time, and structural points of view?

- Have I taken the time to think about the unintended side effects of my change efforts?

- If we streamline this process, what is the implication on the rest of the system of fixing this problem?

competencies around your firefighting—those heroes who do best in a crisis mode and are uncomfortable with a more disciplined, thoughtful, proactive stance. If your addiction is to avoiding the feelings of your middle managers, look for those around you who feel uncomfortable with open and safe dialogue or may be over-functioning to compensate for your weakness. Be sensitive to their discomfort with your changes. Remember, whether we are talking about an organization or a family system, you are not alone in your changes. As you change yourself, you force others to change.

The solution to breaking an addiction is to build continually toward the long-term issues that affect your mission, vision, values, and high-priority goals. Use short-term corrective action only as a means to buy time until the long-term solution works. Are you addicted to firefighting? When short-term crises arise, do not allow them to preempt your long-term improvement activities. Schedule time for both day-to-day activities and long-term improvement activities to assure that both will receive adequate attention. When urgent tasks start to overwhelm important tasks, take heed. You are probably shifting the burden. Are you addicted to "communication avoidance"? When it comes to your middle managers, admit that you have neglected their needs and concerns. Take the time to begin safe and open dialogue, no matter how painful the initial exchange might be. Build toward the long-term vision of respect, value, and credibility that is necessary to the future of your organization.

## Be an agent of change: examine your role in and contribution to the problem

If you think that organizational change is mostly about getting others and the systems around you to change, think again. You too are going to have to change. Organizational change has as much to do with changing ourselves as it does with how we change others. As many people discover, re-patterning the way we think and act, let alone how others behave, is far from a simple task.

When we fail to manage reciprocal relationships, problems can fester and erupt. Event-oriented managers cannot see their contribution to the mess. Instead, they blame their organization's failings on the boss, employee problems, competitors' actions, irate customers' actions, poor-quality supplies, and so on. Likewise, when we watch CEOs and their management teams implement total quality management via lectures, training programs, new recognition and reward systems, or trying to "fix" everybody else, we are watching an event mentality toward change. Closely related to the event mentality is the phenomenon of learned helplessness, a sense that no matter what you do, nothing will change. Allowing yourself to wallow in cynicism or self-pity only gets in the way of your ability to learn new behaviors and influence others.

The sooner we realize that we are part of the problem, the sooner we can move our organizations toward real change. People who are not real agents of change deny their own role in the mess, radiate a sense of helplessness, and often openly finger-point.

Systems thinkers, in contrast, understand and see that they are agents of creation. Being willing to try new behaviors is an important part of the change process—it is only in changing ourselves that we can change others. In changing ourselves, we force those around us to cope with our changed behavior and change in return. As we change, other pieces of the puzzle change with us.

## SUMMARY

There is nothing more challenging than creating and sustaining positive change in an organization. While many managers would like to think that quality improvement can come about by making minor modifications in "business as usual," creating a continuously improving organization requires significant organizational and personal change. That change effort, in turn, depends upon *systems thinking* for its success, not analytic problem-solving strategies.

On a simplistic level, managing your organization as a dynamic system requires attention to three levels of awareness: events, behavior over time, and feedback. Understanding the dynamic structures at play helps us become creators of our future, not victims of circumstance. The object in systems thinking is not to be able to predict the future. This is impossible. Instead, the object is to design a change strategy that is robust to factors that may challenge our progress along the way.

So how do you move from one management system to another with as little disruption as possible? How do you rewire the house with the electricity still on? First, you tread softly. You respect stakeholders and interrelationships, making sure that you effect change in a connected and coordinated manner. Second, you move away from focusing on "events" to actively managing the change process itself.

As you launch your change effort, know that you will meet with substantial resistance. Try to keep that resistance in perspective, remembering that much of it is due less to the diabolical nature of individual members of your organization than to the many structures and management systems that constrain their efforts.

Yet certain questions remain. How can you increase the speed with which you and others learn new behaviors and practices? How can you align the many activities and improvement efforts already taking place within your organization? How can you enable others to act forcefully and appropriately on the front line? Last, but not least, how you can lead others, in an era of consent, to make appropriate strategic choices to create and sustain organizational transformation? The following chapters answer these questions and many more. They are designed to help you improve your probability of success amidst the ambivalence, contradictions, and complexity of organizational behavior and the change process.

| From | To |
|---|---|
| events | structure/behavior pairs |
| analysis | synthesis |
| parts | interrelationships |
| snapshots in time | dynamic processes |
| short term | multi-year |
| linear cause and effect | circular feedback loops |
| immediate consequences | delays |

## Notes

1. David Kreutzer, Gould-Kreutzer, Inc., Cambridge, Mass.

2. Barry Richmond, Steve Peterson, and Peter Vescuso, *An Academic User's Guide to STELLA* software from High Performance Systems, Inc., Lyme, N.H., 1987, 52.

3. Hampden-Turner, Charles, *Creating Corporate Cultures* (Reading, Mass: Addison-Wesley, 1992).

4. Jeffrey D. Ford and Robert W. Backoff, "Organizational Change In and Out of Dualities and Paradox," *Paradox and Transformation,* 127–131.

5. Michael P. Thompson, "Being, Thought, and Action," *Paradox and Transformation: Toward a Theory of Change in Organizations and Management,* ed. Robert E. Quinn and Kim S. Cameron (Cambridge, Mass.: Ballinger Publishing Co., 1988), 125.

6. Peter M. Senge, "Systems Principles for Leadership," *Transforming Leadership from Vision to Results,* ed. John D. Adams (Alexandria, Va.: Miles River Press), 135.

7. Russell Ackoff, "The Second Industrial Revolution," *The Alban Institute Publication* (Washington, D.C.: The Alban Institute, 1975).

8. Daniel H. Kim, "Total Quality and Systems Dynamics: Complementary Approaches to Organizational Learning" (Cambridge, Mass.: MIT Sloan School of Management, 1990), 10–12.

9. Richmond, et al., *User's Guide to STELLA,* 58–59.

10. Ibid., 57–58.

11. Senge, *Fifth Discipline,* 57–67.

12. John F. Kennedy, *Profiles in Courage* (New York: Harper Perennial, 1956), 18.

13. Senge, *The Fifth Discipline,* 57–67.

14. Stalk, "Time," 47.

15. W. Brian Kreutzer and David P. Kreutzer, *Systems Archetypes* (Cambridge, Mass.: Gould-Kreutzer Associates, Inc., 1992).

16. See Kreutzers' *Systems Archetypes* and Senge's *Fifth Discipline,* pages 378–390, for more detailed descriptions of systems archetypes.

17. Colleen Lannon-Kim, "TQM Implementation: An Uphill Battle," *The Systems Thinker,* June/July 1992, 4.

*You can't write a policy manual that would be valid for more than a month. You've got to act, even at the front line, based on what you think is important. Purpose, mission, and values offer the only tools for managing when you're involved with that much speed....*

*The new model of the organization will appear messy, yet it will be solid. The center core—the corporate purpose— will offer more of a rock to grab hold of. The core of the old model is a written policy that nobody ever sees.*
                                   —Tom Peters and Perry Pascarella

# Unity of Purpose:

## Consolidating Good Intentions

T he last time you went to a bus station on a peak travel day, did you notice the people, cars, buses, and taxis in and around the terminal? Did you observe the hustle and bustle as people angled every which way across the station floor? While their movements may at first appear chaotic and random, each individual is seeking a clearly defined outcome. Travelers are purchasing tickets. Parents are trying to find their children coming home from college for the holidays. Taxi drivers are trying to make sure that they get everyone who needs a ride. Young lovers are trying to find their significant others. And so on. These movements appear chaotic because when you put multiple, often inconsistent goal-seeking activities together in a relatively confined area, individual pursuits bump into each other. Nevertheless, independent goal-seeking is taking place. What is remarkable is that anybody can accomplish anything at all.

Does your organization resemble a bus station? Are employees, customers, and suppliers bumping into one another as they work their way through your organization? If so, how can you minimize the chance that they get deflected along the way? The answer is to get aligned. Only through coordinated, rather than competing, action can any organization hope to survive in today's turbulent operating environment.

## Align individual pursuits

Every day, decisions are made that spring from people's ideas about what actions will bring success to the organization. Good things happen when people's choices are based on criteria that everyone accepts as being useful to the organization as a whole. When an individual's criteria are off the mark, however, otherwise good intentions can result in wasted energy and resources. The value of any individual's contribution is directly related to the individual's unique interpretation of the organization's critical success factors.

How do you direct your employees to know which option best fits your organization's needs? How do they know, and how do you know, what is right in any given situation? Some organizations have no guidelines at all for decision-making. It is not that top management in these organizations trusts employees to do the right thing; it is that management has not figured out the right thing to do. Employees in these organizations work in a leadership vacuum. More often, though, organizations rely on written policies and elaborate rule systems to guide employee decision-making. For example, consider the planning department of the New England Telephone Co. in the early 1980s prior to divestiture. At that time, management trainees were expected to learn Bell System practices that pertained to daily decision-making. These rules and regulations filled volume upon volume, and it was overwhelming to wander among them, wondering how to find the rule that applied to a given situation. Rules and regulations emanated from a management which did not trust its people to make the right decisions in a complex business.

The rules-based approach to management has become unworkable in today's fast-paced business environment. Unusual circumstances and problems can crop up at any time. Few employees have the time to consult "the rules" and respond appropriately.

Failing to make a decision quickly, especially when a customer is involved, may be costly. As we saw in chapter 2, every interaction between an employee and a customer is a "moment of truth,"[1] a golden opportunity to create a delighted customer. When people have to search for the "answer," valuable time and opportunities are lost. We cannot afford the paralysis that results from a rules-and-regulations gridlock.

Employees must be armed with an instantly available decision-making framework, one that can help them to respond quickly and appropriately to any new situation. This framework must provide guidance while allowing individuals the freedom to make decisions based on their understanding of the needs of the situation. Call it what you will—participation, democracy, employee involvement—multi-level decision-making is here to stay. The challenge is to turn the participatory element into a positive force, one that works for the organization, not against it.

## CREATE UNITY OF PURPOSE

In these days of participative management, how can you control behavior without resorting to unwieldy rules and regulations? How can you turn individual conflicting goals and objectives into mutually supportive ones? How can you ensure that the skills and behaviors that you want as part of the organizational transformation process will take root in a positive way?

The answer is to take a focused approach to business, one which involves deciding what type of company you want to be, where you want to go, and how you want to get there— and then "hard wiring" that information into each employee. The unified focus approach represents a shift in management from hierarchical dominance (in the way of rules, regulations, and vertical authority structures) to shared accountability, understanding, and common purpose. You can make significant strides in untangling organizational gridlock by breaking the tradition of adversarial relations among internal departments and functions, management and non-management, as well as customers and suppliers, and, instead, developing shared commitment to common purpose.

What exactly do we mean by common purpose? "Unity of purpose" is a small set of unifying principles that bond individuals of varying backgrounds and experience into one operating whole. When the varied talents, experiences, and perspectives of managers and employees are focused on a common set of objectives, an organization is said to have unity of purpose. How are unifying principles different from rules and regulations? Unifying principles have the following characteristics.

- They are directional, not instructional. They show which way to go, not how to get there.

- They are always true, universal, and timeless. They speak to fundamental human values that create inspiration and motivation.

- They precipitate local policy. Once everyone understands the overall purpose of your organization, decisions and actions taken at even the lowest levels will be consistent with its goals.

- They apply to everyone. Unless everyone pulls in the same direction, there will be no alignment, and energy will be lost.

- They apply to daily work.

Building and sustaining commitment to shared purpose is a powerful mechanism to guide everyday behavior, encouraging intuitive and appropriate decision-making to untangle organizational gridlock and provide a context for change. Before you can effectively make partners of internal customers, connect training to business performance, or ask for universal participation in cross-functional problem solving, you first need to lay the foundation for change by gaining commitment to shared purpose.

## The benefits of unity of purpose

In untangling organizational gridlock, unity of purpose builds organizational power and aligns decision-making at all levels of the organization. If you can achieve a consensus on which direction to pull in and if everyone has a clear idea of the goal, you can then create an environment in which the independent actions of people, even at micro levels of the organization, are not only consistent but synergistic. Alignment has several other benefits.

• **Unity of purpose provides a context for other change initiatives.** When changes are introduced within a context that is understood and agreed upon, you stand a greater chance that those changes will take hold and be sustained over time. Investing in training, engaging problem solving teams, collecting data on customer needs and expectations, and focusing on internal customer partnerships all have more meaning when they are linked to a common view of the organization's strategic intent.

• **Unity of purpose simplifies decision-making and facilitates policy-making at micro levels.** Understanding and committing to a common purpose helps people at the micro levels of your organization develop local policies that support rather than sabotage other efforts in the organization. Unifying principles form a set of superordinate goals and objectives that align otherwise diverse, often inconsistent, local goals, thereby reducing the likelihood of goal conflict. When people are guided by a common purpose, they can create appropriate and functional norms, policies, and solutions in an instant, increasing your organization's overall ability to respond to a wide range of problems in a coordinated fashion.

• **Unity of purpose conserves energy.** When you lack a shared purpose, you have little choice but to develop a plan for every idea and problem that comes your way, a costly and wasteful process. Understanding and committing to a common purpose prevents the planning process from becoming a black hole that absorbs infinite amounts of time and energy. A shared purpose gives a focus to your planning process.

• **Unity of purpose consolidates people.** When people understand and are committed to a common purpose, they form a united front. When people are divided in purpose, they may run in different directions and become distracted from taking the actions that count. You can give people all of the skills and resources they need to do the job right, but if they are not pulling together toward a common goal, concerted action and change will be limited. Alignment is necessary for the optimal deployment of all resources, including human resources.

• **Unity of purpose focuses people on something bigger than themselves.** When we are caught up in the moment with something outside of ourselves, time flies. People are often happier and more motivated when focused on something much bigger than themselves. An inspiring common purpose can be compelling. It can unite people, focusing them away from personal concerns and motivating them to work for the benefit of all.

• **Unity of purpose gives intuitive direction.** People united by a common purpose have a kind of equity in their organizations. They internalize the organization's values, mission, and vision to such a degree that they automatically know what to do; they are connected on an intuitive level to what the organization is all about.

If you can build and sustain a unity of purpose in your organization, then you have found a hidden resource, the power of the aggregate. It will give you a real edge over other, less-focused organizations.

## IS YOUR ORGANIZATION ALIGNED?

Unfortunately, few service organizations are truly aligned. At the top of the organization there is often a fragile stability among members of the executive team. It is not uncommon to find angry, though tacit, differences in opinion among members of the executive team on the direction of the organization's priorities or values. At the fringe of the organization, individuals may be pursuing strategies that are several years out of date because the executive team has failed to communicate changes in the intended direction of the organization. Whether at the top of the organization or the bottom, differences in perceptions of the organization's goals dissipate energy through competing internal efforts rather than a coordinated and focused outward expression of organized energy.

One of the biggest mistakes that individuals make in the transformation process is to introduce techniques for which the organization is not ready. Enabling others to act before achieving alignment on common objectives typically only reinforces organizational gridlock. It does not untangle the competing priorities and redundant activities that got you in trouble in the first place. Alignment provides the foundation for change and is critical to the optimal deployment of your resources.

Is your organization ready for the introduction of new skills, behaviors, and practices? Are the members of your organization sufficiently aligned on common objectives to ensure coordinated change efforts? You can begin to assess the degree of alignment in your organization by asking yourself basic questions. Start with these:

- What business are you in?
- What is its purpose?
- Who are your customers?
- Where do you see your business ten years from now?
- What core competencies do you need to achieve that vision?
- What values are critical to the success of your business?
- What are your organization's top priorities over the next five years, or even over the next two years?

You may be able to answer these questions with some specificity, but how many other people within your organization can? Would 100 randomly selected people in your organization have the same answers as you? If your organization is like most service organizations, their answers would vary substantially. Whatever the reasons behind the diverse answers, the mere existence of that diversity reflects a lack of unity. When organizations lack unity, they rarely possess the ability to accomplish their long-range goals.

## UNTANGLING ORGANIZATIONAL GRIDLOCK: MISSION, VISION, AND VALUES FOR ALIGNMENT

High-performing organizations have a systematic way of building alignment of people and their activities through unity of purpose. They take a hard look at the fundamentals of corporate alignment—mission, vision, and values—decide what each of these means to them, and then internalize them. Why does your organization exist? Your mission answers that question—it is your organization's statement of purpose. What does your organization want to be? A vision creates an inspiring description of your desired future state. Finally, how will you act to achieve your vision? An organization's values guide behavior, acting as a kind of social contract between people inside and outside the organization. Mission, vision, and values, when held in common by everyone within the organization, become a powerful and unifying dynamic.

Building organizational alignment is time-consuming and difficult. It's one thing to change an organizational chart, but quite another to change someone's mindset about where the organization should be headed or what values it should demonstrate. Despite the challenge, alignment is essential for other change efforts to take root and hold. Shared mission, vision, and values provide the foundation for all other changes. Let's take a look at each of them in more depth (see Figure 6.1).

## Mission: Who are you? What do you do?

The first step in focusing the energy and activities of any organization is to reach agreement on the overall mission. What business are you in? What business are you *not* in? Recently, I called my local Domino's Pizza and asked the person who answered the phone if she could tell me what the organization's mission was. "Certainly," she replied. "To deliver a hot, tasty pizza at a fair price in 30 minutes, safely, guaranteed." She went on to explain that the organization's mission was so important that it was the first thing employees learned in training. A good mission statement communicates what you do for a living—and what you don't do. The mission statement not only reveals the identity of your organization but also articulates how you want to be perceived by the rest of the world. At Domino's Pizza, the goal of every employee, no matter his or her level, is to deliver their customers a tasty pizza quickly.

Many organizations have never taken the time to clarify their mission. In organizations like these, there is often confusion over priorities. Many other organizations have mission statements that are unfocused and non-directive. Arthur D. Little, Inc., the international technology consulting firm, struggled for many years under a

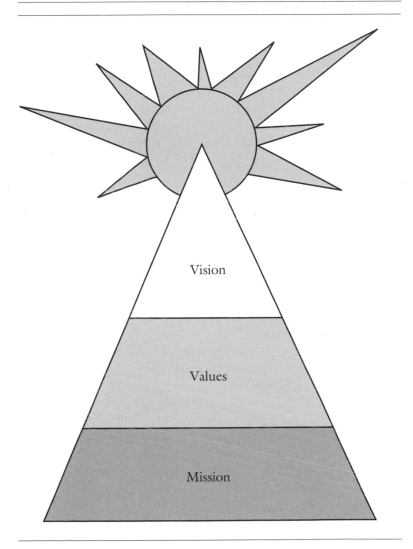

**Figure 6.1:** Unity of purpose

statement that said bravely, "There is hardly anything that is none of our business."[2] Because they said that they did everything, they found themselves focusing on everything rather than on the few things they could do well. Another firm, a large financial services institution, says it wants "to be the quality leader in every area in which we do business." Mission statements like these still leave unanswered the questions "Who do we serve? What business are we in? How are we different from our competitors? What are our priorities?"

There is a limit to what any one organization can do well. When your organization's sense of purpose is clear, then you increase your probability of success. Organizational focus can help you eliminate contradictory activities and keep what's important in front of you at all times.

A mission articulates the unique contribution your organization makes to the marketplace, distinguishes your products and services from the competition, and clearly defines your customer base. In this way, your mission establishes your priorities, dictates the core competencies you need to succeed, and directs you on how best to match your personnel and resources to critical tasks. Your mission statement lays the groundwork for all mechanistic aspects of your business, from organizational structure to control and performance systems.

Let's take a look at a mission statement that clarifies its priorities. This one is from Paine Webber. Contrast this mission statement with those of the other financial services organization above. "Paine Webber is one of the nation's leading securities firms, serving the investment and capital needs of individual, corporate, and institutional clients. By focusing management, time, and resources on four key areas—banking, retail sales, capital transactions, and asset management—Paine Webber is committed to achieving profitable growth, thereby benefitting the long-term interests of its shareholders, clients, and employees."[3]

The hardest part of creating a mission statement is accepting and living with the choices you make. A decision to restrict your organization's activity to one aspect of the industry, for example, can also be viewed as a decision to give up other aspects. Making choices, however, is part of leadership and, ultimately, the force that enables you to succeed.

Creating a mission statement leads to benefits that far outweigh any of the stresses and problems it brings. When people in companies are able to articulate, after long effort and soul-searching, the business that they truly want to be in, the reaction is often akin to fireworks. Having a mission, having something to work toward, unleashes incredible energy. In addition, bringing one's activities into sharp focus, being able to distinguish relevant from irrelevant activities, can *save* enormous amounts of time and energy. In clarifying their mission, some managers decide overnight to eliminate entire product lines. They finally realize that these products no longer fit in with what the company is all about.

You can generate a mission statement that reflects the uniqueness of your organization by asking everyone within your organization to consider the following questions.

1. Who are your target customers? What are your markets?
2. What is your company's self-concept?
3. What is your geographic domain?
4. What are your core competencies?
5. How do you express your commitment to survival? To growth? To profitability?
6. What are the key elements of your company philosophy?
7. What are your primary products/services?
8. What is your organization's desired public image?[4]

Once you have completed this initial process of soul-searching, you will have a better idea of how to position your organization. You can then move on to the next step, which is to determine whether you like what you see—more on that next. Let's move on to shared vision. What is it? How do you get it?

## Vision: define your desired future state

The only constant today is change. If you have your ear to the ground, you can anticipate that change. When you fail to anticipate significant shifts in the marketplace, however, your organization may face a crisis. As we saw in chapter 4, some organizations need crises to change and innovate. Others make innovation a part of their day-to-day operations, seeking to see the world in new ways before being forced to by circumstances.

Many managers believe that, by focusing on the strategic planning process, they will become more future-oriented and create revolutionary products and services. In the absence of a long-term vision, however, strategic plans, rather than providing a means for envisioning tomorrow's opportunities, tend to emphasize responses to the problems managers experience at the moment. As new problems crop up every day, every month, and every year, plans for the future tend to slip aside. Taking the time to focus on the future and taking the actions necessary to shape that future to our advantage never happens.[5]

How can your organization achieve innovation in the marketplace before time and events shift opportunity away? How can managers plan for the future while not short-shrifting the problems of today? The answer is to create a shared vision, a view of the desired state of the organization.

A vision, simply put, is an objective that lies outside the range of planning. As such, a vision includes both a description of the organization's most desirable future state and a declaration of what the organization needs to care about most to reach that future state. It consolidates people of diverse talents and experiences to work toward a common future.

Whereas your mission states "This is who we are and what we do," your vision says, "This is where we are going." Your vision is a more concrete expression of the tangible meaning of the mission over the next several years. Yet a vision is not a goal. Goals state some specific step or strategy that can be achieved when you apply effort toward a particular end. Increasing sales by 20 percent, reducing costs by 10 percent, and improving quality by 30 percent are examples of goals. A vision, while concrete like a goal, expresses a particular view of what the future might be.

Vision works because it utilizes the human capacity for visualization. Visualization uses our powers of imagination and expectation to make our most desired results happen. Creating a mental picture of what you want, then holding an expectation that it will come into being, unleashes powerful internal forces that unconsciously move you to take the steps and adopt the attitudes necessary for success. The thoughts and attitudes you adopt and integrate into your whole being will come to fruition. As Mihaly Csikszentmihalyi discovered in his long-term study of people, documented in his book *Flow: The Psychology of Optimal Experience,* most happy and successful people hold a vision of some desired future outcome. Additional research shows visualization to be an effective tool for anyone who has embarked on a personal quest.[6] Olympic competitors use visualization techniques to envision the successful completion of their event. Downhill racers visualize each race down the slope, mentally negotiating every curve and gate. Javelin throwers envision the feel of the wrist as it correctly propels the javelin through space. Then they visualize the spear's trajectory and see it piercing the ground at a record-breaking point. Have you ever visualized a desired future state and then had that visualization come true? Sure you have! When you hold a strong image of a future condition, every fiber of your being unconsciously focuses on its attainment. Visualization is a powerful tool for change.

Organizations are no different. Once a mental picture of an organization's desired future state is held in the minds of all of its members, the power of visualization will manifest that vision. In fact, the more people who practice visualization within your organization, the better the shared vision. When it comes to visualizing a future state, the more the merrier. There *is* power in numbers.

A good shared vision brings into focus your organization's desired future state. By definition, it highlights the need for change and encourages, legitimizes, and honors the attempts of many people to change the status quo in favor of new ways. A shared vision helps align people with different backgrounds, functional specialties, experiences, and hierarchical positions to channel their unique energies toward the same destination. When people identify with a shared destiny, they build strong organizational commitment to continuous organizational improvement. A vision also assures consistency in resource allocation. Whereas competitive, financial, and political pressures tend to make people and organizations concentrate on short-term tasks and deadlines, a strong vision can help you to better allocate and leverage your resources to achieve your long-term objectives. A vision provides a valuable perspective by looking ahead.

So what makes a good vision? What differentiates an effective vision from a less effective one? In crafting an organizational vision, you need to

- Focus on the future of your customers
- Focus on a higher purpose
- Involve everyone

• **Focus on the future of your customers.** A good vision can help you focus on future possibilities, not current problems. Many service organizations base their day-to-day priorities upon customer complaints. While attention to customers is necessary, this is a rather negative form of management. As we saw in chapter 1, managing the product or service concept based on dissatisfied customers alone is, at best, reactive management. A management that responds to problems after the fact rarely offers exciting options or strategic flexibility.

In crafting your vision, it is important to pay attention to "customer murmurings." Think about your customers' future. What are the trends that affect their business? What are your customers' concerns? As directional signals, customer murmurs can help you identify and understand your customers' latent requirements. These are needs not yet consciously realized, even by the customers themselves; once they are addressed by a product or service, however, they are perceived as obvious. When you focus on latent requirements as a source of innovation in products and services, you focus on what is possible, rather than merely on what is wrong.

Many people think that in focusing on the future, their goal should be to beat a competitor. A vision *can* help you win in the marketplace, but it should originate from your heart, not as an antithetical element. Benchmarking against others is important, but in creating a vision, your goal should be to create your own leadership position through innovation in the marketplace, a position that reflects your organization's unique character and circumstances.

If you are having trouble focusing on the future, pretend that it is five years from now. Your industry's leading journal is about to do a cover story on you. How would the headline read? What would the author chronicle about you and your people? Was your organization in a turnaround situation? Are you famous among your customers? Does your culture invigorate employee morale? What clues are emerging about your future?

• **Focus on a higher purpose.** Typically, many executives approach the vision from the perspective of "being profitable" or "going public." While the parameters for measuring progress toward success should at least be implied in your vision statement, be careful that your vision speaks to a higher purpose. "Being profitable" is important to staying in business, but it does not inspire too many people. As one middle manager observed, "Our CEO's vision is like one of those computer graphics that form visual images out of rows of printed numbers. It is always expressed in terms of sales, market share, productivity, and profit. He just doesn't understand that numbers do not get us out of bed in the morning." The purpose of a vision is to enable people to be a part of something bigger than themselves, to be creators of a desired future state, and to know that they are part of its successful achievement.

Are you having difficulty moving away from numbers? Try this exercise. Imagine that you have fully realized your intentions. Now ask yourself, "If I actually achieve what I am striving for, what will I get out of it?" When answering this question, many people discover the existence of more intrinsic satisfiers and motivators. For example, at the individual level, a person may have a goal of transferring to a particular position—say, account executive. When she asks herself, "What will I achieve from this position?" she may discover that the answer is "respect from my peers" or "more customer contact." By focusing on the higher-order rewards, she can begin to articulate an inspiring vision, which is clearly something quite different from the particulars of this job transfer. Her options become more numerous than she might otherwise have understood, and she has become aware that there may be other positions, both inside and outside the organization, which can satisfy her newly articulated desires.

The same is true when creating a shared vision in an organization. If your organization is profitable, ask: What rewards will that bring? Does it win respect in our industry? Does it mean that our customers are delighted? Perhaps it can lead to leadership status in your community or your industry. Looking at the higher-order outcomes that your organization may realize can provide clues to the rewards you and others truly desire.

• **Involve everyone.** Your organization may already have a great vision, but if top management formed it in a vacuum, it may be worthless. One CEO told me, "We already have a vision." What he meant was that *he* had a vision. While he had a strong sense of personal vision, it was just that—it was personal; it was his vision. Few people had seen his vision statement, and those who had seen it could not remember what it was or tell me how it related to their jobs. Only when the CEO started talking to people about his vision could it become a living reality. He started by gathering their responses to his vision so that he might modify and improve it. Just by bouncing his vision off others, he ended up with a statement about the company's future desired state that was more meaningful to himself and to others. We will look at this important process of involving others in the vision process later in this chapter.

## Values: define how you want to get there

While your organization's mission and vision articulate what you do and where you want to go, your values define the *how*. An organization's values educate its people on which behaviors support its strategic intent and which do not. Unification can take place within any set of values, malevolent as well as benevolent. History is full of leaders who had mission and vision but held reprehensible values. The question is which values in the daily life of your organization will be rewarded or punished.

Values drive the decision-making process. They influence budget allocations, reward and recognition systems, customer relations, daily decisions on the shop floor, and the strategic choices made by senior executives in moments of crisis, among other things. Employees who are backed by a strong set of positive values can work independently, confident that they are conforming to their organization's beliefs and ways of doing things. In this way, values act as a kind of corporate mortar for today's more decentralized organizations. They pull the various units together, tighten the bonds between them, and strengthen the whole.

The extent to which companies consciously manage their corporate values varies greatly. Some organizations are quite deliberate in their efforts to articulate and gain consensus on selected values. Jim Burke, former chairman of Johnson & Johnson, is a legendary advocate of building values into the organization. Burke believes that Johnson & Johnson's values were responsible for the company's rapid action in taking Tylenol®* off the market after a well-publicized poisoning scare.[7] How would some other organizations have reacted? Many senior executives who would have been paralyzed by indecision. A *pro forma* committee would have been appointed, and days would have passed as everyone tried to figure out what to do; in the meantime, people could have been dying. In Johnson & Johnson's case, the decision to remove the product from the shelves was made instantly by a handful of senior executives. Their ability to act decisively and with alacrity can be attributed to a set of strongly held values.

As Jim Burke has often said, Johnson & Johnson's values give the organization a competitive advantage. To prove his point, Burke once commissioned a study of the financial performance of U.S. companies that have had a written value statement for at least a generation. The net income of those 20 companies increased by a factor of 23 during a period when the GNP grew by a factor of 2.5.[8]

## A case history: values

How do you determine whether the values exhibited in your organization support your mission and vision? How do you identify opportunities to leverage the power of values in running your business? Taking the time to gather the perceptions of the people who work in and around the organization is a useful start. I once worked with a small company experiencing declining margins in a niche market which had historically been noncompetitive. Plagued by project overruns, customer dissatisfaction, and low employee morale, the CEO tried management approaches not atypical of

---

*Tylenol® is a registered trademark of Johnson & Johnson.

other CEOs of his generation: replacing senior management, sending employees to packaged training programs, and investing in automation. These efforts failed to improve performance.

The CEO and his top management team then began to implement a total quality approach to business, focusing on customer satisfaction, employee involvement, process improvement, and continuous improvement. In the early stages of this process, the executive team crafted a mission statement that included such phrases as "to be the leader in our market," "to meet or exceed customer expectations," and "to encourage employee involvement."

The executive team decided to conduct a climate survey to see if the existing corporate culture would support such a mission and strategy. In the survey, which produced a 95 percent response, employees reviewed a variety of value statements including "self-interest first," "trust in the goodness of others," "active reinforcement of authority, rules, and regulations," and "change to new procedures, creativity, and growth". Then they scored the presence of these values as rarely/sometimes/often when answering each of the following questions.

1. What values are currently evident in the culture of this company?

2. What values need to be shown in the culture of this company in the future to enhance your effectiveness?

3. What values are currently rewarded in the behavior of the members of your organization?

After we collected and tabulated the data, we used a visual format to display the anonymous individual and collective responses. The visual pattern made it possible for employees at all levels to observe, reflect upon, and discuss specific perceived organizational tendencies lying behind the actual data.

The survey results showed that the current organizational values and behaviors were not congruent with the kind of culture needed to support the executive team's mission and a companywide quality improvement strategy.[9] In fact, the values were all over the map! Some people were rewarded for autocratic behavior, others for participative behavior, and still others for keeping their heads low. The results drew a powerful response from the employees. One front-line employee, looking at the diagram, observed, "It looks like a jungle." A supervisor agreed, saying, "It looks like people are confused." A middle manager announced, "These data show that we are not a club. This is not healthy for a company." The senior vice president of finance, trying to make sense of the whole thing, asked, "But is it reasonable to expect that all employees would hold similar values?"

Much to this man's surprise, the employees actually did have a vision of exactly what values were critical to their business success, and they were the same values regardless of hierarchical level or functional department. The values believed to be "most effective" were tightly clustered around active teamwork: positive people orientation, high task orientation, and willingness to take the initiative. The problem was that top management was not supporting these values on a consistent basis.

The results of this survey impressed upon the executive team that those who are tempted to manage through values had better be prepared to examine their own. For shared values to be meaningful, managers must "walk the talk." Values enter the daily life of the organization through visible actions and behaviors, starting with the CEO and his or her subordinates on the executive team.

In summary, your mission, vision, and values answer the questions *why? what?* and *how?* Together they form the core beliefs of your organization. They focus good intentions. From these shared core beliefs, people develop a sense of which choices and actions will be consistent and supportive of the long-term health of the organization. Mission, vision, and values form the essential foundation of change management. They provide the context for introducing all subsequent change efforts.

## BUILDING A UNITY OF PURPOSE

We have looked at the components of unity—mission, values, and vision—and reviewed the steps that one must take to build each of those components. Now we will turn our attention to the overall organizational effort of creating unity of purpose so that it is sustainable. There are four "must do's."

- Start at the top.
- Keep it simple.
- Cascade direction.
- Apply the PDSA cycle.

## Start at the top

Unity of purpose must start at the top of the organization. Just a hairline crack in executive alignment around the mission, vision, and values can create a chasm in organizational layers farther down. How can executives strengthen unity of purpose in their organization? How can they ensure that everyone in the organization will be singing from the same songbook? They can begin by regularly reviewing their own alignment. They must take the time to uncover potentially significant differences in opinion about direction among themselves.

To be aligned at the top, senior executives must launch a process of self-examination which can be quite painful. But the benefits are enormous, as Sgt. David Couper of Madison, Wisconsin, discovered.

> *Crafting a mission statement was a very important part of our evolution. It put an end, once and for all, to the constant bickering between our top managers. The process of sitting down and examining our values, those things that are important to us as an organization was a very powerful process. People realized that they were not the only ones to hold certain values and started wondering what the fighting had been about. Building a mission statement, examining our shared values, and developing a common vision was hard work, but it pulled the management team together so that we could set a course of action for where we wanted to go.*

Sgt. Couper saw the powerful effect that developing a shared mission statement had on his top management team, an effect that ultimately rippled down through his entire organization.

Alignment at the top increases the likelihood of alignment throughout all operations.

## Keep it simple

I sometimes encounter people who tell me that they have already "done the mission and vision thing." When I ask them about their mission and/or vision, however, they hunt for these statements only to give up in embarrassment. Your mission and vision should be so simple and memorable that everybody can easily remember them and see them as living statements, not just as pieces of paper.

Clarifying the mission, the vision, and values is a consolidating activity. They bring unity of purpose and direction to otherwise disparate persons and groups. The more complex the "unifying" statements, the more diverse the interpretations of the statements. Rather than providing common focus, unwieldy statements about mission, vision, and values only add to confusion; they do not reduce it.

The simpler the statements, the better. But do not confuse simple with easy. It is often easier to leave complexity in "unifying" statements than to do the hard work of concentrating thoughts, words, motives, and feelings. Organizations that do have the discipline to work through the clarifying process are those that communicate the essence of their business in easily remembered and easily implemented operating statements.

## Cascade: incorporate individual vision into the collective visioning process

Knowledge is power. This aphorism has never suited a situation better than in the case of organizations in the process of transformation. If top management wants everyone to be involved in the quality improvement effort, each participant must know and understand the organization's overall purpose and desired future state. They must also understand their unique role in contributing to the successful attainment of those objectives.

The process of creating unity of purpose in organizations is paradoxical; it is both collective and individual. On the one hand, unity of purpose implies a common set of intentions—a central focus for people with differing backgrounds, experience, and hierarchical positions. On the other hand, for a mission, vision, and set of operating values to be truly effective, they must be personal. People must believe that they can create their own outcomes and influence a unique future.

If people are to feel a sense of commitment toward the organizational objectives, then they must have a hand in shaping them. Organizational control is ultimately based on the self-control that comes from each person's individual commitment to the organization. And an individual's commitment to the organization comes from the integration of his or her personal objectives with the general goals and objectives of the organization. If people are not given the chance to participate in the process of developing the mission, vision, and values, they will not feel committed to these "common objectives," even if they agree with them. If leaders do not pay close attention to the process by which the mission, vision, and values are developed, they will never create *shared* purpose. The paradoxical challenge is to make certain that shared purpose is at once an instrument of focus to eliminate certain options and an invitation for widespread participation.

A disciplined consensus building process, one that relies on cascading, can link people's individual objectives with organizational objectives to create commitment to shared purpose. Cascading means that at each level of the organization, objectives (mission, vision, values) are received from above and studied in light of the functions, processes, and operations at that level. By asking "What does this objective mean for us?", supporting objectives are designed from below and sideways. Only after the objectives at one level are defined are these objectives cascaded to the next level.

The cascading process is a powerful way to gain commitment to change. When organizations allow individuals and groups to translate the overall mission, vision, and values into meaningful statements at local levels, they strengthen the overall vision. By building a common framework for all participants, cascading helps to establish a precedent and pattern for teamwork throughout the organization. At the top of the organization, communication and coordination are improved. At all levels of the organization, the

## Building alignment

There are nine steps to building alignment and unity of purpose.

1. Be willing to entertain the notion that you may not have alignment or unity of purpose among members of your team.

2. Create a "safe" environment in which people can share their opinions and differences without fear of retaliation.

3. Create a clear sense of organizational direction, focusing on mission, vision, and values.

4. Start with whatever you have in common. Being able to say "We all believe in X" is a great way to start building a sense of community and common purpose.

5. Cascade this process of self-examination and visioning down the levels of your organization, encouraging each level to participate.

6. Communicate the new direction to every major stakeholder in your organization—employees, suppliers, customers, management, board members.

7. Check for clarity and understanding.

8. Act on any feedback.

9. Start again.

cascading process helps to create a common language and set of expectations. The cascading process ensures agreement on organizational objectives within and among departments before individuals ever get involved in operational issues.

## Live your mission, vision, and values: use the PDSA cycle

Many people view the "event" of crafting a mission, vision, and values as a key characteristic of effective leadership. But building and sustaining shared purpose is an ongoing management practice that must be continually reviewed and improved to ensure that employee and customer experiences bear out these good intentions. Let's take another look at Johnson & Johnson. Its 309-word credo, created over 40 years ago by Robert Wood Johnson, son of the founder, stresses honesty, integrity, and putting people before profits. These values are often found in similar documents of other organizations. What is unusual about Johnson & Johnson is the energy top executives devote to ensuring that the organization lives up to these values; they rigorously manage their process of making these values real. Every few years, for example, the top executives meet specifically to debate the credo's content, a process geared toward keeping their ideals fresh and their values clarified. Executives at this company do not take their values lightly, and they do not tout them merely when it is convenient.[10]

As executives at Johnson & Johnson understand, managing an organization's unifying principles is a process, not a one-time event. As with all quality efforts, this process must be rigorously managed. It is important to monitor day-to-day activities to guarantee that the values espoused are consistent with values in action. And in the event of deviations from expectations, it is essential to take corrective action.

How can you make certain that your mission, vision, and values are living principles in your organization? How can you manage shared purpose as a process rather than merely as an event? You can use the Plan-Do-Study-Act cycle, which we met in chapter 4, to reinforce unity of purpose. Let's take a look at the PDSA cycle as it pertains to building and sustaining shared purpose.

• **Plan: make your operating assumptions visible.** First, analyze the current situation in your organization. Do you have a clearly articulated mission and vision? What values are being exhibited by personnel today? Organizations seldom examine their basic operating assumptions consciously. Yet you cannot manage something that you cannot see! Making visible the unconscious or "assumed" way of doing business (your implicit mission, values, and vision) is key to setting the foundation for continuous improvement. Once you uncover key operating assumptions and make them explicit, evaluate them. Ask yourself, for example, "Are my organization's values helping or hindering? Are these values a tool for competitive advantage, or are they ripping our organization apart?"

This is a time to pull out everyone's secret wish list, a time of selecting the seeds of what you all want to achieve in the future. Your corporate purpose must come from the heart, it must be unique to your organization, and it must be compelling. It must also be meaningful to each person within the organization.

In planning, don't forget your audience. Whom are you trying to motivate? Your employees? Your customers? Your board of directors? Remember, the only way to build commitment among the diverse groups is by involving each group in the planning process. A critical step in clarifying and improving your mission, vision, and values is to invite others to review your objectives and to provide input early in the design stage. If you are just beginning to shape your mission, vision, and values, then bounce your initial attempts in draft form off key stakeholder groups. If the words you use seem too specialized for any group, change them. If your statement is difficult to remember, simplify it. If your customers cannot see a connection between your mission and their business, start over. If you already have shaped your mission, vision, and values, make sure that they are well understood by the stakeholders they are intended to support; otherwise you have just words and no meaning.

• **Do: use your relationships.** What techniques or influences are available to you in moving people and activities in a new direction? Relationships—not arguments, reasons, or methodologies—motivate people. Rational appeals alone are seldom sufficient to move a culture in new directions. For this reason, shared purpose is created and reinforced in a framework of relationships—relationships between leader and follower, manager and subordinate, employee and customer. Modeling our espoused principles in the heat of the action is what makes the difference between words and practice.

Many people believe that promoting shared purpose can be accomplished in memorandum style. Merely publishing mission and vision statements in the company newsletter is not enough. Posting a copy of the values on the bulletin board and on the wall of every office is not enough. As we saw earlier, you must "walk the talk." And you must inquire and listen for concerns and suggestions.

• **Study: seek feedback.** What would happen if you randomly stopped a group of employees in the hallway and asked them to describe the vision or values of your organization? Would you be willing to bet a million dollars that they would all agree? If just one employee does not connect personally to your organization's mission, vision, and values, then you have room for improvement, either in improving communication or in updating your mission, shared vision, or values. This is why you must constantly seek feedback, to check whether unity of purpose truly exists.

• **Act: update unifying principles.** Once you check to see if your vision is shared and if values are living policies within your organization, you will discover opportunities for improvement. Typically, what you discover in the study phase will suggest further action you should take. You may need to spend more time in an informal setting with your employees, talking about how your vision and values translate into daily activities. Or you may need to ask employees how your vision and values might be modified, perhaps by stating them more simply, or by adding or deleting elements. Whatever corrective action is needed, take it.

Once you complete the PDSA cycle, begin again. Remember, crafting vision statements and value statements just once is an event. Making them meaningful for the members of your organization requires two-way communication and is an iterative feedback process.

## SUMMARY

In engineering large-scale organizational change, unity of purpose is the foundation for all other change initiatives. Specifically, a shared mission, vision, and values provide the context for introducing training and deploying scarce resources. Without commitment to common objectives, allocating resources to support change at the local level will only increase the likelihood of redundancy, conflicts in priorities, and false starts. The first step in untangling organizational gridlock is to break the tradition of adversarial relations among internal departments and functions, management and non-management, as well as customers and suppliers, and to develop, instead, a shared commitment to a common purpose.

An aligned organization is a focused organization. All of its stakeholders are not only committed to the overall organizational goals but also share a common mission, vision, language, and set of values. Stakeholders have internalized the organization's purpose and are confident in their roles. Like a person who is centered in life, an aligned organization is focused at all times on what is important. When all stakeholders are aligned around shared objectives, everybody moves in the same direction. You can let others loose to take a greater role in decision-making, because under the guidance of common purpose they will make decisions that are appropriate to your organization's objectives.

Once you are aligned and have enabled others to act, you can accelerate the rate at which you change. Acceleration requires leadership at all levels of the organization, something that we will explore in detail in chapter 8. Contrary to the assumptions of many people, accelerating the change effort is one of the last things a leader should do in trying to effect organizational change. Accelerating the change process comes only after top management understands it's part of the problem, all stakeholders are aligned, and barriers to progress are systematically being removed. Remember the systems principle "slower is faster"? However exciting acceleration may be, it pays to build the proper foundation for future quality improvement initiatives. Once you and others are aligned and enabled to act, you will be truly ready to "step on the gas."

| From | To |
|---|---|
| independent agendas | unified pursuit |
| dispersed energies | concentrated energy |
| inertia | channelled momentum |
| organizational stress | organizational strength |
| ambiguity in purpose | clarified purpose |
| ambiguity in roles | role clarity |

## Notes

1. Carlzon, *Moments of Truth*, 3.

2. Steve Nadis, "The Thought Brokers," *Bostonia*, September/October 1989 (published at Boston University).

3. Paine Webber annual report, 1988.

4. John A. Pearce, II, and Fred David, "Corporate Mission Statements: The Bottom Line," *Academy of Management EXECU-TIVE* 1, no. 2 (1987): 109–116.

5. Gary Hamel and C. K. Prahalad, "Strategic Intent," *Harvard Business Review*, May/June 1989, 66.

6. Mihaly Csikszentmihalyi, *Flow: The Psychology of Optimal Experience*, (New York: Harper & Row, 1990).

7. Rosabeth Moss Kanter, "Values and Economics," *Harvard Business Review*, May/June 1990.

8. Ibid.

9. Michele L. Bechtell, "Finding Order in Chaos: Making Visible the Culture," unpublished paper, 1990.

10. Sara Smith, "Leaders of the Most Admired Corporations," *Fortune*, Jan. 29, 1990.

*The rate at which individuals and organizations learn may become the only sustainable competitive advantage—especially in knowledge-intensive industries.*

—Ray Stata

—◇—

# Organizational Learning:

## Recovering from Organizational Amnesia

How do people acquire new skills and adopt new behaviors? How do organizations and the people in them change? Organizations, like people, grow, change, and continuously improve by learning. Every time you learn something new, you have grown. The question is, do you know how to learn? What is your theory of learning?

I asked this of the CEO of a major financial institution, and he looked at me as if I were crazy. "My beliefs about learning?" he asked. "What are you talking about?" This man had just spent over a million dollars on leadership training for members of his organization. If I hadn't already run into dozens of CEOs like him, the blank look on his face would have shocked me. Truth is, many CEOs today exhibit an appalling lack of knowledge about how organizations and the people in them learn. It continues to amaze me. These are organizations whose very survival depends upon the ability of their people to continuously improve, to learn new things about changing customer needs, to learn how to creatively apply new technology and solve problems. So you would think their leaders would know something about the process of changing themselves and others. You would think that they would have some knowledge about how people and organizations absorb, adapt, and integrate conceptual changes.

You cannot create a continuously improving organization with a brain-dead theory of learning. Today's managers absolutely must understand some basic facts about learning if they are to have any hope of guiding themselves and their organizations into the future and avoiding information indigestion. Whether you are a CEO or a front-line person, you need to understand how individuals and organizations learn. For instance, do you know that individual learning comes about through a series of activities, not just training? Or that individual learning is not the same thing as organizational learning? Or that there are two types of learning that must be managed to continuously improve? If you don't know what I am talking about, then read on.

## WHAT IS ORGANIZATIONAL LEARNING?

More and more, executives can see the need for learning new skills and behaviors to effectively meet the challenges of today's increasingly competitive marketplace. They understand that learning fuels growth and, as such, lies at the heart of continuous improvement. That's the easy part. The hard part has been to get those same executives to stop equating "bums on seats" training with organizational learning.[1] A lot of top executives truly believe, or want to believe, that all they have to do is to put their employees through a one- or three-day training experience. Yes, I know it sounds silly, but it happens all the time. Even if people could really learn during training sessions, individual learning alone does not guarantee that the organization will learn. For an organization to learn, something more has to happen.

## Training does not guarantee learning at the individual level

Organizations want their people to learn new skills. Between the military and organizations, we spend over $78 billion annually on formal training in the United States today. The figure is even higher if you include government and labor union training costs.[2] The problem is that training, by itself, does not guarantee that an individual will learn new skills. Traditional classroom training presents new material in a single lecture or demonstration and assumes that employees will digest it and apply the new knowledge, somehow, somewhere, back in their work situation. But it is difficult to make use of newly encountered material if it is delivered in a way that does not match an individual's natural learning style (see Appendix F). Even if the new material is presented in an appropriate way, it will be forgotten if there is no opportunity to

---

## When training fails

There are several reasons why investments in training often fail to improve quality.

- Training is not tied to strategy and the satisfaction of customer needs and expectations.
- Training is not based on sound learning principles.
- Training is individual rather than group-based.
- Training is lecture-based as opposed to experience-based.
- The work environment does not support the testing of new skills back on the job.
- There is no context to frame the content of the delivery.
- There is an absence of review of the material one month, six months, and two years later.
- There is no PDSA cycle applied to the training process itself.

assimilate it through application in the workplace. Classroom experience contributes to learning; it does not substitute for learning.[3]

Individual learning is a process, not a one-time training event. At a minimum, individual learning requires practicing new skills and obtaining feedback on our performance so that we can adjust our behavior. In the short term, there is no difference in retention between lecture and "experience-based" learning. Over the long term, however, research shows that people who learn through experience-based learning have a significantly higher rate of retention than people who learn via lectures and traditional classroom training.[4] What exactly is experience-based learning? We have already

---

### Individual learning accelerators

Individual learning has certain parameters. While the starting point to accelerated learning is for everyone to adopt a positive attitude toward changing and improving the way they work, key steps in the process of individual learning include:

- Frame the learning in its context. Your memory works by creating networks of associated ideas. By providing an overview or map of what you have learned, you can frame the learning and help put it into an appropriate context.

- Appeal to both sides of the brain. Present each communication to the participant through at least three sensory channels: visual, auditory, and kinesthetic.

- Uncover and test your assumptions using experienced-based learning.

- Briefly review the new material at regular intervals following the learning: one week, a month, six months, a year, and so on.

- Apply the PDSA continuous improvement cycle to what you have learned.

- Aid your intuitive learning by using alternate stimuli, such as visuals. As much as 90 percent of our communication comes at the subconscious level.

seen it in the first part of this book. It is the Plan-Do-Study-Act cycle of continuous improvement: we select an approach, practice new skills, obtain feedback, and adjust our approach. To create an effective learning organization, leaders must shift away from the traditional focus on training to a broader focus on learning. They must create a workplace that facilitates the integration of work and learning on a regular basis.

## The chicken and the bell: the delusion of learning from experience

Many people, once they have gone through the hard work of acquiring one set of skills, resist learning new ones. While leaders clearly understand that their world is rapidly changing, they continue to try to use the same skills that they have always used in the past. At one time they learned new skills, yet now they limit themselves to learning only from experience.

What's wrong with trying to use what worked before? Why should CEOs or anyone else, for that matter, change how they function? It got them to where they are today, didn't it? Yes, but the world has changed, and changed radically. Old methods of "doing" just don't cut it anymore. You may have successfully adopted certain behaviors, attitudes, and skill sets—all elements which led to your past success—but they may have little applicability to or usefulness in meeting today's challenges. In other words, your past successes may bring about a "trained incapacity."[5] In Kenneth Burke's words: "People may be fit by being fit in an unfit fitness." To adopt the barnyard illustration he used in this connection, you can condition a chicken to interpret the sound of a bell as the signal for food, and then use that same bell to summon it to its doom by decapitation.[6] Chickens aren't the only prisoners of their past—we all are. Don't let your past successes incapacitate you for future ones.

As many organizations have already demonstrated, you can adapt to a changed environment. But this requires two kinds of learning. Procedural or *operational* learning focuses on the how. In the illustration above, the chickens relied on their procedural learning abilities to respond faster and faster to their food bell. Relying on procedural learning alone, however, can be dangerous. Had the chickens in this story also relied on the second type of learning, which is at the *conceptual* level, they might have asked why before blithely following that dinner bell to their decapitation.[7] Why is the bell sounding? What is the meaning behind the bell? Conceptual learning, in contrast to operational learning, requires you to examine your theories of action. It requires skills of effective listening, exploring, and building scenarios of alternative futures. While learning at the procedural level is based on experience within the system as you know it today, conceptual learning requires an external focus. One without the other is not sufficient for sustaining high performance over time.

Like the chickens in our illustration, we strive to make operational improvements in ourselves and our organizations. We train in quality tools, leadership, interpersonal skills, and other management techniques to improve our effectiveness, or the *how* of doing. We analyze our problems and take corrective action by applying the PDSA cycle and problem solving skills to each piece of the organizational puzzle. Improving the billing system, resolving customer complaints more quickly, redesigning software, or simplifying an application process all rely on learning at the operational level. As we saw in Part I of this book, continuous improvement at the operational level leads to increased customer satisfaction, reduced costs in the way of rework and scrap, increased revenues, and increased responsiveness.

Not every problem can be corrected simply by improving your methods and procedures. In cases like the chickens', operationally-inspired learning, in the absence of conceptual learning, can kill you. We must examine the *why* of doing things, not simply the *how*, thereby reframing the operational issue as well as our perceptions of reality. Through conceptual learning, we "unlearn"; we break away from the conventional wisdom and our past visions and create new visions of the future. What are some examples of conceptual learning? Conceptual learning occurs when people shift their mindset from "management by results" to "management by process and results," from a short-term focus to a short- and long-term focus, from an internal focus to an external customer-driven focus, and from vertical control to participative management.

In striving for continuous improvement, you want to build an organization that is constantly learning. If your learning process is not focused on both operational and conceptual learning, you run the risk of acquiring life-threatening habits and, ultimately, of being eclipsed by more efficient and effective learning organizations. Organizations which manage the learning process consciously view learning not as a one-time skill-building experience but as a way of life and a way of thinking, a way of reframing the way you think about yourself and your organization. You do not want to just "train" your employees, you want to develop individuals who are capable of learning at both the procedural and conceptual levels. To create a truly effective learning organization, leaders must shift away from a traditional focus on training to a broader focus on learning.

## Individual learning is different from organizational learning

As we have seen, individual learning cannot be accomplished simply by training everyone in the organization. Even if people could really learn during training sessions, what they may have learned operationally and conceptually often remains an unrealized potential for organizational learning. People often "know" but cannot effectively act as learning agents for the organization. Ask yourself the following questions:

- Have you ever concealed knowledge of conflicts or problems from your supervisor or others because they are "undiscussable"?

- How many times in a meeting have you refrained from speaking your mind, choosing instead to keep your knowledge to yourself?

- Have you withheld negative information from someone at work for fear of a direct confrontation or retaliation?

- Have you sought to control a situation unilaterally for fear of how others, with other opinions, may try to influence the outcome of your decision-making process?

- Have you ever withheld information from your supervisor in an attempt to protect yourself or others?

- Have you ever relied on the ambiguity of existing policies to avoid having to deal directly with someone or something?
- Have you ever withheld your fears about someone else's competence?

Interactions like these create and reinforce conditions for error when it comes to improving organizational effectiveness. While individuals may know or have learned, the organization does not. The disposition to treat interpersonal and intergroup conflict as undiscussable, the taboo on public analysis of corporate failures, the wish to avoid direct confrontation—all of these factors and others related to them render otherwise creative and bright individuals incapable of correctly diagnosing and replacing ineffective operating practices with more effective ones. The result? Inaccessible information remains inaccessible. Vague understandings are not clarified. And underlying inadequacies in organizational norms, policies, and procedures remain unexamined. Under conditions like these, individuals are unable to function as agents of organizational learning.[8] While individual learning is necessary for organizational learning to take place, individual learning alone does not guarantee that the organization will learn. For an organization to learn, something more has to happen.

Individuals can become learning agents for the organization only when the organization provides an environment that encourages open inquiry and joint inquiry into ineffective operating practices. Only through joint and open inquiry can mistaken assumptions be reformulated, incongruities be reconciled, incompatibilities be resolved, vagueness be specified, untestable notions made testable, scattered information be brought together into meaningful patterns, and previously withheld information be uncovered.

What does such a learning, or more accurately, an "unlearning" enterprise look like? It is one where dysfunctional behaviors are confronted on a regular basis and replaced with more effective ones in the spirit of continuous improvement. It not only encourages individual learning at the operational as well as conceptual level, but creates the safe and open conditions to channel that learning to reconfigure prevailing organizational mental models, basic operating assumptions, behaviors, and practices. It invites individuals to reveal valid yet previously inaccessible information, to clarify obscure information, and to reconfigure operating norms, practices, and policies. Last, but not least, individuals in a learning enterprise reflect on their earlier attempts to learn, drawing from that reflection a new approach to defining and solving such problems. When you have accomplished all of this, then you will have created a continuously learning organization.

## Team learning is not the same thing as organizational learning

Today, in an attempt to foster joint inquiry into organizational problems, many organizations are using teamwork. Remember the old expression "Two heads are better than one"? Groups provide a forum in which a solid exchange of ideas can occur. Whether they are training in work clusters, cascading new learning, or solving problems with cross-functional process improvement teams, teamwork can help individuals understand how different parts of the organization interact, how select actions have consequences more far-reaching than individual group members would have realized, and why certain basic approaches might be appropriate or inappropriate for the organization as a whole. When various constituencies and viewpoints are represented, this multidimensional view of the business context generates higher quality information, higher risk taking, reinforcement of learning, and a heightened action orientation.

While group learning is certainly one form of joint inquiry, group learning is not synonymous with organizational learning. How can this be? At the local level, group problem solving often leads to mere "ecological adjustment."[9] That is, small groups work to solve problems that are important locally, perhaps working on problems that are caused by the solutions other groups have found to their own problems. These groups do not confront the more fundamental conflicts in basic assumptions and operating norms in the larger organization. Receiving messages from the executive team that "quality is job one" while receiving messages from management that "month-end shipment schedules and delivery of services must be met or else" is one example of conflicting operating objectives that can impede collective progress yet can never be solved by local work teams.

"Well, what about cross-functional teamwork?" you might say. "That ought to do the trick." While cross-functional group problem solving teams may help address some issues of wider concern to the organization, they too are not sufficient to ensure organizational learning. Just because you have numerous cross-functional teams working on quality improvement does not mean that your organization is learning. It just means that you have a collection of quality improvement teams. You are creating an organizational culture of many task forces working on quality improvement, but not a continuously learning culture. Organizational learning is something more than a fixed number of learning groups. It is the ability to regularly replace dysfunctional operating norms with more competitive ones.

## Organizational learning is the development of shared mental models

Organizational learning is different from individual learning and group learning. It is a process in which members of an organization uncover and challenge deeply rooted assumptions and norms. They detect dysfunctional behavior patterns, correct them, and embed the results of their inquiry into new organizational maps and images that are the operating policies, practices, procedures, norms and behaviors, resource allocations, and staffing of the organization. It is the process of converting "old scapes into new maps."[10] The configuration of these organizational maps describe organizational memory. In *Organizational Learning*, Chris Argyris and Donald Schon describe the organizational learning process.

> *Hence our inquiry into organizational learning must concern itself not with static entities called organizations, but with an active process of organizing which is, at root, a cognitive enterprise. Individual members are continually engaged in attempting to know the organization, and to know themselves in the context of the organization. At the same time, their continuing efforts to know and to test their knowledge represent the object of their inquiry. Organizing is reflexive inquiry.*[11]

An organization learns when the individuals within it have changed their shared mental models about how the organization should behave. Ray Stata, CEO of Analog Devices, Inc., a successful semiconductor firm in Andover, Massachusetts, goes a step further and talks about how organizations learn.

*First, organizational learning occurs through shared insights, knowledge, and mental models. Thus, organizations can only learn as fast as the slowest link learns. Change is blocked unless all of the major decision-makers learn together, come to share beliefs and goals, and are committed to take the actions necessary for change. Second, learning also builds on past knowledge and experience—that is, on memory. Organizational memory depends on institutional mechanisms (e.g., policies, strategies, and explicit models) used to retain knowledge.[12]*

A learning organization is one in which individuals, teams, and the enterprise itself are continually learning (see Figure 7.1). This requires a shift away from the elite and individual training mentality to create an organizational culture that interlaces work and learning. It is a process by which individuals are able to confront inconsistencies in organizational theory in action which have become organizational dilemmas. How do you know when you have a learning enterprise? Your policies, norms, and practices are changing. "Business as usual" is changing. Your espoused theories are changing. And there are smaller and smaller gaps between your espoused theories and your theories in action as evaluated by others.

## Benefits of individual and organizational learning

Organizations used to view human resources as "costs" that had to be factored into the overall scheme of things. Today, most organizations view their people as valuable assets which must be nurtured, developed, and "grown." When learning takes place at the individual, group, and organizational level, the organization will experience sustained improvement.

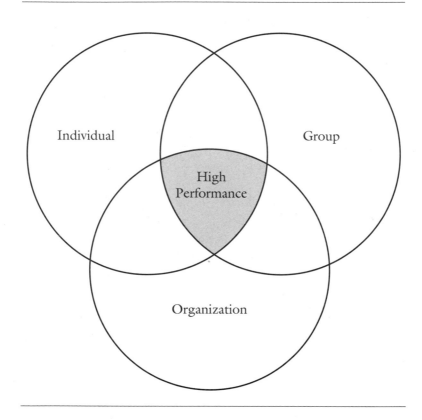

**Figure 7.1:** There are three levels of learning

Are you and others in your organization openly questioning prevailing assumptions? Are you open to having your personal opinions, behaviors, and practices challenged, discarded, and replaced by new ones? Are you testing your plans against alternative future scenarios, conservative ones as well as those that stretch your imagination? If you cannot answer yes to these questions, then you have not yet successfully combined conceptual and operational learning. Real learning at the conceptual level only happens when you can change certain basic operating assumptions in response to or in anticipation of changing external conditions, and when you can manage incremental and breakthrough improvements at the same time.

# "OLD SCAPES, NEW MAPS": KEYS TO ORGANIZATIONAL LEARNING

So how can you and your organization avoid being caught by surprise by the meaning of the bell? How can you move from skilled incompetence to fit fitness? If you can no longer count on your own experience, a series of successes that you are particularly proud of, then what can you do to ensure success in the future? The answer is threefold. First, recognize that, indeed, you have a performance problem. Are you working on the same problems this year as last year? Have you been unable to sustain early gains in quality improvement? Facing your performance problems honestly and forthrightly is a prerequisite to learning. Scary, maybe; necessary for learning, definitely. Second, recognize that you cannot correct your problems by doing better what you already know how to do. Be open to alternatives. Accept that you must initiate a process of inquiry which is radically different from inquiry in the past.[13] Third, create an environment in which individuals can be effective learning agents for the organization.

The bottom line is that you need to learn how to learn. You need to learn how to change shared mental models, not just those of one individual or a small group of people. What are the basics of changing shared mental models? There are six underpinnings or principles necessary to build a learning organization: (1) start at the top, (2) make sure that learning permeates the entire organization, (3) study failure, (4) reconcile differences between espoused theory and theory in action, (5) maintain goals despite adversity, and (6) review, review, review. Let's look at each of these principles in more depth.

## Start at the top

Top management must not only be the first to "learn about learning" but it must be the first to change learning styles. Top managers today seem to have trouble learning. In some cases, CEOs will surround themselves with non-challengers, people who see the world as they do and who conveniently and safely agree with their perspectives. By surrounding themselves with non-challengers, CEOs do themselves and their organizations a tremendous disservice. Not only do they rarely hear divergent viewpoints, but they reinforce their own limited assumptions and behaviors. They don't give learning a chance.

At the executive level, many senior managers believe that top officers do not need training in leadership and management skills. "I try to teach my executive team through example," the CEO of a major insurance organization once said to me. "And besides," he added, "they are all college trained." The problem is that few people are born knowing how to manage or lead. Fewer still pick up skills in problem solving, interpersonal relations, customer issues, technology issues, or delivering feedback, among other things, in college. Industry leaders need to end the arbitrary association of education with 12–16 years of youth schooling. In some cases, their last exposure to education may be 10–20 years out of date.

Besides getting back into the learning mode, another challenge for every executive team is to connect individual learning at the boundary of their organization to top management decisions. As John F. Kennedy noted in *Profiles in Courage,*

> ...*I question whether any Senator, before we vote on a measure, can state with certainty exactly how the majority of his constituents feel on the issue as it is presented to the Senate. All of us in the Senate live in an iron lung—the iron lung of politics—and it is no easy task to emerge from that rarefied atmosphere in order to breathe the same fresh air our constituents breathe. It is difficult, too, to see in person an appreciable number of voters besides those professional hangers-on and vocal elements who gather about the politician on a trip home. In Washington, I frequently find myself believing that forty or fifty letters, six visits from professional politicians and lobbyists, and three editorials in Massachusetts newspapers constitute public opinion on a given issue. Yet in truth, I rarely know how the majority of voters feel, or even how much they know of the issues that seem so burning in Washington.*

Executives must get out of their box to learn. Executives who are disconnected from the everyday vagaries of their operations (customer murmurs, employee-cited production constraints, malfunctioning systems) can miss market opportunities or produce elegant strategies that are inappropriate for their organizational capabilities. Every day, employees at the boundary of the organization learn a lot. Their learning, however, whether it is on customer issues, supplier constraints, or environmental changes, does not automatically make it to the top of the organization. Perhaps you have heard the phrase the "iceberg of ignorance." This phrase reflects the fact that top management only hears about four percent of all the problems affecting the organization. A lot of complaints and discordant information occur at the bottom of an organization, where people have a lot of customer contact. Unfortunately, these ideas are too often tamped down in many organizations. In other cases, employees simply do not know how to communicate their information upward. Employee disgruntlement usually starts when people with better ideas about how to do things are ignored.

The only way top management can make wise decisions is if it can gain access regularly to learning at the boundary of the organization. This means that top management must come up with a reliable method to learn from the margin. How you gather the intelligence of your service, marketing, and engineering people, just to name a few, can have a profound impact on the ability of you and your enterprise to learn.

Before top managers can expect employees at other levels in the organization to learn, they must learn first. A lot of management literature says that everyone must learn, no matter what level or position they hold in the organization. The cold reality is that you cannot have organizational learning without top management learning; you cannot delegate learning. When a top management team demonstrates the ability to truly learn new behaviors, it inspires others to follow suit. If managers fail to learn first, however, then no matter how much other individuals in the organization learn, their improvements will be uncoordinated and unsupported at the top. The result? An aborted change process.

Does this mean that only those at the top need to learn? Absolutely not. We all need to learn, and the learning process is the same at every level of the organization.

## Learning must permeate the entire organization

If continuous improvement is the name of the game in today's competitive business environment, and if learning lies at the heart of the continuous improvement, then everyone must learn how to learn. Joseph D. Williams, chairman of the board of Warner Lambert, is one CEO who has grasped the importance of learning at the individual level. He says,

*The multidimensional manager understands the big picture and the full implications of the word* global. *This person is adaptable to a series of work environments, each one different*

---

### Organizational learning accelerators

- Pick one theme each year. Such themes may include "partnership for customer focus," "PDSA for process improvement," or "management by data."

- Use visuals to communicate the company strategy.

- Apply the PDSA cycle to everything you do, including the overall quality improvement strategy itself.

- Annually review your key operating assumptions as part of your planning process. Generate at least two alternative sets of assumptions.

- Get top management to immerse itself in the learning process.

- Examine failures.

- Create an operating environment in which it is safe to challenge others.

- Identify and discuss the undiscussables.

- Get top management to exchange roles and listen to boundary agents such as front-line employees and sales personnel.

- Get top management to collect and review employee feedback on challenges, missed connections, and opportunities for improvement in top management behavior.

---

*from the one before. Most important, this person is willing to learn—and to keep doing so throughout his or her career.*[14]

In today's rapidly changing market, individuals must be encouraged to learn new skills and behaviors. Learning must permeate the entire organization. Unfortunately, many senior managers do not make a commitment to investing financial resources or time in the learning process.

While some organizations exclude top management in their training and education efforts, other organizations limit their training and education to top management to the exclusion of everyone else. In the United States today, sadly, 89 percent of American workers receive no training from their employers at all.[15] Truth is, top management cannot learn *for* the organization; every employee must become a learning agent for the organization. People have an unlimited ability to learn, yet many organizations seem blind to their employees' capabilities. What a waste of resources! And remember, training does not equal individual learning. PDSA is needed, but it is still not enough. Individuals must be encouraged to challenge the organization at the operational as well as the conceptual level.

## Embrace failure: admit that you do not have all the answers

A practitioner at a major management consulting firm recently said to me, "We are finding in our consulting practice that more and more of our clients already tried the quality thing and failed. So in these organizations, we call our work something other than total quality management." But the solution, in the wake of a failed first attempt at implementing continuous, customer-focused quality improvement, is *not* naming it something new. That is a copout which strikes at the heart of a healthy learning process. The solution, instead, is to admit that you failed the first time around.

As we saw in chapter 5, quality improvement is not a program, it is a *process*. It is a learning process. And learning entails making some mistakes along the way. A top management team that finds the courage to admit that it failed the first time around will gain more credibility with employees, customers, and suppliers than it can ever hope to accomplish with the sham of a new label. In trying to fool others, the executive team demonstrates to members of the organization that it still does not understand the basics of continuous quality improvement. In being a role model for learning, you must demonstrate humbleness and take responsibility for the mistakes you make in trying to learn something new, especially something as difficult as implementing continuous quality improvement.

Before you start any change effort, let your people know that you don't know everything and that you, as well as they, are bound to make lots of mistakes along the way. Shocked? If you are like many managers, you may initially reject this suggestion. For many people, admitting that they are not omnipotent is a foreign concept. Some can never say it. They believe that not having all of the answers is viewed as a weakness. No one can have all of the answers, because, as we have seen, no one has an all-knowing godlike view of the world. This is important for upper management as well as those at lower levels of the organization to fully appreciate.

Some of the most effective people in the world are those who openly embrace their failures. They view problems, mistakes, and failures as powerful tools for learning, not just as vehicles of disappointment. Whereas success confirms that you were right in your expectations, failure can provide you with a broadening revelation by telling you what you didn't know. Aleta Holub at First Chicago notes:

> *Quality improvement is all about making mistakes. It is looking at where you are not meeting customer expectations, analyzing what went wrong, and correcting it to make sure that it doesn't happen again. In the banking industry, people only give their money to those who have the greatest integrity and are beyond reproach. So it is very difficult to admit mistakes. Yet it is a paradox, because when you are talking about something that has happened to the customer, who are you hiding it from? Certainly the customer knows that the mistake happened. But in banking, there is the prevailing inclination to hold our cards close to our chests. In turn, the partnership that is needed in TQM with vendors and customers is not as easily grown as in some other industries.*

How do people treat success and failure in your organization? Do they avoid talking about failure? Are you only allowed to revel in your successes? In many organizations, it is safe only to speak of success. But people who limit their focus to their successes tend to be limited people. If the managers in your organization focus only on their successes, they may have unwittingly stepped onto a carousel from which they cannot escape. Round and round they go, repeating their behavior (it worked before, didn't it?), behaving the same way day after day, and, eventually, becoming deaf from the repetition of it all. They remain blind to "bad" news, such as falling sales, unhappy customers, and unhappy employees. Focusing on success means focusing on sameness.

In most organizations, while people gladly share their successes, they work overtime to hide their failures. Given that "failure information" often provides the greatest source for learning, this coverup can have major, disastrous implications for organizations. Failures which start small, as most failures do, have an insidious way of growing humongous, systemic, and chronic if left alone. You don't have a big earthquake without some little tremors along the way. So be sensitive to potential problems when they are still small.

Kathleen Lusk Brooke, director of the Center for Success in Boston, notes that people who are successful over the long term tend to look at failure differently than others.

*After having interviewed many people over the years on this topic, the only difference that I have been able to discern between successful people and people who are not successful has to do with their view of negative information. Successful people see negative information as information. On the other hand, failure-oriented people see it as a much-feared confirmation of their own self-doubt. Successful people may have strong egos, but they are not very involved in themselves. They are more outwardly focused in getting the thing done, not in whether they are right. Successful people see negative information as the leading edge of information because they are looking for ways to make things work. They will elicit negative information quickly.*

The challenge for all of us is to learn how to gain wisdom from failure. Absorbing negative information can be hard; the trick is to create a mechanism for collecting and delivering negative information. Here's how:

• **Manage failure in a longer time frame.** Many of us function within a time frame whereby if something is not of immediate use, we deem it useless. When you operate within an urgent time frame, it's easy to interpret "failure" information as useless when the opposite is very often the case. Information about failure is often leading edge information that we have yet to figure out, incorporate, or internalize. When you take enough time to absorb information, failure has a funny way of eventually turning into or contributing to a future success. Successful salespeople know this well. A no from a customer today may become a yes next year. When your goals are less immediate, formerly undesirable information and experiences can become new avenues of learning and growth. What does this mean for your business? Stretch out your learning period. Take your learning out of context and examine it for usefulness.

• **Take the time to harvest your "failure information."** The only way a farmer can benefit from a corn crop is if he or she harvests it. So it is with failure information. There is a lot of failure information out there; you need to make the effort to harvest it in a non-threatening manner from every member of the organization. Pay particular attention to people in the boundary positions, such as customer service, sales, service, and administration. When you set out to harvest information, do so at a leisurely pace. Only by pausing in your daily activities, stepping out of time, and taking a long-term view can you transform negative information into positive information. Organizations need to take these pauses. Using the PDSA cycle to dissect each failure can help you get beyond the emotionality of each "negative" outcome and make explicit the criteria for achieving the next success.

To create a continuously improving organization, we need to experience both success and failure. Taken alone, success or failure can warp your sensibilities. Together, they form a dynamic learning process that can guarantee long-term success.

## Identify and reconcile discrepancies between espoused theory and theory in action

"Walking the talk" cannot be overemphasized. The difference between what you say and what you do is one of the most common learning traps for an organization. Consider what happened at one firm in the early 1990s. This small human resource management consulting company promulgated an elaborate and glitzy code of behavior for its employees, an acronym made up of words like *respect* and *empathy*. It was very seductive, and people tried to adhere to it. There were many management exhortations about the importance of these behaviors, and a chairman's award was given each year to the employee whom peers identified as most exemplary of this code of behavior. Customers were very impressed with the apparent zeal with which employees believed in the code. The curtain came down when, without notice, 25 percent of the employees were laid off with minimal severance pay. Their phone-mail boxes were eliminated from the system, and the network was shut down for fear of retaliation. Many consultants found out that they had no job when, while on-site with a customer, they called in to collect messages from their phone-mail boxes only to find that they no longer had an extension number.

It was not so much the fact of the layoff but the manner in which it was handled that was so revealing about the values held by the senior management of this company. In one moment, the true values of the top management were made visible to all members of the organization. For those who remained, the company morale felt like scorched earth. The credibility of senior management plummeted internally as well as externally in the consulting community. To this day, the company has not fully recovered. Had the senior management of this firm been sensitive enough to see that its espoused values and its behaviors were so far apart, perhaps this disaster could have been avoided.

Many executives, however well-intentioned, unconsciously deliver daily anti-quality and anti-learning messages to their people. Saying one thing and doing another, they confuse themselves and others with the differences between their espoused theories and their behaviors—their true theories in action. In creating a learning organization, it is these very gaps that offer the greatest opportunities to make significant strides in organizational learning.

As you examine your shared mental models and operating assumptions, notice the difference between what you say you believe and what you actually do. Often, we think·we believe something, only to realize upon closer examination that we never put our money where our mouth is. This isn't surprising. There usually is a gap between our espoused behavior and our actual behavior. For example, senior management may talk about employee involvement or customer focus but consistently fail to back espoused theories with action.

How do these gaps arise? It is generally not because we intend to deceive others. Instead, it is more often because in acting in accordance to one espoused belief, we come into conflict with other espoused beliefs, norms, or practices.[16] For example, many managers espouse employee empowerment until empowerment challenges their fundamental beliefs that the supervisory role is to make and control the important decisions. Examining such gaps and closing them puts us on the road to real learning. Being honest about the fact that employees in such a situation are not empowered, and taking the time to explore the nature of the underlying beliefs controlling the situation, defines the path to progress. In this example, redefining the value of the supervisory role as that of mentor and coach is more effective than simply ignoring employees who complain that they are not empowered.

Closing the gap can be difficult. First, many people are genuinely blind to the difference between what they say they believe in and what they exhibit in their day-to-day behaviors. Second, even when people are aware that the gaps exist, the organizational culture within which they have to function often dictates that these gaps are undiscussable. The consulting firm cited above regularly conducted its own employee survey. When asked by one timid junior employee what, if anything, senior management had learned from the employee survey, how did a senior vice president respond after the layoff? The survey suggested that the company was just fine; there really wasn't anything that the company had to work on! What a learning disability in this organization.

The very inconsistencies in organizational behavior which lead to organizational dilemmas are often taboo subjects within the organization. In these organizations, people are conditioned only to detect errors which can be corrected so as to maintain the status quo. When you are not allowed to confront deeper taboo issues, you can never reframe some of your most significant operating problems. To narrow the gap between intentions and experience, top management needs to create an environment where its people, especially subordinates, feel free to confront others on their discrepancies. Confrontation and feedback are the secrets to top-level learning.

## Maintain your goals in the face of adversity

Change may not feel natural to you. Whenever organizations are on the road to real change, the people within them frequently experience great discomfort and chaos. When this happens, people frequently beat a hasty retreat because they are either confused or afraid to admit that they do not have all of the answers. Making fundamental change is frightening and unsettling; not only do you not know what the future state will look or feel like, but you will have to obtain new competencies and form new alliances.

You can gain an edge if you know, going into the learning process, that you will probably feel uncomfortable, but that it will pass. People actually learn in distinct stages. Initially, we may be unconsciously incompetent. Then, once we have launched a learning process, we may enter a phase of conscious incompetence, during which we are painfully aware of how many mistakes we make. Later, as we learn more, we become consciously competent. Finally, after we have lived with our competence for a while, it becomes unconscious. Eventually, of course, our conscious competence becomes unconscious incompetence, and the cycle starts anew.

Moving from one stage to another can be quite painful, which is why many people, and therefore a lot of organizations, work hard to look like they are changing when all they are really doing is standing still and making noises. So many of us abandon our ambitious goals when the going gets tough! We don't have the courage to see them through, and our goals erode over time. (See the "eroding goals" archetype in Appendix E for a description of this phenomenon from a systems thinking perspective.) What's tragic about giving up at this point is that when life becomes uncomfortable, it usually signals an impending breakthrough.

## Test your assumptions

When you test your assumptions, be brutally honest with yourself: How have you contributed to the problem? As we saw in the last chapter on organizational transformation, individuals are never divorced from the problem context. We are all part of the problem. How do you know when someone is not taking responsibility for being part of the problem and therefore part of the solution? The signal is the "they" word. One of the biggest initial hurdles for learning is the "they" word. "They (the employees) are not really committed." "They (the customers) need to be educated in the insurance business." "They (top management) are not walking the talk." "They (the people in the next department) are not responsive to our concerns." And on and on.

By using the "they" word, people absolve themselves from taking any responsibility for the problem at hand and create an atmosphere of learned helplessness. Blame will never be a part of any solution. When you can view yourself as an agent of creation, capable of taking the initiative for resolving underlying problems, you empower yourself to seek enduring solutions. Being able to ask "What am I doing that contributes to this problem?" is a starting point. Being able to ask "What can I do differently that might lead to the resolution of this problem?" is another step.

At the level of the individual, there is a powerful yet very simple technique called internal dialogue which can help you see how your assumptions and mental models create and reinforce operating problems. Before you read on, take a look at the boxes on pages 225–226 to see how this technique works.

As you can see in the dialogue between the two associates, George assumed that Roberto was not being helpful and lacked a sense of urgency in solving the problem. Perhaps some of George's assumptions were true; perhaps not. What counts is that before Roberto even had a chance to provide meaningful input, George made some damaging assumptions, assumptions which not only showed a lack of respect for Roberto but which virtually incapacitated George's ability to learn about the problem and solve it once and for all.

## The internal dialogue technique

• **Step one.** The next time you talk on the phone to an internal customer about a problem, take out a piece of paper and draw a line down the middle of the paper, vertically.

• **Step two.** Once the conversation gets going, start writing down everything you both say in the right column. You are recording a script of the conversation, if you will. If you know shorthand, great! Otherwise, paraphrase as best you can.

• **Step three.** This is where it gets tricky. While you are talking to your associate and writing down your script, also examine what you are really thinking—and write that down too, on the left side. No one will see this when you are done, so be brutally honest with yourself: What are you really thinking?

| **Internal Dialogue** *(George's thoughts)* | **External Dialogue** (Roberto and George) |
|---|---|
| *Roberto is inexperienced. And he is often difficult to deal with. He and his people do not like to be held accountable when there are problems. They just are not committed.* | **George:** Do you have any suggestions on how we might solve this problem? |
| *I do not like what he is saying nor his delivery. This is not what I asked.* | **Roberto:** I've known about this problem since yesterday. I assumed that you would make a unilateral decision, as usual. |

*continued, next page*

## The internal dialogue technique (continued)

| **Internal Dialogue** *(George's thoughts)* | **External Dialogue** (Roberto and George) |
|---|---|
| *Yes, he is right. But I want results now. Only I know how much pressure is on me from above to make this look good. Besides, the root cause problem-solving process works best when there is plenty of time. This is a crisis; there is no time.* | **George:** I think we should... |
| | **Roberto:** I hear what you are saying, but I think that we should take time to solve this problem once and for all. We have had this problem before, and we always end up putting a Band-aid on it. I think we should form a team to solve this problem at the root cause level. |
| *This is what I am going to do.* | **George:** What would you say if I were to...? |
| *This is exasperating. I've got to get Roberto and his people to commit to this approach immediately.* | **Roberto:** That might work. Without seeing some hard data, though, I can't be sure. |

Rather than facing their problems squarely, Roberto and George talked around the subject. The result? They ended their meeting with no fundamental solution, let alone a clear definition of the problem. By operating on preconceived notions, George only made the problem worse. They never got the opportunity to correct false assumptions or lay out an approach to solve the fundamental problem.

The challenge, then, for George and Roberto (and for most of us) is to learn how to conduct an open conversation with someone who doesn't necessarily share our point of view. For a conversation to be truly productive, each party must remain neutral and suspend judgment throughout the interaction. Only by trying to understand each other's viewpoint can you collect valid information, launch the process of learning, and develop a joint solution.

## Invite challenge: suspend judgment

A word of warning: when solving problems, people often make the big mistake of choosing only people with whom they feel comfortable. Often, the person whom you initially identify as being a barrier to change can be the key to true change. And the person who shares your views may be a barrier to appropriate and effective change. The only way to find the most appropriate solution to a challenging problem is for individuals with diverse experience and skills to learn together, ultimately building a common base of shared beliefs and goals.

Encourage contradictory thinking. Invite people from different camps not only to interact but to question each other's assumptions. Successful change agents not only initiate a reframing process for others but also accept the diverse perspectives that naturally arise from sharing leadership. Specifically, they encourage others to challenge them. Internal debate can help people appreciate that there is no "right" way to do anything, only a number of complementary ways. The more perspectives you have in the planning process, the more appropriate and innovative your thinking will be.

It can be a real challenge to learn how to hold and act upon conflicting perspectives simultaneously. This is the difference between inquiry and advocacy. Inquiry requires one to remain somewhat neutral during the learning process. Advocacy, on the other hand, is the pushing of a particular opinion in the context of problem solving. Being able to balance inquiry and advocacy is critical to effective learning at any level. If individuals evade the conflicts that inevitably creep up, they will be unable to convert their decisions into day-to-day practice.

The more you can encourage varying perspectives to emerge, the better quality the decision. Once the group can foster an ability to *understand* differences in the way of inquiry, rather than to *negotiate* them as part of advocacy, its members are better positioned to interact creatively in terms of those differences.

Gaining a true understanding of the nature of the problem means that you must invite challenge. Asking others, including your subordinates, to participate in the decision-making process is not a sign of weakness. If you look at feedback in that light, then you are caught in a learning trap baited by your ego. It actually takes a lot of courage to ask for and listen to opposing viewpoints and other truths. Feedback can help you test your assumptions: assumptions about what your employees need from you, about what works and doesn't work, and about their assumptions.

## Discuss the "undiscussable"

Unfortunately, some of the biggest problems and therefore the most significant opportunities for organizational learning are topics that are "undiscussable." Discussing the undiscussable means going public with some very sensitive issues. While the idea of publicly testing one's views may be perfectly acceptable and actually encouraged, the danger is that it can lead to others taking advantage of the openness.

Consider what happened in one advertising firm. At a special off-site meeting, the CEO stood before a group of division managers and announced some less-than-encouraging financial performance. Revenues were off by a substantial amount from projected bookings, and people were genuinely discouraged. In this public setting, a courageous division manager raised his concern that the divisions were under pressure to make their projected bookings look as favorable as possible, and perhaps this could account for inflated estimates. The CEO, upon being challenged on his assumptions about the validity of the sales forecasts, challenged any division manager who did not have complete confidence in his or her projected bookings to stand before the group—an embarrassing challenge to say the least. Only this one man had the courage to stand.

The double bind in which this CEO placed his managers cost him and the organization dearly. As you might suspect, few divisions came in on plan that quarter, and the company went into a management spin. The result was a significant layoff; a companywide review of the forecasting process, including redefining what qualified as a "certain" booking; and as a result of this review, substantial adjustments in the annual corporate plan to discount the "inflated" bookings of the past. This demonstrates what can happen when top management doesn't want to hear the truth as others might see it and uses a public forum to shoot down the courageous.

In summary, the culture in a learning enterprise encourages individuals to confront the basic assumptions behind the views of others and invite confrontation of their own basic assumptions. In this way everyone's underlying hypotheses are brought to the surface, publicly confronted, tested, and redefined. The result? Discovery that leads to continuous improvement. Through joint inquiry, individuals produce a final position based on the widest possible exploration of views and to which people at all levels feel internally committed.[17]

## Clarify ambiguous theories in action

As we have seen throughout this book, one of the greatest obstacles to organizational learning for continuous improvement is ambiguity. Lack of clarity of organizational objectives in the mission, vision, and values; lack of good data on customer expectations and employee concerns, lack of clear criteria for performance management—all these vagaries contribute to misinterpretation, false assumptions, and inappropriate and ineffective actions. Simply collecting the facts goes a long way toward improving the quality of basic operating assumptions.

To help reduce ambiguity and misinterpretation, more and more organizations are using visual management. Bulletin boards and posters can help to communicate the mission, vision, values, company strategy, and performance to all members of the organization. When data are displayed publicly, every employee can view them, appreciate them, and participate in their message. The visual display of data can also provide your people with an active form of learning in which the viewer is involved with the data and related measures of performance. It encourages discussions outside formal performance review meetings and is available to all employees—not just a few select managers—during coffee breaks, while passing in the halls, or while chatting with others.

## Frame the information in its context

People often plunge into a new subject without an overall notion of what it involves. Yet, understanding the context is fundamental to integrating new information into long-term memory. If you familiarize yourself with the material that you have to learn and develop a cognitive map of its boundaries, vocabulary, areas of knowledge, and essential points, you will be better able to assimilate that material. Once you have examined the whole context, you can create a cognitive structure that takes you outside of your internal preoccupation and puts you in a relevant and dynamic context that you can understand and act upon.

How does a frame help organizational learning? In a training context, you can help build the proper framework by including some thought-provoking exercises that enable people to discover a personal relationship to an idea before it is formally introduced. At the level of corporate communication, you might start tying your quality improvement activities and corporate communications to a five-year business strategy. At the team level, you might work to see where a particular problem fits in the whole organization. Regardless of application, take the time at the beginning of every project to review the overall purpose of the project, your criteria for its success, the time frame, and how you will know when you are done.

Framing can help you see problems inside and out. It can cure our tendency to be too internally focused, help us make sense of new information, and give us a mental model in which to retain new information longer so that we can integrate it with our day-to-day activities. Whether it is training, alignment for unity of purpose, or simple corporate communications, taking the time to frame the new information in context is invaluable. When training is managed properly, and by this I mean grounded in real business issues and provided to everyone within the organization, it has a chance to take root. If you have not linked your training to strategy, you can bet that there will be a lot of waste, ineffectiveness, and starts and stops. One way to change your perspective about training, and therefore about learning, is to stop thinking in terms of training costs and to think instead of investment costs. In building a learning organization, you are making a strategic decision to invest in your people.

Tie learning to strategic business issues. Whether it is in the form of training, education, feedback, or even the development of a common working vocabulary, learning is less effective if it becomes separate from the way the company is actually run or if there is no plan for guiding the effort. To help make the connection between business issues and skill base, and to get a long-term perspective, take the time to develop a five-year training plan.

## Give yourself time to learn

Too many of us want to see immediate results. We need instant gratification. When some managers do not see results right away, they tend to overcompensate by adding more training. Remember, cause and effect are not always close in time. There may be a time lag between when you initiate the learning process and when you begin to see results.

How can you slow down your expectations of the quick fix?

- Be willing to change yourself.
- Seek feedback from others in a nonthreatening way to determine opportunities for improvement.
- Invest in the education and training of yourself and others in your organization.
- Tie your education and training to our strategy and business performance measures.
- Practice new habits.
- Start again.

There are many time-tested learning techniques for individuals. Get to know these techniques and start applying them to yourself and those around you today.

## Review for continuous learning

Successful learners frequently review what they have learned. Poor learners usually say that they "just don't have the time to go over all that old stuff." Never underestimate the power of reviewing what you already know or what you think you know. Reviewing provides a systematic way for individuals to examine their basic operating assumptions. What assumptions were made in good faith that later turned out to be inaccurate? What new assumptions will be pursued the next time around? Was the environment supportive of the learning process? The answers to these questions are essential to continuous improvement.

We need to review at the individual, group, and organizational level. Assumptions must be reviewed on a regular basis, whether they are private assumptions about the behavior of individuals, working assumptions used as part of the problem solving process by a local work group or a task team, or organizational assumptions used in setting strategy or defining organizational structure. You can use the PDSA cycle, which we met in chapter 4, to conduct a systematic review.

Reviewing material does not mean rote learning; it means reviewing what you have learned *over time,* and repeatedly. Many people assume that they will automatically retain new learning. So they fail to structure review into their daily operations. Without significant, repetitive review, your learning cannot make the trip into your long-term memory and will be lost forever. Or, at least, it will be lost until you re-learn what you thought you had already learned.

Review is the most conspicuously absent aspect of most training programs today. Numerous companies spend millions of dollars on putting their people through training courses with absolutely no follow-up, treating training as an event, not a process. When you view learning as a process, you will intuitively include review as part of that process.

You can use the PDSA continuous improvement cycle to check and review anything new that you have learned. You can also build the habit of review into your daily life. For example, if you attend a training course, revisit the material one month later. Six months later, revisit the material again, and so on. To create a truly powerful review process, go over the material with others who have also been exposed to the same learning. Better yet, design an official review period for all training courses and strategic planning processes. You can never review enough.

## THE "UNLEARNING" ORGANIZATION: HOW TO MEASURE PROGRESS

How do you know when your organization is learning? What are some shared mental models that document continuous improvement? What are the "maps" that we need to unlearn to ensure conceptual as well as operational learning? There are four key indicators of organization learning: language, work standards, alternative future scenarios, and customer feedback.[18] If these shared mental models are changing, then your organization is changing (see Figure 7.2).

### Language

Strong cultural norms are the basic assumptions and habits that characterize our everyday interactions. They help everyone know what is important and how things are done without expending much conscious energy. We do not have the time or the energy to think through every detail of every interaction every day, so we adopt certain norms to do the job for us.

Some norms are explicit. For example, dress codes describe one aspect of "the way things are done around here." But when it comes to organizational change, the most powerful norms are often implicit. In fact, we become so reliant on these norms that they frequently become unconscious.

Language is such one set of norms. We use language to "map" key concepts and connections that we need to communicate on a regular basis. For example, when we say *home* or *parents* or *children*, we share meaning with others. We don't have to think about the meaning of each of these words each time we use them. We use them because others know what we mean. In this way, words simplify our lives. It is easier to say *children* than it is to say *those little human beings that we produce when a man and a woman procreate.*

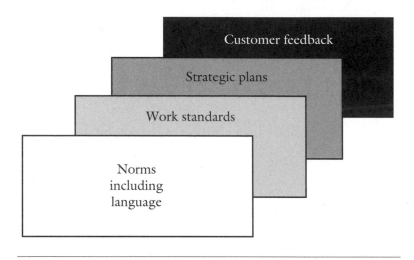

**Figure 7.2:** There are four types of shared mental models that document change

Words like *home* and *parents* are common to many people. But in more technical areas of life, vocabulary is more specialized. The language of a tax accountant to describe work issues is different from that of a car mechanic, nurse practitioner, or pet groomer. Their varying vocabularies describe the unique frame they use to construct the world. Regardless of application, language is a means to communicate the basic assumptions behind our shared mental models.

Organizations are changing when they acquire new vocabulary. As they change their vocabulary, they are changing shared mental models. They are hard-wiring new concepts into "business as usual." Consider the case of a total quality management implementation. When everyone in the organization understands a similar definition of the word *quality* (such as "meeting or exceeding customer needs and expectations"), when employees throughout the organization begin to use the language of *Pareto charts, fishbone diagrams,* and other statistical methods, when you begin to hear the words *feedback loops, cycle time, benchmarking, trust,* and *partnership,* you are witnessing an important aspect of the learning process. You know that you are moving from old ways to new ways when new concepts emerge as shared vocabulary, a form of "unconscious competence."

## Work standards

We may share the same language, but we have little else if we do not agree on what the exact product or service should look like from a practical point of view. We need consensus on what qualifies as an acceptable product or service before it is delivered to the customer. We need to make certain that the product or service provided by one employee is consistent with the quality that is provided by another employee on a different day.

This requires an ability to be self-critical, to adjust for quality control and inspection. To what do employees adjust themselves? Accepted work standards. Work standards are the definition of the actual material goods as we wish to deliver them to our customers. They capture or "map" consensus on the best practices known to the members of the organization.

Changing work standards (how it is really done, as opposed to how it is supposed to be done) means that shared mental models are changing and the organization is learning. As we saw in chapter 4, if work standards are out of date, then the organization cannot effectively and consistently improve in any meaningful manner. Getting your work processes under control requires that you identify common cause and special cause variation, key opportunities to advance individual and organizational learning. So revisit your work standards. In the absence of standardizing process improvements, there is a tendency to regress to the old way of doing things.

## Alternative future scenarios

How have so many service organizations missed key competitive opportunities? How is it that so many management teams react to changes in the marketplace with less strategic flexibility than they would like? In many cases, it is because they were wedded to the status quo. They believed that they understood well the needs of the marketplace, international politics, and the likelihood of new entrants in their industry.

As Arie deGeus of Shell Oil observed years ago, planning is an important part of the learning process. Taking the time to consider various scenarios about the future and test our current operating practices against those possible futures is a key to long-term survival and adaptation—the essence of organizational learning. We may have our own ideas about what it takes to produce a quality product or service and about our own long-term goals, but there are other organizations with other operating norms and goals that are creating new competitive situations for us every day.

Building future scenarios requires getting out of your box on the organizational chart as well as getting out of your current organizational mindset. How can you do this? Use the wisdom of people at the boundary of your organization—sales representatives, customer service representatives, and other front-line employees—as well as those accessible outside the walls of your institution—individuals representing new technologies or other geographic regions—to help you create challenging if not "outrageous" scenarios of alternative futures. Then test your current practices against them to design a robust strategy for the organization.

Generating alternative scenarios is critical to survival. If your visions and fantasies about the future are changing and are being incorporated into your strategic planning process, then your organization is stretching and growing.

## Customer perceptions

What happens when we ask for performance feedback from others? Sometimes we receive information that confirms our suspicions about our operations. More often, we receive information that challenges our assumptions about how we operate, our mental models of reality.

Feedback can be startling. Perhaps our customers tell us that we are doing a very poor job at something that we feel particularly good about. Or perhaps our employees tell us that they are unhappy with the behavior of senior management, something which flies in the face of our belief that our organization is filled with happy campers. Depending on the nature and magnitude of the discrepancy, this "failure" information can be difficult to accept. Some people reject the feedback outright. They find excuses for why the individual(s) giving the feedback are wrong. But more and more organizations are beginning not only to accept but also to seek feedback from customers, employees, and others to ensure future success.

Feedback is a powerful means to revise our shared mental models; we can learn from objective perceptions, however nonrational they may at first appear to us. In trying to understand the operating assumptions or mental models that control customer and employee behavior, organizations can reduce their unconscious incompetence. It isn't always easy. With new stimuli or viewpoints there is often confusion. Many people are uncomfortable when they are confused. But confusion is part of the price of transition and learning. New learning occurs while making new pathways and new connections.

In this way, feedback provides a directional map for changing behavior. Are you staying abreast of changing customer needs and expectations? Those who communicate with their customers view their business in a radically different way than they did a few years back. They are changing their mental models about how to run a successful business. These new mental models are changing the basis of competition with other firms in the same industry.

## SUMMARY

In mastering the art of continuous improvement, vibrant organizations must master the art of learning. What are the hallmarks of a learning organization? Learning organizations know that training, by itself, does not guarantee individual learning and that individual learning by itself does not guarantee organizational learning. Organizational learning is the changing of shared mental models and maps related to operating policies, operating norms, and performance criteria.

For organizational learning to take place, there must be a supportive environment in which individuals and groups can safely share important information, reduce ambiguity, and talk about gaps between espoused theory and theory in action. Learning organizations understand that the real breakthroughs in organizational learning occur when the undiscussable topics are brought out into the light in an environment characterized by inquiry, not advocacy or blame.

What does the life cycle look like in a dynamic learning organization? First, the life cycle is just that: a cycle. It never ends. An organization may start off in a relatively stable state, but it does not stay there for long. To prosper and grow, it must continuously leave stability and seek out chaos. Organizational learning is not about simply eliminating error or streamlining operations; it is instead evident in the way business practices are continually analyzed and revised, incompatible organizational norms are continually engaged, and conflict is continually confronted and resolved.

How do you know when you have it? Ask your customers, employees, suppliers, and other stakeholders, both within your organizational boundary and outside. You will be known as a leader in creating your own future, not a victim of external forces. You will continually update your shared mental models of how the world works, reframing the *why* behind your actions, not merely improving the *how.* You will have created a learning organization, a systems thinking organization.

| From | To |
| --- | --- |
| learning is limited | learning is unlimited |
| logical left brain | multiple intelligences |
| isolation | interaction |
| discussion | dialogue |
| individual training | group training |
| gaps are not discussable | gaps are explored |
| operational learning only | operational and conceptual learning |
| personal mastery | team learning |

## Notes

1. Bill Ford, "The Learning Enterprise: Integrating Total Quality Management and Workplace Reform and Renewal," Proceedings, Second National Conference, Total Quality Management Institute, August 21–23, 1991, World Congress Centre, Melbourne, Australia.

2. Training figures on dollar amount spent are from Nell P. Eurich, "The Learning Industry," the Carnegie Foundation.

3. Michele L. Bechtell, "Teaching Management for Quality Improvement," *Journal for Quality and Participation*, June 1990, 92–96.

4. Donald F. Van Eynde and Roger W. Spencer, "Lecture Versus Experiential Learning: Effects on Long-term Memory," *The Organizational Behavior Teaching Review* XII, 4, (1987–1988).

5. This analogy is attributed to Thorstein Veblen by Robert K. Merton in his introduction to "The Ambivalence of Organization Leaders: An Interpretive Essay," *The Contradictions of Leadership* by James F. Oates, Jr. (New York: Appleton-Century-Crofts-Meridith Corp., 1970), 4.

6. Merton, "Ambivalence," 4.

7. Daniel H. Kim uses this terminology in "Toward Learning Organizations: Integrating Total Quality Control and Systems Thinking", 30 June, 1989, to describe the difference between single loop learning and double loop learning, two distinctions made by Argyris and Schon in *Organizational Learning*.

8. Argyris and Schon, *Organizational Learning*, 46–58.

9. Ibid., 37.

10. Hoffman, *Old Scapes*.

11. Argyris and Schon, *Organizational Learning*, 16.

12. Ray Stata, "Organizational Learning: The Key To Management Innovation," *Sloan Management Review*, Spring 1989, 64.

13. Argyris and Schon, *Organizational Learning*, 13.

14. Joseph D. Williams, "Multidimensional Managers," Warner Lambert.

15. *The Wall Street Journal,* 22 October 1991, 1.

16. Argyris and Schon, *Organizational Learning,* 11.

17. Ibid., 43.

18. Michele L. Bechtell, *Living with Paradox.* Forthcoming.

*Myth associates leadership with superior position. It assumes that when you are on top you are automatically a leader. But leadership is not a place, it is a process.*
    —James M. Kouzes and Barry Z. Posner

— ✧ —

## CHAPTER 8

# Management, Learning, and Leadership:

## Are They Different?

I recently met with the CEO of a financial services company who needed help in rejuvenating a companywide quality improvement effort; it had lost the "magic." He was desperate for assistance. "My people just are not getting involved," he complained. "No matter how hard I push, people just aren't making the changes needed to improve quality at their own levels in the organization. I have spent money on training, given speech after speech, and written memo after memo. Push, push, push. I am exhausted from always being in a 'hard sell' mode." This CEO, discouraged but still committed to the change process, wanted to discover what he might do differently.

Over the next several days, I heard many complaints from employees about senior management. The employees, while excited about quality improvement, were still waiting for direction from the top. "Nothing has really changed," I heard over and over again. "It's just the same old stuff from top management. They say that we are going to change 'business as usual,' but where are the significant changes? We got sent for some training, and some of us got put onto quality improvement teams. But nothing much else has happened." Although they disagreed on the reasons, top managers and others alike saw the same result— organizational paralysis. The old ways prevailed, and there was disappointment on both sides.

Mid-level managers say that the leaders aren't leading. Top management says that no one is following. Who is right? They both are. The organization is stuck in a leadership gridlock. The problem is one of semantics.

Why is understanding the nature of leadership so difficult? In the more stable operating environments of the past, many people in service organizations made it to the top by making astute political moves, being methodical, or making significant individual contributions. Their success depended, in large part, on their ability to maintain and manage the status quo. Service organizations can no longer afford to be merely maintenance oriented. No matter what level you are at in the organization, if you are attempting to achieve total cultural transformation, you need more than good management skills. You must be able to move yourself and others from inertia to initiative—you must know how to lead.

## LET'S DEBUNK SOME LEADERSHIP MYTHS

What exactly is leadership? Let's first take a look at what leadership is not.

• **Leadership is not pushing.** Many people think that the only way to motivate others to action is by pushing, and pushing hard. We will look at this concept of pushing later in this chapter. For now, suffice it to say that if you are seeking long-term, lasting organizational change, you cannot push intelligent people in directions that they do not want to go, nor can you force your opinions, ideas, and decisions onto them. Intelligent people *choose* to follow.

• **Leadership is not being a hero.** Many people view the leader as a daring but isolated achiever. In reality, leadership has less to do with heroics and individualism and more to do with altering fundamental relationships. To alter any key relationship, you need the active participation of all relevant parties, leader and followers.

• **Leaders do not have to be business school graduates.** Some people think that effective leaders must be well-versed in traditional business skills, such as those typically associated with graduate business school curricula. Truth is, effective leadership has less to do with number crunching and more to do with taking people to places they have never been before. Rational thinking, while necessary for effective leadership, is not sufficient. Effective leaders motivate people to action by appealing to their emotional and visceral sides.

• **Leadership is not creating shared vision.** Creating and sustaining shared vision is critical to success, but it is a form of management, albeit a macro form of management. Whether managing local budgets, participating in cross-functional problem solving efforts, providing recognition for a job well done, or creating shared vision, the function of management is to consolidate and maximize *existing* resources.[1] Leadership has more to do with making choices, acting upon new options, and generating *new* sources of revenue.

• **Leadership is not synonymous with learning.** Many people confuse leadership with learning, describing the leader as learner and teacher. Learning is an adaptive and alternating function designed to increase flexibility and to improve the quality of individual and group thought processes and skills. While learning is necessary for change, it is *preparatory* to effective leadership. Leadership is not about being a perpetual student, devoting time to always "getting ready," or generating and understanding new options and alternatives. Leaders make the choices from *among* the alternatives. The difference between learning and leadership can be likened to the difference between ambivalence and choice.

• **Leadership is not just a relationship between leaders and followers.** Many people think that leadership only takes place in the context of interactions between leaders and followers. This micro focus on personal interactions ignores the equally important macro aspects of leadership, such as selecting the design of the organizational structure and selecting a competitive strategy. Leadership requires a micro focus as well as a macro focus at every level of the organization, from the CEO's office to the clerk at the front desk.

• **Leadership is not the same as being at the top of the organization.** Many people believe that the sole responsibility for leadership rests at the top of the organization. Nothing could be further from the truth. While leadership is indeed necessary at the top of the organization, it is not sufficient for companywide continuous improvement. Such a leadership myth can be fatal to organizations because it encourages people at lower levels to abandon any leadership capabilities they might have in favor of learned helplessness. Everyone has leadership skills and must be given the opportunity to use them. Leadership is a practice and is related to behavior, not position.

## LEADERSHIP IS A UNIQUE AND NECESSARY FUNCTION

Organizations need leadership to jump from old and comfortable ways to new and untested ways. While effective management and learning skills are certainly critical to organizational transformation, they are not sufficient to ensure continuous quality improvement if there is a lack of leadership. What is the unique contribution that strong leadership makes to every change process? Whereas management specifies the *what,* and learning suggests the *how,* leadership provides the *why.*

Much of today's confusion over the nature of leadership arises because many people combine management, learning, and leadership activities into just two categories: management and leadership. Abraham Zaleznick, in a now-famous *Harvard Business Review* article entitled "Managers and Leaders: Are They Different?", argued that managers and leaders were different in the way they approached problems, human relationships, and their organizations.[2] While the distinction between leaders and managers was an important contribution to human resource development, this distinction is limiting for today's organizations.

The question for today's managers is "Management, leadership, and learning: Are they different?" The answer is a loud yes. Management, leadership, and learning are unique and necessary elements of the change process (see Figure 8.1). Whereas learning concerns widening our scope of alternatives to create new possibilities, and management focuses on consolidating and maximizing our existing resources, leadership is about strategic choice.

What value does leadership bring to an organization that learning and management do not? The answer is change. Leaders propel their organizations into the future. They take you on a journey to new places, and in so doing, you discover new talents and capabilities in the adventure. Learning is an adaptive role, preparatory to effective leadership. Management creates order out of chaos to put strength and muscle behind leadership. But leadership is progressive direction. Leadership is the process of activating change; it is the decisiveness to move resources from areas of lesser to greater productivity.[3]

## THE CORNERSTONES OF LEADERSHIP: GETTING AT THE "WHY"

In debunking some common myths about leadership, we have already launched an inquiry into its true nature. We have seen that leadership differs from management and learning. We have seen that leadership is a practice, not a position on the organizational chart. Leaders lead the way; they take us on a journey to new places. Now, let's look at what makes an effective leader. Strong, effective leadership depends upon the following behaviors:

- Leaders make choices.
- Leaders pull as well as push.
- Leaders redefine boundaries.

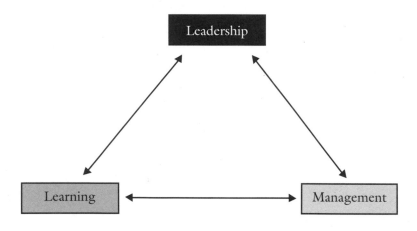

**Figure 8.1:** There are three requirements for continuous improvement

- Leaders are catalysts.
- Leaders manage at the margin.

Let's look at each of these principles in more detail.

## Leaders provide meaningful choices

Today's operating environment is turbulent. Rapid changes in market conditions, technology, and strategic partnerships often make people feel vulnerable and hesitant. In such an uncertain environment, effective leadership becomes a critical success factor. The director of personnel at Olivetti, Daniele Mosca, explains:

> *We have experienced that a management team without a leader, or with a leader who has limited power, even if composed of members of great worth and individual personality, leans more to a search for equilibrium within the team than to making real choices and decisions faster than competitors.[4]*

Leaders start the change process by making the difficult choices that enable the organization to survive. Whether it is selecting priorities for organizational focus, making a commitment to develop a new product or service, reorganizing for the $n$th time, or knowing when to break the rules, the leadership role involves strategic choice. Leaders make the hard choices of how to allocate or reallocate organizational resources to create change. Peter Senge, professor of management at the Massachusetts Institute of Technology, describes the nature of choice:

> *Choice is different from desire. Try an experiment. Say "I want." Now, say "I choose." What is the difference? For most people, "I want" is passive; "I choose" is active. For most, wanting is a state of deficiency—we want what we do not have. Choosing is a state of sufficiency—electing to have what we truly want. For most of us, as we look back over life, we can see that certain choices we made played a pivotal role in how our life developed. So, too, will the choices we make in the future be pivotal.*[5]

As Peter Senge indicates, choice allows you to operate from a position of power and control. For most people, however, making strategic choices is not easy. Why? Because it means that they can't have it all. To choose one option means that you must give up on another. Robert Frost, in his poem "The Road Not Taken," ties together the concepts of choice, paths, and journey.

> *...And both that morning equally lay*
> *In leaves no step had trodden black.*
> *Oh, I kept the first for another day!*
> *Yet knowing how way leads on to way,*
> *I doubted if I should ever come back.*
>
> *I shall be telling this with a sigh*
> *Somewhere ages and ages hence:*
> *Two roads diverged in a wood, and I—*
> *I took the one less traveled by,*
> *And that has made all the difference.*[6]

Choices are critical to progress. If we sit at the fork in the road and do not make a decision, we will never know what lies along either path and we will never move forward. We may imagine all we like; we may analyze the advantages and disadvantages of each path ad nauseam; we can prepare for our journey indefinitely. Do what we will, if we never get down to the hard work of making choices, we achieve nothing but stasis.

Leaders are decisive, and in this way they create the future. Only through choice do we discover previously unknown capabilities that we have yet to use or fully leverage. Certain conscious as well as subconscious capabilities emerge and develop when we are confronted with the trials of our journey. But we restructure our skills and talents to survive and succeed along the way. In this way, leadership and choice are linked directly to transformation.

## Leaders pull as well as push

You can don a handsome uniform, carry a shiny baton, and march down Main Street—and be all alone. To have a parade, people must line up behind you. Whose fault is it if the people don't start marching? Is it their fault? Is it the training department's fault? No. It is the leader's responsibility to draw people forward. You can't force intelligent people to follow you, nor can you push them forward against their will. In the short term, of course, some people may follow you, if they fear for their jobs, but they will withhold real commitment to the bitter end. In the long run, all of the threatening and coaxing in the world will get you nowhere.

Our Western culture typically associates aggression (pushing) with strength and virility. This attitude has led to the "I say, you do" school of management. People who take a linear approach to achievement assume a direct link between cause and effect. They believe that if only they push harder, they will get better results. But pushing harder is not the solution. In addition to pushing, effective leadership requires many passive and nonlinear skills.

The difference between active and passive may be thought of as the difference between *pressing* and *assessing*. Active, assertive leaders push for change. They force their choices upon others. More passive leaders take a selective approach to accomplishment. Whether it is choosing the best person for the job or developing a subordinate to take on new responsibilities, there are important selection tasks that have nothing to do with pushing but have everything to do with initiating and supporting transformational change.

Leadership is not as simple as setting direction and then telling others to follow. It requires creating the conditions for change, and this often takes place in indirect ways. Is nonlinear leadership slower than more aggressive styles? Not in the long run. While a more aggressive approach may give some people a sense of immediate satisfaction, their "good" strategies may never get fully implemented. If others are not given the opportunity to exercise individual choice in the decision-making process, they may comply, but their hearts will never truly be committed.

## Leaders redefine boundaries: be a systems thinker

The third cornerstone of strong leadership is boundary specification. Whereas learning requires that we traverse existing boundaries, and management is about building strength within well-defined boundaries, leadership is the act of changing the boundaries on the map. Leaders do not get caught up in the constraints of the status quo. Instead, they operate from outside the system, changing boundaries and relationships much like one manages the pieces of a large jigsaw puzzle.[7]

Boundaries give meaning to action. Every day we make distinctions and assign labels that define, identify, and evaluate things and people. And then we take action accordingly. We make important decisions based on distinctions like "urgent," "competitive," and "cooperative." And we evaluate success based on distinctions like "quality," "profitable," and "costly." Such descriptions require that comparisons be made, that things be put in relation to other things.

At a minimum, relations are established through the presence of the boundary *not*. Management, for example, is best understood in relation to non-management. Similarly, competitors are best understood in relation to non-competitors. *Before* is best associated in relation to *after; out* is best understood in relation to *in*. The remarkable thing is that *A* and non-*A* are actually part of the same unity. Without one, the other does not exist. By defining *A*, we also define non-*A*.[8] In this way, reality is socially constructed.

The very act of leadership involves drawing distinctions. At any particular point in time, members of the organization view their situation, individually and collectively, through a select frame. Change is manifest when a new frame or paradigm is used to view the same world in a different way. Whether it is the rearrangement of the organizational chart, a merger, or a new customer/supplier partnership, fundamental change follows altered boundaries.

Leaders challenge the existing frame and provide us with the means for constructing a new one. They can challenge it through argument, human development, structure, or individual action, but the bottom line is that they get people out of their perceptual traps. In this way, leaders get people to redefine their own boundaries. The leader's challenge is not to find a niche within the existing space as perceived by others, but to create new space that is off the original map.[9]

How do you redraw the map in your favor? Leaders focus on four main boundaries. By stepping out in front, they redefine before and after. In this way, leaders change the boundaries of experience through personal action. In changing boundaries specified on the organizational chart, leaders challenge structure—"my authority versus yours." Through strategic moves, leaders challenge external boundaries that differentiate the organization from its competitors—us versus them. Last, but not least, leaders redefine the "family" boundaries by deciding which people have membership and which requirements have priority in daily affairs—in versus out. As you will see shortly, managing each of these boundaries is critical to strong, effective leadership.

## Leaders are catalysts

Leaders initiate. They start the change process and then let it go. They know that while they are decision-makers, they are not *the* decision-makers. A leader does not own the change process, because he or she is but one of many intelligent decision-makers. Organizational transformation can only occur when all decision-makers commit to the plan. And the only way people can commit is if they struggle with old and new perspectives on their own.

For many people, one of the greatest leadership challenges lies in releasing their hold on outcomes. Leadership requires that you give up control, at least in the traditional "I say, you do" sense. For many managers, giving up control is counter-intuitive. Sgt. Couper of Madison, Wisconsin, describes:

> *Some managers initially think that giving their employees the opportunity to participate in the decision-making process will only result in the same decision that the managers would have made. They say, "I am the boss, and 99 out of 100 times I come to the same conclusion that my employee teams did. What the hell do I need employee work teams for?" Well, it is because of the carry-out phase. If you are the only one who came to the decision, then all your time has to be spent trying to kick them in the tail to try and get them to implement your ideas. When you empower work teams, once they see what needs to be done and you give them the authority to do it, your work is all done and you can get on to more important things instead of being the cop of the workplace.*

Even the most elegant strategies can fail if there is no commitment from every individual who is responsible for implementing the plan. And people can only commit if they have choice. Besides, who really knows best? Not the people who are one or two layers of management away from the action. Only those individuals who work in the system are qualified to determine what is achievable at their level.

## Leaders manage at the margin

Effective leaders manage from the margin. This requires that leaders pay attention to the state of "organizational readiness" for change. One of the greatest gifts a leader can have is sensing when people and systems are at a breaking point—or a starting point. Like the straw that broke the camel's back, a small, almost imperceptible quantitative change can result in a significant qualitative change in outcome.[10] The trick is to sense, in advance, which straw in the $n-1$th one and which is the $n$th straw.

Effective leaders understand that there are thresholds of change—critical levels of energy—which must be reached for boundaries to move and change to happen. So they are sensitive to the readiness and willingness of others to participate in the change process.

## REWRITING THE LEADERSHIP SCRIPT: SEEKING CATALYSTS, NOT HEROES

So how can you lead in this era of consent? How can you direct action if you cannot control the outcome? The answer is to be a catalyst for change. Effective leaders understand that people must choose to change themselves, so they work hard to create the conditions under which natural and appropriate change may occur.

Leaders can set direction in many ways. While some current leadership theories advocate a single approach to leadership such as consensus over control or inspiration over practicality, a single style just doesn't exist. Leading others amidst the complexity of today's operating environment requires adeptness at active as well as passive interactions, emotional as well as rational appeals, objective as well as subjective perspectives, and proactive as well as reactive skills. Rather than style, it is progressive action that counts.

The leader, as catalyst, creates conditions in which appropriate change can be guaranteed to take place. As agents of change, effective leaders use four decision-making processes to move themselves and others from inertia to action (see Figure 8.2). These following four leadership practices are necessary at every level of the organization.

1. **Benchmark.** You can inform strategic choices by interpreting or benchmarking the competitive environment. Leaders pay attention to what "they" are doing.

2. **Organize.** You can use structure to match the critical tasks with your available skills and resources and to channel decision-making. Leaders shape relationships based on what "we" need to satisfy our long-term goals.

3. **Nurture.** Leaders develop and nurture their people. They know that the more they understand and respond to their people's fluid needs, the greater the probability that their

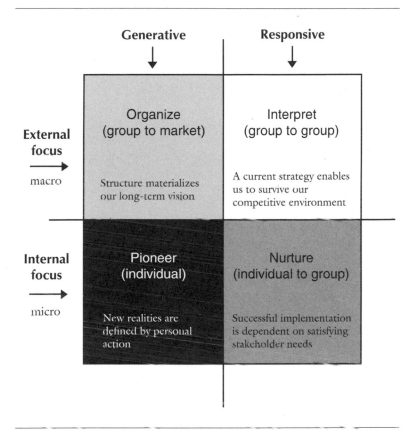

**Figure 8.2:** There are four key leadership practices

strategies will be implemented. Leaders supply what "you" need to get the job done.

4. **Pioneer.** Leaders pioneer the way. By stepping out in front, they model the way for others. Leaders act in good faith with what "I" believe.

Although you may feel more comfortable with some of these leadership skills than with others, all four leadership practices must be pursued simultaneously. Let's examine each of these leadership practices in more detail.

## Benchmark: interpret the context

In the year 500 B.C., a Chinese general named of Sun Tzu wrote, "If you know your enemy and know yourself, you need not fear the result of a hundred battles."[11] Today, we are in an economic war, and these words are just as relevant for today's leaders as they were to others long ago.

Strong leaders possess keen comparative capabilities. In the capacity of a four-star general, making astute comparisons of strengths and weaknesses to select competitive strategies is critical to success. Effective leaders take the initiative to collect external as well as internal information to assess the strengths and weaknesses of their organization in the larger competitive context.

Good information is key to selecting competitive strategies. As we saw in Part I of this book, conventional management decisions based on the vertical organization chart often err on the myopic side, emphasizing parochial decision-making and short-term perspectives. But in an increasingly competitive environment, it is critical to understand people and issues outside the boundaries of your organization. Keeping an eye on the big picture, especially the activities of your competitors, enhances your chances of survival and gives you strategic flexibility in the long run.

How do leaders determine which strategies are most promising for their organization? They benchmark the procedures and practices of their organization against others in their operating environment. Once they know their own internal operations and the operations of others, they move to incorporate the best practices to gain superiority. Armed with timely and relevant information, they weigh their competitive strengths and weaknesses and then go on to select appropriate strategies. The benefits of benchmarking are several:

• **Competitive benchmarking can help you differentiate a wise strategy from a foolish strategy.** Managers who fail to understand critical factors at play in their organizational context may lead their people in the wrong direction, with catastrophic results for the work unit and the company.

• **Benchmarking can help you identify advantageous partnerships.** This will help you compensate for your weaknesses.

• **Benchmarking can help you identify areas within your company which need improving.**

• **Competitive benchmarking can provide you with real-world data.** This indicates how well you are doing in the eyes of the customer relative to other service organizations.

• **Benchmarking helps you to get away from autocratic decision-making.** Most people will line up behind a leader when there is an enemy to fight or an industry-best practice to beat. Unlike an edict, which is externally imposed, seeing the competitive challenge is an automatic and consensual direction-setting practice. In my work with executive teams, I notice that benchmarking plays a beneficial role in helping top managers change their perspectives; benchmarking can provide individuals a graceful way to reposition without invalidating themselves.

Benchmarking is an objective, rational, responsive, and active leadership practice. It is objective by being externally focused. It is responsive by making strategic choices and allocating resources in reaction to developments in the competitive arena. It is rational in that interpretations are based on facts, not emotion. It is active in that benchmarking requires initiative.

Benchmarking is an urgent leadership requirement. Your competitors have already benchmarked you, and they are working to capitalize on your failings! So the more you know about yourself, them, and other high performers, the more you know what is possible and the better defense you can prepare.

Unfortunately, benchmarking is frequently underutilized. Many people believe that benchmarking only works against direct competitors whereby you make specific competitor-to-competitor comparisons for the product, service, or function of interest. But benchmarking is a generic process. The object of benchmarking is to identify management practices, processes, and methods that you can copy, innovate around, or leverage. You can benchmark within your own organization by comparing various internal operations to identify best operating practices. You can also make comparisons between similar functions within the same broad industry. Are you unique in your industry? Then look at other industries! Many business functions or processes like training, performance management, finance, and legal services are the same regardless of industry. You can benchmark against any company or organization that has a proven track record in continuous improvement. Good management practices are good management practices, regardless of industry.

Wise leaders never take their eyes off the competition. Many people believe that benchmarking is "spot checking," something you do when you feel like it or happen to have the time. But benchmarking is a leadership process. Benchmarking requires constant updating because, over time, every other organization is making changes to improve its operations. Benchmarks indicate a relative position, and updates are needed to keep them current.

Benchmarking is a leadership practice that you can do yourself. Many people believe that they have to hire third parties to collect comparative data. Nothing could be further from the truth. Not only can benchmarking be done by yourself and others in your work unit, but it is actually most effective when you are personally engaged in the data collection process. How can you begin? Regardless of whether you are benchmarking an administrative process or the design characteristics of your products and services, there is a simple method for benchmarking that you can do yourself. It incorporates the PDSA cycle that we saw for continuous improvement in chapter 4:

- **Plan.** You can start the planning process by asking yourself the following questions.

   —Which processes are we going to benchmark?

   —Which organizations are we going to benchmark?

   —How will we collect information about our target organization(s)?

- **Do.** Now you are ready to launch the data collection process.

   —Collect data.

   —Visit other organizations or internal functions.

   —Make phone calls, and so on.

- **Study.** Next, study your collected data.

  —Is this other organization better than ours?

  —How much better?

  —Why are they better? What are they doing that we are not doing?

  —Can we do it too?

  —Should we do it?

- **Act.** Finally, you are ready to incorporate lessons learned during the benchmarking process. Using the standard PDSA process for continuous improvement, you can develop, implement, and then evaluate your action plans.[12]

In summary, benchmarking is an important leadership practice. Through benchmarking, leaders gather information on themselves and others to make strategic choices that move resources from areas of lesser productivity to other, more effective ones. Through benchmarking, a leader can act as a catalyst, letting the competitive information do the talking. One note of caution: To make the most out of the interpreting leadership practice, any opportunities for improvement that are uncovered in the benchmarking process should never be considered a reflection of any person's failure. Benchmarking is done in the spirit of competition and continuous improvement. The leader, as catalyst, provides the means by which all people can get access to competitive information and then provides the support for implementing new practices identified during the benchmarking process.

## Organize: match scarce resources with critical tasks

As Chris Argyris, professor of management at Harvard Business School, once noted,

> *The mob is a collectivity. It is a collection of people who may run, shout, and mill about together. But it is a collectivity which cannot make a decision or take action in its own name, and its boundaries are vague and diffuse.[13]*

Leaders organize. They add value by selecting the strategic structure that channels individual activity and allocates scarce resources. Through structure, they turn a collection of otherwise inert and undifferentiated resources into working entities.[14]

In this way, leaders are architects. They are designers. Through organizational design, hierarchical reporting relationships, staffing, and governing policies, leaders define the cause and effect that crystallizes our activities into the status quo; they make something work in practice. Structure brings several benefits:

• **Structure defines your organization and the markets you serve.** Setting goals, choosing the form of the organization, and defining authority structures are ultimately tied to ambitions in the marketplace. Every organization wants to generate demand for the organization or work unit's products or services. In defining critical tasks, priorities, and staffs, leaders make the choices that materialize the collective long-term vision.

• **Through structure, leaders can force change.** A change in context—structure, reporting relationships, staffing patterns, and/or management systems—can stimulate and sustain new management approaches by altering the information that employees receive, the interactions they must manage, and the roles they must play. By itself, reorganizing will not accomplish much unless such action is supported in other ways. But changes in attitude generally follow and reinforce new organizational designs.[15]

• **Organizing reduces complexity.** Leaders use structure to reduce the number of decisions and factors that must be considered simultaneously. None of us can remember every detail of our lives. We have to organize information so that we can easily find it when necessary. Similarly, organizational designers think hierarchically when facing complex problems. They break down tasks into relatively simple units and then regroup them for ease of recognition and control. By providing a template which makes organizational priorities clear, leaders reduce chaos.

• **Structure communicates resource allocation priorities to all members of the organization.** Structure helps lower level managers understand the logic behind resource allocations. And it helps people at the top of the organization understand their roles and responsibilities for managing scarce resources.

• **Organizational structure increases delegation and enables others to act more swiftly and appropriately.** Every organization needs an authority structure to shape key roles and tasks. A solid organizational structure defines the rules of the drama—not only your obligations, but what you must do to get everyone else to play their roles on the same stage.

What are some structures that can force change in the context of continuous quality improvement? Organizing along process lines rather than product lines is one way. Introducing cross-functional process improvement teams, decentralizing decision-making through self-managed work teams, introducing new performance management systems, updating information systems, physically moving offices closer to internal customers, and creating quality steering committees are just a few of the structural changes that are frequently associated with positive change.

Organizational design requires considerable technical knowledge of how to analyze, modify, and simulate the behavior of complex human systems. Unfortunately, few managers ever receive such training in business school, and fewer still learn from their immediate supervisors. There are some specific organizing principles that make the difference between poor organizational design and more effective design. These include focus on the long-term vision, sequential thinking, careful selection, and personal involvement.

• **Focus on the long-term strategic intent.** Whereas competitive benchmarking is a necessary leadership practice, it is not enough. Competitive benchmarking is an objective leadership practice that focuses on responding to the current competitive threats. Organizations are indeed controlled by the situational constraints of their competitive operating environment. But ceaselessly focusing on others with a view to comparison leads only to greatness by contrast. Focusing only on today's competitive realities can obscure or distort potentially useful partnerships that may be relevant to the organization's success over the long term. In contrast, organizing is a proactive leadership practice that looks beyond today's problems; it crystallizes the long-term strategic intent into the status quo. Rather than merely react to the strategic initiatives of others, leaders use structure to force their environment to fit their own long-term strategic intent. They look forward with structure as well as look sideways with competitive information.

• **Demonstrate skill in sequential thinking.** The purpose behind organizational design is mechanistic. In the organizing role, leaders are orderly and systematic. To select an appropriate structure, the leader applies a logical, rational thought process, placing people and activities in a causal sequence. This sequence is based on the leader's perception of a series of cause and effect events; that is, the leader views certain events as preceding or causing other events.[16]

• **Demonstrate skill in integrated thinking.** Skills in sequential thinking must be supported with systems thinking skills. Effective leaders understand that the parts are not only internally connected to one another but are also connected to the external environment. They focus not only on the internal structure but also on the industry systems that define the larger environment in which they operate.

• **Involve others.** How a structural change is introduced is very important to its ultimate success. Changes imposed from the top without the involvement of individuals affected by them usually fail. Bring together in a committee or task force those people who might ultimately work together. Give them the task of examining the interdependencies between their departments and ask for recommendations for managing those interdependencies. Incorporate their recommendations in the final scheme.

• **Be careful who you pick for the job.** The design of the organizational chart defines authority. But when it comes to appointing an individual to fill a position of authority, the leader must do so carefully. A poor "pick" will reflect directly upon his or her leadership as a whole. Effective leadership does not exist without followers. A particularly powerful leadership tool is the placement and promotion of individuals who support the transformation with what they do, not just with what they say. The people to whom you delegate tasks and authority must inspire confidence and gain the respect of those around them. The more competent and respected the people are who have been put in charge, as evaluated by others in the organization, the more favorably others will feel toward the directives they issue.[17]

• **Stay involved.** In too many cases, delegation becomes an excuse for abdication. In and of itself, delegating does not constitute leadership. You must remain an active catalyst, constantly revisiting the structuring process matching individual skills and capabilities to tasks.

When all is said and done, how do you know whether you have an effective organizational design within your firm? When everyone knows

- where the organization is headed: its objectives
- what tasks have to be done on a regular basis to achieve those objectives
- who is responsible and has the authority for accomplishing those objectives
- how the parts are to work together

In summary, whereas benchmarking suggests an appropriate strategy for surviving current competitive realities in the short term, leaders actively shape the design of the organizational structure and its governing policies to fulfill their long-term strategic intent. In the organizing role, leaders continually match people, skills, and critical tasks with organizational resources to ensure mission accomplishment. In this way, a leader acts as a catalyst, allowing those in their assigned positions to make appropriate decisions on behalf of the organization. Organizing is not a one-time event; instead, it is a process of constantly revisiting the mission and goals in light of changes in market issues, resource constraints, and strategic intent.

## Nurture: remove the limiting factors

Structure and strategy are indeed important leadership practices. But what happens if you try to lead others through these purely objective and rational means? You may fail to implement your strategy. The best of strategies can fail in the face of unexpected circumstances unique to every situation.

A critical leadership question that is often neglected is "Can this strategy be implemented?" People who strictly go by the rules, who never rely on common sense or exhibit flexibility in the face of the unexpected, can lead their organizations to the brink of disaster. Consider this experience related in C. Woodham-Smith's biography of Florence Nightingale.[18]

> *In January 1855 when the army before Sebastopol was being ravaged by scurvy, a shipload of cabbages was thrown into the harbor at Balaclava on the grounds that it was not consigned to anyone. This happened not once but several times. During November, December and January 1854 to 1855, when green coffee was being issued to the men, there were 173,000 rations of tea in store at Balaclava; 20,000 lbs. of lime juice arrived for the troops on December 10, 1854. But none was issued until February. Why? Because no order existed for the inclusion of tea and lime juice in the daily ration.*
>
> *Again at the end of December there were blankets enough in store, says Miss Nightingale, to have given a third one to every man. But the men lay on the muddy ground with nothing under them and nothing over them since their blankets had been lost in battle or destroyed in the hurricane, because the regulations did not entitle them to replacement.*
>
> *At Scutari, the Hospitals Commission recorded in January 1855: "Goods have been refused although they were, to our personal knowledge, lying in abundance in the store of the Purveyor. This was done because they had not been examined by the Board of the Survey."*

Horrible things can happen when the rules we have designed to guide us are applied indiscriminately. While rules and reporting relationships are essential for the general class of situations we expect to encounter, hierarchy alone ignores the dynamic aspects of growth and evolution.

In reality, business conditions are fluid. Supplies aren't always delivered on time. Employees don't always have the requisite skills. And family emergencies crop up that remove valuable people from the scene at the worst possible moment. Every day, issues arise from the constant interaction between suppliers, employees, and customers which create subtle variances in expected behaviors.

When these things happen, leaders do not get a free day off. Leaders are expected to make wise decisions as conditions change. While popular opinion is to think of the leader as a first starter, successful leadership is equally determined by the ability of individuals to act decisively in response to situational constraints, to meet the unique needs of the circumstances and the people and, yet, fulfill the mission. In these emergent situations, not only must leaders make the most of an awkward situation, but they must also turn every situation to their advantage.

In this way, leadership has personality at its center. In addition to formal structure and competitive strategy, effective leaders "fill in the sketch of collective purpose with color and detail," to save it from narrowness, incompleteness, and waste.[19] An effective leader understands the importance of each and every individual who touches or is touched by the organization, including the employee whose child is diagnosed with cancer, the individual customer whose expectations for service are disappointed, and the employee who is fulfilling responsibilities but is not having fun on the job. The most effective leaders are the most human of all. For them, the goal of all is tied to the goal of one.

This necessitates an informal decision-making process to fulfill the needs of others at the moment. Knowing when it is appropriate to bend the rules to accommodate a particular situation and sensing when others who are essential to the accomplishment of the overall mission need special support is critical to success. While we may like to think that our world is predictable, effective leaders know that they cannot rely on the formal authority specified on the organizational chart alone—they also seek to satisfy the personal needs of others on an ongoing basis.

This informal side of leadership differs from the formal organizing side in that the nurturing aspect of leadership is a result of behavior rather than organizational structure. It is less of a vertical relationship and more of a horizontal one. In contrast to managing from behind a desk in the large corporate office, it is MBWA, management by walking around. Informal leadership requires knowledge of how people interact and respond in different organizational situations.

This nurturing aspect of leadership requires an informal decision-making style, one that is passive, subjective, nonlinear, and responsive. It is nonlinear in the sense that circumstances arise that are not necessarily rational or sequential in nature yet which still require strategic choices to be made. It is passive in that the strength of this type of leadership rests in the leader's ability to selectively prune, weed, and nurture individuals and resources to enhance their natural talents. It is subjective in that the focus is on the individual, not the institution—when people can fulfill their own needs, they can ultimately service the organization as a whole. And it is responsive to the needs of the moment.

Nurturing, developing, economy—call it what you will, this informal aspect of leadership requires employee focus for its success. Successful implementation of any strategy, no matter how omnipotent the leader may think he or she is, depends not on what you accomplish but on what your employees accomplish. Making others feel secure in the knowledge that their needs will be met is an important leadership practice. Others feel that they are "in" the family of concern, not "out" in the cold, abandoned like the soldiers in Florence Nightingale's story. Leaders are receptive and responsive to others' personal and professional issues. They are interested in any concerns others might have about their ability to get their jobs done. When you respect your people, they will respect you.

To be successful, leaders know that they need the full participation of all of their key stakeholders. They do not behave as isolated individuals. They understand that authority is not simply assigned from above, it is also conferred by the people with whom they interact on a daily basis. In this way, leaders exhibit both individualism and interdependence, the ability to sensitively gauge how actions and events will influence others. This leadership practice does not involve unidirectional "telling." Rather, it is a circular process of giving and eliciting feedback in an environment of safety, openness, and trust.

## Pioneer: model the way

Beyond organizing, benchmarking, and nurturing, strong leaders take the lead in the truest sense. They step out in front and illuminate the path to show those behind them which way to head. In this respect, leaders *lead* the change, they do not simply direct it. They go first; they change first. You can always tell when individuals have tried to go about the change process without changing themselves first; you hear murmurs that the top team does not "walk the talk."

If you must push at all in the leadership process, push forward as a pioneer. This does not mean pushing others, it means pushing yourself. Pioneers actively define new frontiers. In contrast to explorers, the first people to venture forth as part of the process of inquiry, and settlers, the ones to develop and enhance the areas already established, pioneers are the ones who establish roots. They activate ideas, converting the partially known into the definable. There is a claiming connotation to pioneering. There is also the spirit of adventure of going into territory where you have never been before.

Pioneering is a unique but essential aspect of leadership. It is active, in that pioneers learn by doing, and it is nonrational, in that pioneers base their actions on faith and spirit, not data or prior experience. Pioneering is venturing off into the unknown, there is no model to copy. Let's take a look at how it differs from the other three leadership practices.

• **Pioneering differs from organizing in that it lacks hierarchy.** A pioneer is frequently out there alone. Whereas organizational architecture focuses on material resources and organizing principles, pioneering takes place as a result of sheer will and often in the absence of significant resources.

• **Pioneering differs from the benchmarking aspect of leadership in that its every action is unmeasureable and unknowable.** Pioneers are driven by visions of greatness, and they continually make one leap of faith after another. Whereas strategies focus on making the most of your operational constraints, when you pioneer, you force current resources, circumstances, and surroundings to fit your vision. Consider the small plant pushing up out of the earth in springtime. Just by emerging, the plant redefines the environment. Just like the seedling, pioneers change the environment for others. They are proactive and make progress through their own sweat equity.

• **Pioneering differs from the nurturing aspects of leadership in that it lacks interdependence.** Stepping out in front is purely personal. Pioneering involves self-initiative, and, as such, is the most individualistic aspect of leadership.

Pioneering leaders are persistence in action. Change, especially in longstanding relationships and institutions, does not happen overnight. It requires repeat attacks on the status quo. Many people think that they can take assertive action once and that that should fix things from then on. But pioneering leaders know that "hit and run" maneuvers never bring lasting change. They are constantly battling the forces that try to get them to revert to the more familiar and comfortable way things were for the others before the change.

Through individual action, pioneers challenge the status quo. They disturb the equilibrium. This can be difficult for others. In changing yourself, you force others to change. This can make people feel downright uncomfortable and anxious. Depending upon how much you challenge their comfort level, they may do or say things to encourage you to revert to your old ways. You may be accused of disloyalty or disregard for others' preferences. Or you may receive verbal threats that the other person will terminate a working relationship. These countermoves, while stressful, are no surprise to pioneering leaders.[20]

Pioneers do not take countermoves as a personal affront; in fact, they expect them. They know that other people do not make countermoves simply because they are dominating, controlling, or mean-spirited. They may be these things, but that is almost beside the point. Countermoves are par for the course when we begin to challenge the system and others around us. When you are up against the status quo, you are disturbing the equilibrium; otherwise you would not be pioneering.

The pioneering leadership challenge is to remain firm in the face of countermoves. Most of us want to take individual action, but we also want others to like our decisions. We want to challenge the status quo, yet we still want to receive praise and positive strokes. But this is not always possible, especially when you are challenging the very systems and people that chose you for your old and familiar ways. Countermoves test how well you understand your own position. It takes time for others to learn new behaviors to cope with the changed behaviors that you are demonstrating.

How can you be a pioneer? How can you create change? Through personal involvement. Specifically:

• **Concentrate on your own actions.** Do not blame others for your problems. You cannot change others, but you can change yourself. You are responsible for your own behavior, so examine your contribution to the problem and begin there. Blaming and fighting are often just ways of preserving familiar dysfunctional relationships, not changing them. Our own resistance to change is a limiting factor that cannot be underestimated.

• **Speak out in meetings.** If something bothers you, speak up about it. If you keep your opinions and beliefs to yourself, how will others learn? Speaking out helps you and others clarify issues and realities in organizational life. Remember, often negative reactions are due not so much to what is said but to how the message was delivered. Be clear in your message, but offer it in as positive a way as possible. A lot of positive change occurs when people build relationships in which others can be candid, not complicit in all of our craziness.

• **Use countermoves to achieve greater self-clarity.** When you challenge the familiar systems and the people around you, they may work hard to get you to change back. Countermoves challenge your commitment to your new behavior. The most challenging countermoves, the toughest questions, and the most irritating situations are those that test our mettle to the very core. Use countermoves to clarify what you want and how you want to do it.

• **Lead by doing.** You cannot pioneer from your armchair or by reading a book. But you can pioneer by letting your appointment calendar do the talking. How you spend your time, what activities have priority, and where you spend your energy are the strongest messages you can deliver about what you think is important. Pioneers are powerful role models. Everything that you say, do, or reward *is* the strategy.

• **Be entrepreneurial.** Pioneers are entrepreneurial and proactive rather than merely accessible or supportive. They take risks, encourage risk-taking in others, and support courageous decision-making at all levels. Encourage your people to jump on the bike and fall off a few times so that they can eventually ride it with ease. If you encourage a maintenance orientation, you end up with the status quo. Pioneers jump in and start doing.

• **Assure others that they are important to you.** When you confront others with your new behaviors, it is important to affirm your commitment to the organization and those around you. Explain that, while you value them and understand that they may have beliefs that are different from yours, you must be true to your own beliefs.

In summary, pioneering is a critical and unique aspect of leadership. Beyond interpreting your current operating environment for competitive advantage, organizing your resources for long-term effectiveness, and catering to the needs of others, pioneering is the heat of action. You need more than information, resources, and nurturance to be a leader—you need boundless energy, motivation, and independence to spearhead new efforts and endeavors. Pioneering is not a one-time event—it is an ongoing leadership practice.

## The leadership paradox

Leadership is inherently paradoxical. In advancing the change process, leaders select structure based on what "we" need for the collective good. At the same time, they seek to satisfy the unique needs of every emergent situation by focusing on what "you" need right now. Always watchful for what "they" are doing, leaders select strategies to survive competitive threats. And, knowing that no one person can ever change another—we can only choose to change ourselves—leaders take action based on what "I" believe to be true. In the aggregation and over time, these four leadership challenges are not only interrelated, they can often appear contradictory.

It is difficult to focus on the "I," "you," "we," and "they" at the same time. Yet emphasizing one leadership practice at the expense of the others will only abort the change process. The leadership solution is not in the or's: Focusing only on hierarchy can lead to bureaucratic paralysis. Focusing solely on individual needs can lead to anarchy. Focusing only on what others are doing leads to looking over your shoulder as you run and will cause you to trip on the path ahead. And challenging the status quo, just for the sake of it, will needlessly distract others. The solution to effective leadership is in finding the balance.

Leadership is the artful balancing of the pioneering, nurturing, organizing, and benchmarking requirements for change. The leader's solutions require both rational and nonrational considerations, passive as well as active behaviors, micro as well as macro perspectives, and proactive as well as responsive attitudes. Leadership is knowing when to break the rules to preserve the intent behind the rules. It is creating flexibility through structure, stability through change, innovation through "business as usual," and individual contribution through group interaction. Effective leaders create change amid the paradoxical realities of everyday existence.

## SUMMARY

Effective leadership is a unique and critical requirement for transformation. You cannot manage yourself into battle; your people must be led. Nor can you make significant progress by becoming a perpetual student. While learning provides flexibility and is preparatory to effective leadership, and management maximizes existing resources to perpetuate direction, leadership creates the conditions for change. You need leadership to move from inertia to action.

Where do you start? By releasing your hidden leaders. Your organization is full of people who already know how to lead. As we have seen, organizing, interpreting, nurturing, and pioneering are four key leadership practices. And not one of these skills is related to position on the organizational chart. Leadership is not concerned with telling others what to do; it concentrates on the *why*. Why do we pioneer? For the sense of adventure, to find new frontiers. Why do we benchmark? To survive, to beat our competitors. Why do we organize ourselves? So we won't fall apart, so we can meet the needs of the market, so we can materialize our long-term vision. Why do we develop and nurture others? So that all of our stakeholders will feel included, committed, and able to implement our strategies.

Most simply put, leadership, in an era of consent, requires being a catalyst. It involves providing conditions and processes which guarantee an appropriate outcome no matter who the decision-maker and no matter what the nature of the decision.

## Notes

1. Bechtell, *Living with Paradox.*

2. Abraham Zaleznik, "Managers and Leaders: Are They Different?" *Harvard Business Review,* April/May 1977, 67–78.

3. Noel M. Tichy and Mary Anne Devanna, "The Transformational Leader," *Training and Development Journal,* July 1986, 27–32.

4. Allison Farquhar, Paul Evans, and Kiran Tawadey, "Lessons from Practice in Managing Organizational Change," *Human Resource Management in International Firms: Change, Globalization, Innovation,* ed. Paul Evans, Yves Doz, and Andre Laurent (London: The Macmillan Press Ltd., 1989) 45.

5. Senge, *Fifth Discipline,* 360.

6. Robert Frost, "The Road Not Taken," *You Come Too* (New York: Holt, Rinehart and Winston, 1959), 84.

7. A complete model of the differences among leadership, learning, and management is presented in *Living with Paradox.*

8. Jeffrey D. Ford and Robert W. Backoff, "Organizational Change In and Out of Dualities and Paradox," *Paradox and Transformation*, 86.

9. Hamel and Prahalad, "Strategic Intent," *Harvard Business Review*, 73.

10. Thompson, "Being, Thought, and Action," *Paradox and Transformation*, 127–131.

11. Camp, *Benchmarking*, 3.

12. A more extensive description of the benchmarking process is provided throughout *Benchmarking*.

13. Argyris and Schon, *Organizational Learning*, 13.

14. Ralph H. Kilmann, *Beyond the Quick Fix* (San Francisco: Jossey-Bass Publishers, 1984).

15. Michael Beer, "The Critical Path for Change," *Corporate Transformation*, 17–45.

16. R. E. Boyatzis, *The Competent Manager: A Model for Effective Performance* (New York: John Wiley and Sons, Inc., 1982), 109.

17. Peter Block, *The Empowered Manager: Positive Political Skills at Work* (San Francisco: Jossey-Bass, 1987).

18. C. Woodham-Smith, *Florence Nightingale* (London: Fontana, 1964).

19. Charles H. Brent, *Leadership*, William B. Noble Lectures 1907 (New York: Longmans, Green and Co., 1908), 26–28.

20. Harriet Goldhor Lerner, *The Dance of Anger* (New York: Harper and Row, 1985), 33–39.

— ✧ —

*A life extended in a thousand directions risks depression and madness.*

—May Sarton

— ✧ —

*If you don't know where you are going, you might end up somewhere else.*

—Yogi Bera

# Policy Deployment:

## Focus on the Critical Few

"The will to succeed is worth less than the will to prepare." This age-old expression often pops into my mind when I come across a friend, colleague, or client who seems hesitant to do the hard work of planning. Yet the only way to create and sustain continuous quality improvement is to leave as little as possible to chance. We have all met people who have fire in their eyes, know where they want to go, and are full of passion. They are on a mission! They have a vision! Some of these people go on to achieve greatness. Others, however, fade away, seemingly incapable of scaling the heights to which they aspire. Anyone can dream. Only those who take the time to plan, however, can make their dreams a reality.

Continuous companywide quality improvement and organizational learning are closely related to planning.[1] When asked "How do you improve quality on a companywide basis?" many managers answer, "By having everyone work on quality improvement projects." But this is not enough. It is an approach to quality improvement which is neither reliable nor able to be systematically replicated or sustained throughout the organization.

How can you create a *reliable* quality improvement process? The answer lies in taking the time to plan, execute, monitor, and control a quality improvement strategy. Rigorous planning and review can help you answer important questions: Did we achieve our desired outcome? Which strategies worked for us? Which ones did not? Which assumptions proved valid? Which ones proved false? Careful planning brings focus and strategic control into the organization, ensuring that everyone knows what to do and how to learn from doing.

## TRADITIONAL PLANNING METHODS ARE INADEQUATE

Some organizations do not plan for quality improvement; they trust in Lady Luck for positive outcomes. But most organizations do plan to some extent. Despite good intentions, however, even the most committed planners often fail to attain their hoped-for results. You can have the most elegant strategy in the world and yet, as one CEO complained to me, "When I turn on the switch at the top of the organization, the lights don't go on below." Designing a nice strategy is one thing. Making it happen is another.

A variety of strategy implementation techniques exist, but the most popular one employed these days is the practice of Management by Objective, sometimes referred to as MBO. In this traditional approach to planning and performance management, top management establishes an objective—say, to improve quality by 20 percent by quarter's end—against which it measures a person or department's performance. MBO is hierarchical in nature, with each level of the organization providing plans and objectives which loosely reflect those "above" them.

As we saw in chapter 2, managing solely by the organizational chart can lead us to overmanage the individual boxes on the chart and undermanage important business issues that require cross-functional coordination. Vertical management systems like MBO can lead to suboptimal results for the enterprise as a whole. Specifically, MBO frequently fails as an effective performance management system for a number of reasons.[2]

• **MBO leads to "management after the fact."** Management by Objective focuses on results. But failure to achieve revenue targets, improved customer satisfaction, and/or cost reductions are lagging indicators of performance. They shed little light on the means by which these results were accomplished. When people focus more on the outcome and less on the means, they can get caught in the trap of short-term, reactive thinking. The performance of individuals against "top-down" objectives becomes more important than the performance of the system.

• **MBO lacks buy-in.** The best-laid plans are only as good as an employee's commitment and ability to implement them. Yet in the traditional MBO planning process, people plan for other people. Employee input, if it exists at all, is usually limited to upper management. In the absence of employee participation, the very people most critical to the success of the overall strategy often do not understand or agree with the merits of the plan. What happens if you attempt to force your ideas on others? At best, people may comply with what they perceive to be top management's goals. At worst, they may complain forcefully, and if they feel unable to influence top management, they may overtly or covertly persist in established ways, resistant to the bitter end.

• **MBO does not connect strategy and performance metrics.** When was the last time your organization's strategy changed? When was the last time your organization's performance metrics changed? Typically, in organizations that practice MBO, strategies may change but performance metrics do not. When you fail to tie your performance metrics to the strategy, you cannot know whether your strategies have been implemented as intended nor whether they were successful.

• **MBO lacks cross-functional coordination.** The traditional MBO planning process defines functional objectives. Unfortunately, these often are not integrated horizontally, missing out on important cross-functional linkage issues. In many service organizations, departments limit their focus to their own isolated and frequently incongruent internal objectives. The result is an internal win/lose mentality and adversarial isolationist attitudes which undermine performance of the enterprise as a whole.

• **MBO does not advance group learning.** In service organizations that practice MBO, the review process is rarely structured well enough to ensure that all goals and operating assumptions are regularly reviewed. The result? Managers rarely catch deviations and, therefore, rarely fix them. Strategic planning becomes an event, not a process that is continually revisited to ensure learning at the individual, group, and organizational level.

• **MBO lacks focus.** Organizations which rely on MBO frequently toss their well-laid plans out the window to focus on the crises of the moment. Rather than consciously focusing scarce resources on a few target areas, these organizations end up dissipating their efforts and suboptimizing their resources. They end up working on the trivial many at the expense of the critical few.

In summary, for all its popularity, the Management by Objective approach to strategy implementation fails to provide the leadership and learning required to sustain continuous improvement. Simply deploying goals and objectives throughout the organization does not guarantee that they are implemented or achieved. In the absence of role clarity and meaningfulness at the local level, MBO, by default, leads to "managing by instinct," an outcome that is neither reliable nor able to be systematically replicated throughout the organization.

## Organizations need to build focus, commitment, and communication

If Management by Objective is so deficient in providing direction and cross-functional coordination, how can managers develop, communicate, and monitor their corporate road maps? How can they guarantee that the means are deployed as systematically as are their objectives? How can they coordinate their many quality improvement activities to achieve continuous incremental improvements as well as strategic breakthroughs? The solution is to find a planning process that can (1) mobilize an entire organization toward the achievement of key business objectives, (2) interpret a companywide vision at the local level, and (3) support continuous improvement. In a world of increasing distractions, individuals must be able to focus quickly on things that are congruent with the long-term aspirations of the enterprise. They must understand how their attempts to improve quality integrate with others to make significant breakthroughs in performance improvement.

Such a planning process already exists. The Japanese call it *hoshin* planning. *Hoshin* is a Chinese word for "shiny metal showing direction"—a compass.[3] To many Western organizations, however, hoshin planning is known as *policy deployment*. The term policy deployment is sometimes confusing, because in the United States policy is associated with company rules and regulations. But in this context, *policy* means the objectives as well as the means and methods organizations use to achieve them. Objectives alone are merely slogans, management exhortations, and wish lists. In the context of policy deployment, policy is not policy unless objectives are visible as theory in action.

Policy deployment is a time-tested planning and implementation process that translates a customer-focused vision into action. It combines the concepts of customer focus, shared vision, management by facts, universal participation, leadership, and continuous improvement—all concepts you have seen in prior chapters of this book—to execute strategic breakthroughs. How does it work? It weds the positive aspects of MBO (autonomy, creativity, and flexibility in accomplishing strategic objectives), the PDSA cycle for continuous improvement, and cross-functional employee participation to manage the top-down and sideways implementation of organizational priorities. The result is an organization which consistently focuses on a few priorities, identifies key systems that need to be improved to achieve strategic objectives, and then clearly communicates that focus throughout the organization. Policy deployment yields many other benefits.

- Policy deployment makes planning and execution of selected strategies a reliable process.

- Policy deployment provides meaning by connecting day-to-day quality improvement activities to organizational objectives.

- Policy deployment builds commitment and buy-in through participation.

- Policy deployment increases communication and understanding, providing (1) top management with an efficient method of staying in touch with the realistic capabilities of the organization, and (2) employees with the means for providing input into strategy selection.

- Finally, by emphasizing the importance of planning, review, and management by fact, policy deployment facilitates organizational learning.

In summary, policy deployment, as hoshin, *is* a compass. It keeps an organization headed in the right direction, focusing everybody's attention on the final destination, and pulling everyone toward that destination in a smooth, coordinated, and focused way.

## UNDERSTANDING POLICY DEPLOYMENT: THE CORNERSTONES

Policy deployment takes a three-pronged approach to ensure targeted business results. First, it focuses on a few critical customer-focused priorities (as opposed to the trivial many). Second, it directs continuous improvement throughout the organization by focusing on the means (as opposed to measuring performance after the fact). Finally, it builds organizational commitment to shared objectives through universal participation in the planning process. This approach translates into three management principles.

1. **Keep it simple.** Policy deployment is a direction-setting leadership process which helps you select key customer-focused priorities on which to act.

2. **Continuously improve.** Through the PDSA cycle and management by fact, policy deployment links continuous improvement to customer satisfaction. It does so through a

rigorous review process that keeps you focused on customer priorities and makes sure that you plan, execute, monitor, and control your management processes to achieve targeted business results.

3. **Involve others.** By involving employees in the planning process, policy deployment builds employee commitment and communicates corporate objectives to the entire organization. This process relies on the concept of cascading priorities from above while defining the means through consensus from below. Objectives and means are deployed together based on the true capability of the organization.

Policy deployment integrates many of the principles and processes described throughout this book. For example, as we saw in chapter 1, priorities need to be directed by the voice of the customer. In chapter 3, we learned how building organizational commitment requires universal participation in planning and implementation efforts. In chapters 4 and 7, we saw how the PDSA cycle supports continuous improvement and organizational learning. And in chapter 8, we learned that choosing priorities requires strong leadership. Policy deployment is key to making it all work. Let's see how.

## Keep it simple: focus on the critical few

Given the rapid changes and increasing distractions organizations face today, individuals must be able to focus quickly on things that are congruent with the long-term vision of the organization. From the outset, management needs clear priorities so that it can establish a leadership process to evoke purposeful, business-directed activities from everyone in the organization. If you have too many priorities, you risk defeating your purpose, diluting everyone's energies, and becoming "a jack of all trades, master of none." The clearer your priorities, the easier it will be for people to focus their energies on what really counts.

Selecting priorities requires strong leadership. John Hudiburg, former chairman of the board and CEO of Florida Power and Light Company, winner of the prestigious Deming Prize awarded in Japan for total quality performance, emphasizes the importance of making those hard decisions.

*One of our early mistakes in policy management was a common one: we tried to work on too many things at once. The first time we went through the process, if someone suggested dropping an item from the quality element (customer requirements) list, they were looked at as if they were proposing murder. Our counselor's way of putting it was that we were chasing too many rabbits at the same time. Eventually we narrowed down the number of things designated for major improvements to just the vital few....There were only eight elements on the list for the entire organization....Moreover, any given department would only work on about three of these at the same time.[4]*

The first step to harnessing corporate energy is to select two to three "vital few" strategies upon which to focus. Why? First, few managers have the capability to focus on more than three "major impact" items at a time. Second, focusing on too many objectives can dilute the overall effort.

Vital few strategies represent areas or capabilities that require significant improvement. They should have a high impact on the ability of the organization to improve performance in the eyes of your customers, shape the environment, utilize resources effectively, and/or strengthen organizational effectiveness. Because the vital few are organizationally so significant and usually require a new way of managing and possibly new resources, they are often referred to as breakthrough strategies.

It is important to select the vital few issues before specifying departmental goals. In general, every functional department supports continuous improvement through (1) quality in daily work—the application of the PDSA cycle to daily work, and (2) cross-functional management to maximize coordination and cooperation with other functions. But only certain groups can significantly affect the "vital few" objectives. The vital few objectives will determine specific functional and cross-functional groups that must be mobilized to ensure breakthrough performance. Together, policy deployment, quality in daily work, and cross-functional cooperation, work to translate the vision into action (see Figure 9.1).

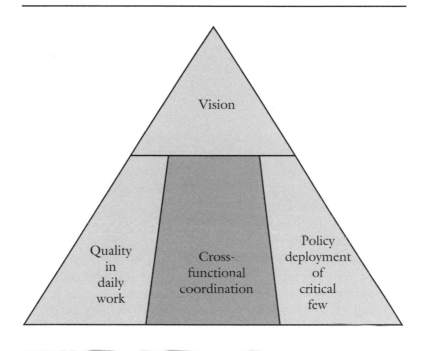

**Figure 9.1:** Translate the vision into action

How do you select the vital few issues? The best breakthrough strategies are customer-focused and based on facts. By using data from customers and analysis of the strengths and weaknesses of your enterprise, you can identify key areas which require improvement and promise the greatest impact. John Hudiburg stresses the importance of managing by facts.

*Another early mistake we made was relying almost entirely on gut feeling and not nearly enough on data in priority setting. Too often the person with the strongest opinion or the loudest voice decided the close ones, and I myself was absolutely one of the worst offenders. But as we began to obtain more accurate and useful data and to insist on speaking with facts, this became less and less true. Once we had learned to discipline ourselves in this manner, we were amazed at how much more we were able to accomplish in a much shorter time. We actually began to end meetings early, with much better communication and decisions having taken place. You certainly still need to exercise judgment, but judgment based on data—on facts—produces a better result.*[5]

The case for keeping it simple and focusing on a chosen few is clear: If you never take on the hard job of choosing what to focus on, you will dissipate your energies and underutilize precious resources. Customer focus and leadership are critical to the process of creating continuous quality improvement.

## Continuously improve: use the PDSA cycle

Planning is a process. And like any other process, it can be continuously improved. How can we improve the process of continuous improvement? How can we ensure that we translate our vision into action? Once again, we turn our attention to the PDSA cycle, the disciplined management tool developed by W. Edwards Deming.

Using the PDSA cycle at the strategic planning level, senior managers can answer such questions as: Were our quality improvement plans indeed implemented? How well did we do? How much improvement did we make? Which operating assumptions were correct and which were faulty? What did we learn? Only by gaining insight into these issues can organizations continuously improve performance. Through PDSA, which ensures results by focusing on the means and not just the ends, we can drive improvement throughout the entire organization. John Hudiburg observes

*Any organization that has existed for any length of time is probably good at "plan-do"; at FPL we had always done a pretty good job of this. But back in 1985 the "check-act" part was virtually nonexistent. "Check-act," as we came to learn it, means using data to analyze whether the actual results of "do" were the ones planned, and then taking action to improve the next PDCA cycle. (At that time we would have said we did this, but in hindsight it is clear that any attempts we made were pretty superficial.) And PDCA is applied not only to improve problem-solving skills but also to improve the quality improvement process itself; this application is probably the most important use of the PDCA cycle.*[6]

How does the PDSA cycle support companywide continuous improvement? You can apply the PDSA cycle to the strategic planning process in the following way.

• **Plan.** Map your quality commitments. Top management defines where it wants to go but not how it is going to get there. Because the change process does not belong to top management, only those responsible for implementing the plan will define the means to achieve the objectives. In the planning phase, a lot of negotiation takes place. Truly effective planning takes a long time, requires a lot of hard thinking, and depends on open communication among all parties concerned.

• **Do.** Execute the plan. Top managers act as facilitators and catalysts. They monitor implementation deviations, evaluate the performance of the process against top-down objectives, and do whatever they can to support others in the implementation process.

• **Study.** In the study phase, systematically and visually track and evaluate your progress. Did you achieve what you set out to do? If not, why not? Were there any surprises? If so, why? How can you capture that learning? Monitor your actions not once but at regular intervals during implementation.

• **Act.** Analyze how well you implemented your new strategies to control your results. If, in the checking phase, you decided that your strategies need to be modified, now is the time to do it. When you identify improvement opportunities, start the PDSA cycle anew: Incorporate your findings into a modified plan. Implement the revised plan. And then check it all over again.

As you apply the PDSA cycle to your corporate quality improvement process, you begin to align various companywide quality improvement efforts with the long-term vision (see Figure 9.2). John Hudiburg recounts the instruction and analogy that he and others at Florida Power and Light received from their quality counselor from Japan:

> *Dr. Asaka likened a company just getting started to a group of arrows dropped on the floor randomly, pointing in all directions. The arrows represent the efforts of the different departments—forceful and well intentioned, but uncoordinated. After the first attempt at policy deployment (that is, the first PDCA cycle), the arrows look like the spokes of a hand-held fan, more or less pointing in the same general direction but still not perfectly aligned. After another iteration of the PDCA cycle, the arrows are parallel and all point in the same direction but have gaps between them. Finally, after one more turn of the PDCA wheel, the arrows are all aligned in a bundle, mutually supporting each other, with a third dimension: depth. The arrows in the bundle support each other and produce greatly enhanced strength. Likewise, in an organization, the various elements of the company work together cross-functionally to produce greatly enhanced results. Today I use the same description to explain the effects of policy management at FPL.[7]*

It takes discipline to apply the PDSA continuous improvement cycle to strategic planning. But as we saw in chapter 7, people and organizations only learn when ambiguity is eliminated and valid information is supplied. The PDSA cycle, applied to strategy implementation, forces operating assumptions to be publicly uncovered, documented, tested, and revised. As with anything, practice makes perfect: the more you can plan for change and understand your successes and failures, the easier continuous improvement will be. While to some extent change will occur as a trial and error process, the PDSA cycle provides you with a reliable, time-tested tool for managing improvement.

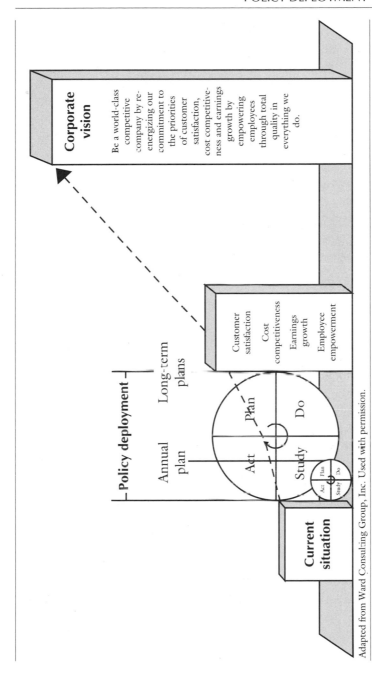

**Corporate vision**

Be a world-class competitive company by re-energizing our commitment to the priorities of customer satisfaction, cost competitive-ness and earnings growth by empowering employees through total quality in everything we do.

Customer satisfaction

Cost competitiveness

Earnings growth

Employee empowerment

**Policy deployment**

Long-term plans

Annual plan

Plan

Do

Act

Study

**Current situation**

**Figure 9.2:** Translating the vision into action

Adapted from Ward Consulting Group, Inc. Used with permission.

## Involve others: cascade and percolate to build commitment

As we saw in chapter 3, only when you involve others in planning and decision-making can you build organization-wide commitment to action. There is a Chinese proverb which underscores the importance of employee involvement:

*Tell me, I forget.*
*Show me, I remember.*
*Involve me, I understand.*

There is also an apt expression, "The transfer of knowledge is power." Nothing could be truer, and nothing builds employee commitment faster. Unfortunately, too many managers are reluctant to share important knowledge with the majority of employees. To these managers, knowledge is power, a power they are too scared to share. How does this play out in the planning process? In many organizations, the planning function is designated to a planner, who plans for others. The resulting plans are then communicated to those who are supposed to *do*.

This approach to planning often results in little or no commitment to the tactics or actions specified. Middle managers and others knowledgeable about the realities of their business are traditionally excluded in the initial stages of the planning process. Yet they can often immediately spot the weaknesses, inefficiencies, or outright impossibilities of the plans thrust upon them. In the traditional planning process, people close to the process and the realities of the business have no way, and certainly no incentive, to share their knowledge with the planners. The valuable knowledge of these individuals is never included in the development of the plans. The result? A plan with gaps, weaknesses, inefficiencies, and sometimes, outright impossibilities—all results that could easily have been avoided had the "hands-on" people been consulted. Only by involving the people who are expected to implement the plans can you gain the alignment and commitment you need for successful implementation and learning.

You can build organizational commitment, gain increased role clarity, and learn your true organizational capabilities by bringing

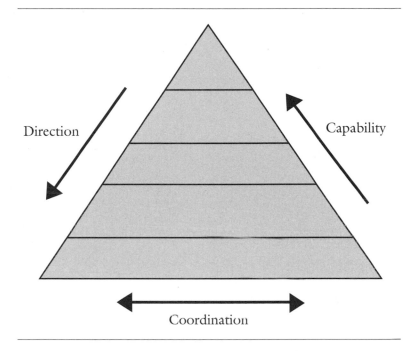

**Figure 9.3:** Deploy goals and actions plans
based on the true capability of the organization

the entire organization—both top-down and bottom-up—into the
strategic planning process by using a process to cascade plans and
objectives. Cascading is not a unidirectional process of telling.
Instead, it is an invitation to those at all levels of the hierarchy to
participate in the development of ambitious yet realistic plans for
quality improvement (see Figure 9.3). For example, senior managers may solicit information directly from mid-management to
identify areas for quality improvement as well as to obtain input on
quality improvement goals.[8] Heavy participation by employees
ensures that the organizational focus is rationally developed, well
defined, clearly communicated, monitored for compliance, and
based on system feedback.

How does cascading work? Once top management defines the
key objectives, it cascades those objectives down to the next layer of
management. Since only those individuals who are closest to the

business can define the most appropriate strategies, it is the lower layers of the organization that specify the "how." In designing appropriate strategies, employees at every level are careful to take into account their subordinates' inputs as well as those of their peers. Their goal? To zero in on their final destination from every conceivable angle. This cascading process means that at each level of the organization, objectives (ends) are received from above and strategies (means) are designed from below and sideways to support them.

In policy deployment, objectives are promulgated down the organization in an ends-means, ends-means, ends-means fashion whereby the means for one hierarchical level become the ends for the next. How is this cascading process different from MBO? Cascading ensures that the knowledge and ideas of individual employees are woven into the company plan. While a manager in a traditional organization practicing MBO is given the freedom and responsibility to develop the means or method to achieve objectives, the manager in an organization that practices policy deployment adds knowledge exchange and consensus to the objective-setting process.

Policy deployment ensures that you gain agreement on your strategies every which way: up as well as down through the departments, and sideways across departmental lines. This helps prevent various departments from implementing strategies which may be suboptimal from the point of view of other departments in the company. And it ensures that goals and action plans are cascaded based on the true capability of the organization.

Cascading reflects the consensus-building aspect of policy deployment. Achieving consensus is different from voting. *Consensus* implies that individuals voluntarily give consent. In contrast, voting means that the majority position wins while the minority loses. Sometimes when losers feel threatened or angry, conflict, divisiveness, and sabotage may ensue. Although a decision by vote may be made within a quick and limited time period, the result is usually an organization that is not aligned. In contrast, when you use the cascading process to build consensus, you keep the discussion going until everyone agrees on a course of action. The outcome of the process is frequently not one side's position or the other's, but a creative third solution that incorporates and addresses the concerns expressed by all. Cascading coupled with consensus offers a win/win approach to decision-making. Everyone may not share the same degree of enthusiasm over the resulting decision, but they will at least go along and help carry it out.

As members of the organization gain confidence in the policy deployment process, typically there is increased employee contribution. Mr. Sasaoka, president of Yokogawa Hewlett Packard, recalls that during the company's first year of implementing policy deployment, virtually all directives emanating from top management came back unchanged. Today, he estimates that what is eventually implemented is only 60 percent intact; the remainder is modified according to lower level management input.[9]

You can tell that your policy deployment process is effective when all of your employees know and understand

1. the mission of the operation

2. the customer-focused corporate priorities

3. how you measure quality

4. your role in improving quality

5. the tools necessary to ensure and improve quality

In summary, a quality improvement strategy requires input from everyone; it cannot be a staffer's job. It is directed by a few customer-focused priorities. It applies the PDSA cycle for continuous improvement. And it uses a disciplined consensus-building process by cascading a few key strategies down through the entire organization.

## DEPLOYING YOUR QUALITY OBJECTIVES

Active employee involvement may strengthen the strategic planning process, but it can also be its greatest undoing. For most managers, the first step in policy deployment involves choreography—the process of getting everyone to dance together, and to the same tempo. Just like the traffic cop who directs traffic to break up a jam, so too must managers choreograph their people's parts to keep the planning process out of gridlock. Sound a bit overwhelming? It does to many managers. But in the absence of a systematic, disciplined, participative process for planning and review, it is just a fantasy that you have control over your people, your processes, and your organizational performance.

Just how can we integrate the PDSA cycle, cascading, and setting direction? What follows is a seven-step process for analyzing, developing, testing, and deploying your policy (see Figure 9.4). Step 1 is related to the act phase of the PDSA cycle. Steps 2–4 tell you how to "plan your plan." Step 5 executes your plan (the "do" step). The sixth and seventh steps are the checking phase.

1. **Diagnose external and internal performance to create a three- to five-year plan.** Before turning on the PDSA engine, warm up by taking a hard look around you. Do you agree on where you are going? One of the greatest compliments managers bestow on one another is to say that someone has vision, the ability to see the future. Many organizations, however, are hindered by their inability to look beyond the current quarter. Good quality planning depends on your ability to think and see long-term.

Before you can get on with planning, you may need to revisit your corporate mission. Given that your mission guides your every step, now is the time to take a fresh look at it. Do you still agree with the stated purpose? Can your mission statement be clearer? Once you have satisfied yourself that your mission is on target, revisit your vision. Focus on the next five years. Is it customer-focused? Does everyone understand it?

With your mission and vision in place, you can now determine exactly what you need to accomplish to attain your vision. Translate vague terms like "pre-eminent" and "quality" into specific objectives. Using data from customers, internal corporate groups, and the corporate strategy, analyze the organization's strengths and weaknesses, identify several key areas for improvement, and separate issues which require significant, breakthrough improvement from those which represent day-to-day continuous improvement. From this list, select three to five fundamental objectives which you hope to accomplish within the next five to seven years. You may define your fundamental objectives within broad areas such as customer satisfaction, organizational effectiveness, environmental safety, utilization of resources, and utilization of people.

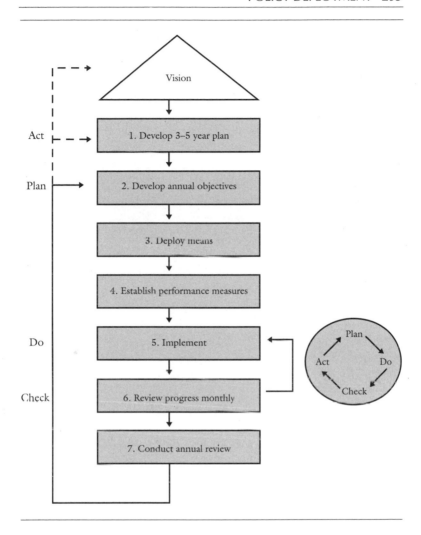

**Figure 9.4:** Policy deployment is a process

With your vital few objectives in hand, you are now ready to determine the short-term specifics. Here's where the planning step of the annual PDSA cycle starts.

2. **Create a one- to two-year plan.** Keeping your updated vision in mind, analyze the current environment and needed breakthroughs as

well as any lessons learned from last year's plan. Your goal is to roll your fundamental objectives back into a short-term plan, asking yourself, "What do our breakthrough objectives mean for next year?"

Given these objectives, what areas and issues could thwart your plans? Once you identify these areas, prioritize them. Which require immediate attention? Which have the greatest impact on the customer? Once you identify problem areas, define your short-term goals accordingly.

Upon completion of this step, you will have a list of short-term goals that are specific, measurable, feasible, and significant. These detailed short-term objectives are the mechanism to translate your fundamental objectives into departmental objectives.

3. **Deploy the means.** Once you identify your one-year goals, build organizational commitment toward them by cascading them in a top down-sideways manner. Employees at each level translate the one-year objective of the level above them into local strategies, answering the question, "What does this mean for us?" They select their own areas on which to focus, determining for themselves to what degree they can or want to influence each fundamental objective (see Figure 9.5).

4. **Establish performance indicators.** Once you have cascaded your plan down to every level and reviewed it sideways, people will need performance indicators and related targets so that they will know if they have achieved their stated objectives. Among other things, the value added by policy deployment is that there are no surprises come performance review time. How do you know when you are done? You will be done when your annual plan includes the answers to *who, what, how much, how,* and *how we will know when we get there.*

5. **Implement your plan.** Strategies come to life in the implementation and execution stage. Assign a measure to each task, such as a completion date or progress target, and designate who will be responsible for carrying it out. As facilitators, top managers take on the responsibility for monitoring the implementation deviations and the interactions of these on the overall performance of the

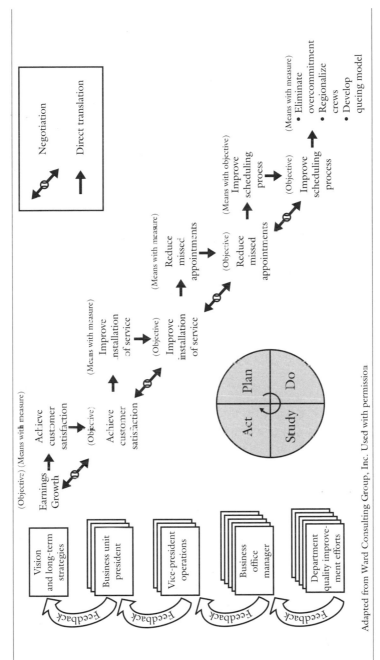

**Figure 9.5:** Cascading the means and objectives

Adapted from Ward Consulting Group, Inc. Used with permission

organization. The object is to evaluate and act on the performance of the system or the means as opposed to the performance of individuals against top-down objectives.

6. **Audit your plan monthly.** Through periodic progress checks, management can verify that strategies are correct, implementation is progressing according to plan, and goals will be met. A monthly audit helps to detect problem areas early so that you can root them out. Also, the more you can document your successes and failures, the better the assumptions you will make in your next planning cycle.

7. **Audit annually.** A monthly audit, while necessary to keep on track, is not sufficient. You need to make a thorough review at least once at year. The annual review is an analytical assessment of the prior year's objectives, accomplishments, and lessons learned. In this way, the annual review is grounded in management by fact. In the spirit of continuous improvement, the job is never over. Once you complete the annual audit, you begin the PDSA cycle again.

As you can see, policy deployment differs from MBO in that the manager takes on the roles of leader and facilitator, not dictator. In policy deployment, managers develop a plan and negotiate differences, a role which requires that each manager take a systems, versus a parochial, view of the organization. Top management sets the direction by specifying a few key breakthrough objectives, and then assesses and monitors implementation deviations to form the means for continuous improvement. When this is done correctly, results become an outcome of the means rather than an end in themselves. Results, in the end, indicate how well policy deployment is working.

## PREREQUISITES FOR POLICY DEPLOYMENT

While policy deployment is a powerful management process that virtually guarantees continuous quality improvement, as you might suspect, members of an organization need certain skills and capabilities to be successful. Prerequisites for policy deployment include

- companywide knowledge and experience with basic principles of total quality management, including where policy deployment fits; the PDSA cycle; and knowledge and use of analytical quality control tools (topics covered in chapters 1–4 of this book)

- leadership to (1) establish customer-focused priorities and communicate them to everyone, and (2) remove system barriers, as we saw in chapter 7

- participative management skills and cross-functional coordination, as we saw in chapter 2

---

## Criteria for evaluating a good quality plan

After you have developed a preliminary quality improvement plan, you can ask yourself the following questions to make sure you are on the right track.

- Have you translated the vision into concrete corporate objectives?

- Does your plan focus on three to five issues—the critical few versus the trivial many?

- Have you established measures to quantify corporate goals? Can you measure your success every step of the way?

- Is the process for establishing corporate priorities repeatable?

- Have you analyzed the trends or gaps in prior years' results?

- Can you cascade your strategy?

- Can you draw a picture of it?

- Are there specific targets and goals related to each objective?

- Can everyone understand the strategy?

- Have management reviews of progress against plan been included in the schedule?

- Have you standardized improvements?

- Is the planning process reviewed and improved at the end of each cycle?

Policy deployment is something that organizations work toward; it is not something that can be accomplished in one swift management move. Building the base skills and designing the choreography requires some experience on the part of top management with customer focus, problem solving skills, PDSA for continuous improvement, and employee involvement. Without these basic skills, policy deployment and management control are just a pipe dream. Policy deployment is a rigorous disciplined way of ensuring continuous companywide quality improvement.

## SUMMARY

When it comes to quality improvement, many executives cite as the cause of their problems the sea of middle managers who resist change. Yet middle managers in these same companies usually complain that senior management has failed to clearly articulate priorities and/or the linkages between policies and procedures, thus creating confusion, lack of coordination, and waste. Although they disagree about the cause, both groups agree that the biggest obstacle to change is lack of connection between day-to-day activities and strategy.

When most organizations initiate a companywide quality improvement effort, it is not uncommon for employees and CEOs to experience quality improvement activities as an add-on to business as usual. Collecting data on customer needs, attending training sessions, and participating in process improvement teams are time consuming, and in an environment where work load is already an issue, this can create stress. While all of these quality improvement activities are necessary, the key to success is in moving from an activity-based approach to quality improvement to an effort which is driven by a few critical priorities. Failure to link quality improvement activities to strategic business issues is why so many organizations fail to achieve the full benefits of what customer focus, process improvement, universal participation, and continuous improvement have to offer.

Policy deployment is a structured and disciplined method to ensure communication of organizational priorities among horizontal functions as well as among vertical levels in the hierarchy. It depends on a circular feedback process that travels both down and up the hierarchy to tie daily work and quality improvement activities to critical long-term customer-focused business issues. Using policy deployment, you can translate critical organizational priorities into practical, implementable actions by inviting those who are responsible for implementing the plans to join in the process of creating them and measuring their success.

| From | To |
| --- | --- |
| lengthy strategy document | cascadeable policy |
| ends | ends and means |
| MBO | MBO plus cross-functional collaboration |
| directives | participation in implementation plans |
| results through targets | results through process |
| evaluation of individual performance | evaluation of the management process |

## Notes

1. deGeus, "Planning as Learning," 70.

2. A. Richard Shores, "Leadership Through Planning and Review," *Survival of the Fittest* (Milwaukee, Wis.: ASQC Quality Press, 1988).

3. "Hoshin Planning: A Planning System for Implementing Total Quality Management (TQM)" (Methuen, Mass.: Goal/QPC Research Committee, 1989), 1.

4. John J. Hudiburg, *Winning with Quality: The FPL Story,* (White Plains, N.Y.: Quality Resources, 1991), 45–46.

5. Ibid., 47.

6. Ibid., 44.

7. Ibid.

8. George H. Labovitz and Yu Sang Chang, "Learn from the Best," *Quality Progress,* May 1990, 81–85.

9. Goal/QPC, *Hoshin,* 11.

*There is nothing more powerful than an idea whose time has come.*

—Victor Hugo

# Quality Is Not a Destination; It Is a Journey

A s long as there is a dynamic marketplace where customer needs and expectations are changing, there is room for improving the quality of our products and services. As customer expectations and preferences change, a commitment to total quality excellence requires an operating philosophy and system designed to continually improve the quality of everything we do.

Beneath the quality label, there is a wide spectrum of experience and practice. Some of this variety is the result of genuine experimentation, development, and specialization. Some is due to the initial symptoms of poor quality, blind spots, and misconceptions of the management team. As in all things, you have to find your own way, trust your own heart, and above all, be humble.

Despite the variety of experiences in implementing continuous companywide quality improvement, significant improvement requires adherence to nine operating principles:

1. *Focus on the customer.* Every employee should know the customer requirements (internal and external) for his or her output.

2. *Streamline the process.* Understand that everything is a process and that variability in the process is a source of waste.

3. *Use partnerships and teamwork to solve problems and reduce waste and costs.* Every employee plays an important part in bringing about continuous quality improvement, because each person has a piece of the solution.

4. *Create a system to achieve continuous improvements in quality.* Every employee must believe that what exists today is just not good enough.

5. *Managers must work on the system.* Quality improvement requires a systems perspective, focusing not merely on the parts but also on how they interact.

6. *Provide constancy of purpose.* Create a compelling and exciting shared vision of what the organization can be.

7. *Invest in creating a learning enterprise.* Every employee deserves the chance to act as a learning agent for the organization.

8. *Take the lead, thereby serving as an example to your subordinates and peers.* Be a catalyst for change, and create a sense that change in the right direction will be recognized, rewarded, and reinforced.

9. *Focus on the critical few, not the trivial many.* Combine vertical direction-setting with cross-functional coordination to focus the collective energy on a few breakthrough objectives.

While these are the basics of continuous improvement, total quality itself is a process, and processes can always be improved. As Dr. Shoji Shiba of Tokyo University says, "There is a need to improve the total quality process itself, in contrast to just increasing the intensity of its application." How will total quality evolve? Today, more than ever, people in organizations can determine what quality will mean for society. When it comes to issues of national education, health care services, environmental protection, and the establishment of global partnerships, quality improvement is a must in what is rapidly becoming our global village. Total quality breeds respect for others, a search for excellence and discovery, and a more human set of ethics to direct the process of value change in our society.

When you set out to improve the performance of your organization, be forewarned that you are committing yourself and your organization to an enormous investment of time and energy. It can easily take several years to establish the habit of continuous companywide quality improvement. Why? You will be asking yourself and the people around you to do some initially counter-intuitive things. Abandoning old management styles and behaviors is hard; your progress may often seem slow and painful.

· In the end, customer-focused quality improvement is more of a personal practice, a way of living, than it is a business methodology or solution. It is something that you do with others, not to them. The fundamental principles are as appropriate at home as they are at the office, as relevant to large organizations as to small, as beneficial for a for-profit firm as for a nonprofit organization, and as pertinent to front-line employees as to top management. Customer-focused quality is more than a specific type of management practice, it is a way of life.

## How to do things wrong

1. *Be unfriendly.* Treat unanticipated actions of customers or clients as breaches of contract. Snarl. Insult. Mumble unintelligible verbiage. Use peculiar idiosyncratic language or abbreviations.

2. *Blame others.* Blame all your problems on other departments, unreasonable customers, and difficult employees. Do not accept any responsibility for being even a little part of the problem. Act like you are a victim and feel good about it.

3. *Ignore employee suggestions for improvement.* Label employees who complain about the system or identify problems or inconsistencies as "difficult" or "troublemakers." Make certain that you exclude them in the development of plans. Do not communicate upward their concerns about feasibility of implementation of the plan.

4. *Be controlling.* Believe that you are the only person capable of making an informed decision. Do not give employees the authority to make their own decisions about resource requirements and system changes. Demonstrate in your actions that you do not trust their capability to conduct important meetings, make key sales calls, or make wise decisions on the future of the company.

## How to do things wrong (continued)

5. *Demand instant results.* Go for the quick fix. Choose the symptomatic solution over the root cause. Do not allow your employees to take the time to do it right the first time.

6. *Demand allegiance to your way.* Treat disagreements expressed by your subordinates as insubordination. Equate their efforts to inform you of possible problems in your ideas with a lack of commitment to the organization.

7. *Be defensive.* Create an environment in which employees and customers are afraid to come forward with suggestions for improvement, organizational inconsistencies, or problems. Interrupt them before they finish what they came to say, or change the subject.

8. *Be secretive.* Don't have a mission. Don't have a vision. And if you do have them, make sure that they are not made public. Have them be known only among the executives in the organization, if at all. And don't continue dialogue about the vision or mission after you have done the "vision" thing. Make sure these documents stay in employees' drawers or filing cabinets.

9. *Be unfocused.* Insist that everything is a priority. If you do set priorities, make sure that you change them as soon as possible.

# The Customer Requirements Matrix

I f you had infinite resources and time, you would seek to satisfy every customer desire you could identify. But that is not the real world. During the design process, tradeoffs may be necessary due to constraints in the availability of technology or resources. The good news is that not all customer preferences are equally important. In making design decisions, the voice of the customer can be used to help set priorities.

The customer requirements matrix is a powerful management tool that can help you bring common sense, discipline, and most important, the customer's voice into your service design process (see Figures A.1 and A.2). This technique is one of several management matrices contained in a methodology known as quality function

**Figure A.1:** Product service design characteristics

deployment.[1] Originated in Japan, this methodology is now being used by companies worldwide. The customer requirements matrix can help you quickly highlight the inadequacies in your current data collection methods. A proactive and culturally unbiased method, the customer requirements matrix can also help you select customer desires that promise the greatest return in customer satisfaction and provide a disciplined approach to structuring information on customer desires and perceptions.

A systematic approach to design, the customer requirements matrix forces you to answer four questions:

- Which attributes does your customer want?
- Do customers prefer all attributes equally?
- What does your customer think of your performance?
- Which attributes offer competitive advantage?

Put yourself in your customer's shoes and pretend that you are about to purchase one of your organization's services. In column one of Figure A.2, list six key product or service attributes that will satisfy you as a customer.

Since not all preferences are equally important, in the second column, score the relative importance of each of these attributes on a scale of 1 to 5, with 5 being the high end of the scale.

In the third column, determine your perception (as the customer) of your organization's performance. Assign a value of 5 if

| Customer desires | Relative importance | Customer perception of performance | | | Targeted performance | Improvement ratio | Added sales appeal | Priorities |
|---|---|---|---|---|---|---|---|---|
| | | Our company | Competitor X | Competitor Y | | | | |
| | | | | | | F/C | | BxGxH |

| A | B | C | D | E | F | G | H | I |

| | | | | |
|---|---|---|---|---|
| A | Customer desires | | G | Our percentage improvement ratio |
| B | Relative importance to the customer (1–5; 5 = very important) | | | Percentage = targeted performance where we are today |
| | Customer perception of performance (1–5, 5 = excellent) | | H | Incremental sales appeal 1.0 = no additional sales appeal |
| C | Our company | | | 1.2 = moderately attractive to the customer |
| D, E | Our competitors | | | 1.5 = very attractive to the customer |
| Γ | Our target performance (1–5; 5 = excellent) | | I | Weighted benefit Relative importance x (percent improvement required) x added sales appeal |

**Figure A.2:** Customer requirements matrix

you perceive the organization's performance to be of the highest quality, and a value of 1 if it is extremely poor.

Follow the same process for each of two competitors.

Now switch hats and pretend that you are a top manager of your company. Look back over the range of customer performance ratings to see how they differ. On some attributes, your customer may perceive that all competitors perform at roughly the same level. If you and your competitors are all low on perceived performance and this attribute is extremely important to the customer, you have identified an improvement opportunity that could gain you competitive advantage.

You are now ready to select the performance levels or *target performance values* that you wish to achieve. The ratio of your target performance value to your present level of performance is called your *improvement ratio*. When you calculate an improvement ratio for each product or service attribute, you can compare across attributes and determine where you have the farthest to go to improve your competitive performance. This approach is congruent with a scoring and tracking management system.

Now look at your real situation. Can you fill out even the first column of customer wants and desires? Only companies that are already customer-focused can answer this question in the affirmative. Do you presently collect detailed information on the service attributes your competitors offer, rather than simply comparing overall customer satisfaction company by company? Many service organizations do not. And yet discovering customer desires, determining their relative importance, and knowing whether you meet expectations is a commonsense and profitable approach to doing business. You can start by asking some real customers to complete the first five columns of this matrix. Look for gaps between what you and your management team assume is true about your performance and what your customer really thinks about your performance.

## Note

1. Bob King, *Better Designs in Half the Time: Implementing QFD Quality Function Deployment in America* (Methuen, Mass.: GOAL/QPC, 1987).

# The Costs of Poor Quality

Typical areas of waste in service organizations include

- lost time
- unnecessary labor
- complexity
- uncoordinated transportation
- unused data
- idle people
- sales time spent on unfruitful prospects
- lost accounts
- management's time
- unnecessary administrative time (spent on additional accounting, purchase orders, and so on)

- employee turnover
- corrective actions
- cost of disposal
- reprocessing of orders
- investigation time
- legal costs
- bad debt collection
- billing error costs
- field service costs
- service contracts—insurance policies against poor workmanship
- complaint resolution time
- rework
- screening
- sorting
- long information retrieval time
- disorganized meetings
- telephone tag
- unnecessary motion
- confusing numbering schemes
- confusing notices
- unnecessary memoranda
- too much concern over who gets the credit

# Nominal Group Technique

In using this version of nominal group technique, be certain to complete all six steps. What may at first appear to be a shortcut will only cost more time and create confusion in the long run.

All you need to start is a single question that captures the problem at hand. Your question can be as simple as "What are the internal barriers to improving quality in our working group?" "How can we improve morale in our department?" or "What are our expectations of the billing department?" Whatever the issue, it must be presented as a question. It must be placed in full view of all participants at the beginning of the session and remain there the entire time. For your first time, pick a topic that is manageable in size and not too controversial.

Once you have defined the question, decide who should attend the working session. In a company that is unfamiliar with employee involvement, managers frequently leave out individuals or representatives who are deemed difficult, negative, habitual complainers, troublemakers, and so on. Not so in the use of nominal group technique! These are the very people you want to have as participants in the brainstorming session. The key to a successful working session is that all individuals who affect the process from cradle to grave must be represented on the team. A good number to have in the group is about five to nine members.

Prior to the start of any meeting, it is a good idea to involve as many people as possible in active roles. It is also a good idea to ask for a volunteer to be the nominal leader for the session. The difference between this and other ways of running meetings is that the nominal leader is an equal. Next, ask for a volunteer to assist the leader in putting flip-charts on the wall and tallying votes during the working session. Third, ask for a timekeeper to keep everyone honest. Give an overview of the structured process that you will follow during the remainder of the session. It is often helpful to list the six steps on a board in full view of all participants, along with the amount of time that will be allotted for each step. It is useful to warn people that at times the time frame may seem to be shorter than one would expect, especially for discussion, but that this will give discipline to interactions that you might not have otherwise.

• **Step 1: silent generation (10 minutes).** Given pencil and paper, participants are asked to list everything that comes to mind regarding the problem, including politically sensitive or personal issues. Although they are not required to share these lists with the rest of the group unless they choose to do so, this step is essential to get each individual focused on the problem at hand and on his or her part in it.

• **Step 2: round robin (20 minutes).** Meeting participants take turns sharing items from their list. Each idea is recorded on a master list at the front of the room. When participants run out of new items to share, they say "pass." As new ideas strike them, they may re-enter the round robin at any time. The round robin is over when everyone in the room says "pass."

This is a time for the listing of ideas only. No one may discuss the practicality of any idea at this time. The contribution must be recorded exactly as it is given. Some groups, trying to shortcut the seemingly lengthy process of going around the room one by one, alter this step by having each person give all of their items at once. But one of the benefits of going one at a time is that within one or two rounds, participants are no longer able to identify which ideas are theirs and which belong to others. Instead, they begin to identify with the group and its master list.

• **Step 3: clarification (15 minutes).** With the master list in front of the room, ask everyone to review the list for clarification. Again, there is to be no discussion about the merits of any idea or suggestion. The purpose of this step is to build a common understanding of each issue and to develop a shared vocabulary. An item may not be edited without the consent of the individual who offered it. If there is any discomfort at all, a new item should be added to the list to reflect the difference in meaning. Sometimes, two items are combined as a result of this clarification process.

• **Step 4: initial scoring (10 minutes).** Few organizations have infinite time and resources; therefore they need to set priorities. Ask each participant to pick from the list their five favorite ideas and to rank them, with 5 being the issue of highest priority to them and 1 being the lowest. Ratings are anonymously recorded on 3" x 5" cards. The leader and an assistant collect the cards and record the scores on the master list. Through this ranking process, the original list, which may have had between 60 and 100+ items, is pared down to manageable handful. Without discussion, you have achieved group convergence on some key issues. This brings a sense of group ownership of the list and builds the foundation for consensus.

• **Step 5: discussion (20 minutes).** Finally, discussion time! Group members now discuss each of the items on the short list, remembering to stick to the time frame originally agreed upon. The timekeeper should remind people of the passing time and give a 10-minute warning of the close of the discussion period.

• **Step 6: final scoring (10 minutes).** Following discussion, there is a second scoring. This second scoring is conducted exactly the same as before. Each team member once again silently selects and ranks five of the items on the list. Once again the scores are collected and recorded on the chart at the front of the room. The degree to which first and second scoring differs often has to do with the quality of the information shared during the discussion stage. When groups have roughly the same information available to them prior to the meeting, there may be little change. On the other hand, if a group has had relatively unequal participation by members in prior interactions, nominal group technique by its very nature of structured participation pulls out privately held and rarely expressed ideas and viewpoints. As a result of this new information and shared insights, such groups are apt to exhibit greater swings in importance ratings following discussion.

## Next steps: roles and responsibilities

Use the nominal group technique just once and you will get hooked on it. If you follow each step, participants will leave the meeting feeling energized and motivated, with an improved sense of common vision and hope for the future. As a bonus, all the material generated during a nominal group technique meeting is in an easy format for immediate documentation, distribution, and recognition. This includes the question as recorded at the beginning of the work session, the complete list of suggestions with the final priority ratings (recorded on the flip charts), and a record of the participants.

# Analytical Quality
# Tool Kit

- Where are the data? *checksheet*
- With what frequency are our problems occurring? *histogram*
- What has happened over time? *line graph*
- Is the process in control? *control chart*
- Which problems are most prevalent? *Pareto chart*
- What are the contributing factors? *fishbone diagram*
- Is there a correlation between factors over time? *scatter diagram*
- What does the process look like? *process flow diagram*

# Description of analytical tools used to identify and eliminate problems

### 1. Where are the data? Use a *checksheet.*

A checksheet is a form that facilitates the collection of data to clarify the nature of a problem being solved. It can be used quickly and easily to compile data in a format that can be used later for quantitative analysis. Data are collected using ticks, check marks, or numbers to record how often something happens in a given time period or to measure things. A checksheet is frequently used to gather data on defective items, defect locations, and defect causes.

| Defective copies | March | | | Total |
|---|---|---|---|---|
| | 1 | 2 | 3 | |
| Missing pages | 3 | 3 | 3 | 9 |
| Muddy copies | 7 | 11 | 5 | 23 |
| Show through | 15 | 10 | 15 | 40 |
| Pages out of sequence | 5 | 5 | 4 | 14 |
| Partial copies | 5 | 6 | 6 | 17 |
| Total | 35 | 35 | 33 | 103 |

**Example:** Checksheet for defective copies

### 2. With what frequency are our problems occurring? Use a *histogram.*

A histogram is a bar graph showing the frequency of occurrence of a measured characteristic. The variation of observations is called the distribution of variable data. A histogram is used to make decisions about where to focus initial improvement efforts. It is useful for visually communicating information about a process and helping to make decisions about where to focus improvement efforts.

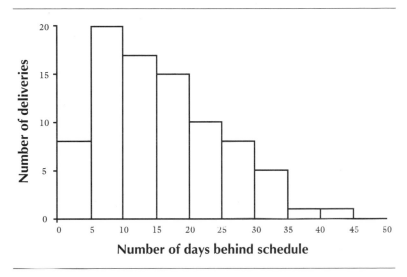

**Example:** Histogram showing distribution of delivery delays

### 3. Which problems are most prevalent? Use a *Pareto chart.*

A Pareto chart can be used to sort raw data into several categories and rank order causes from most to least significant. It can be used to display, in decreasing order, the relative importance of each cause to the problem. Relative contribution may be based on the number of occurrences, the cost associated with each cause, or another measure of impact on the problem. A line graph indicates the cumulative value of the data, ending at 100 percent. A Pareto chart can be used to choose the starting point for problem solving, monitoring success, or identifying the basic cause of a problem. This technique is based on the Pareto principle, which states that a few of the problems often account for most of the effect. By distinguishing the critical few from the potentially less significant causes, you may get maximum quality improvement with the least effort.

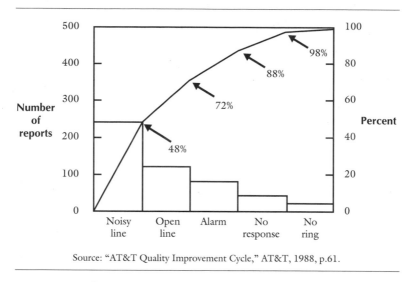

Source: "AT&T Quality Improvement Cycle," AT&T, 1988, p.61.

**Example:** Pareto chart depicting customer complaints

## 4. What has happened over time? Use a *run chart.*

A run chart is a graphic display of observed data points as they vary over time. It can be used to identify meaningful trends, patterns, or shifts in behavior over time.

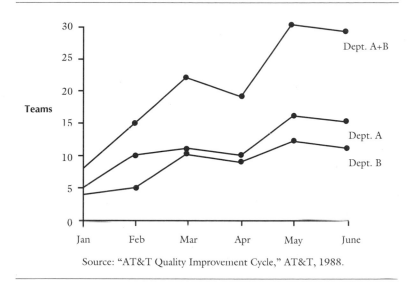

Source: "AT&T Quality Improvement Cycle," AT&T, 1988.

**Example:** Line graph representing quality improvement teams

### 5. Is the process in control? Use a *control chart.*

A control chart is a run chart that has control limit lines at the top, bottom, and middle of the display. It is used to detect whether variation in data is due to the inevitable variations that occur under normal conditions or to a specific cause or abnormal condition.

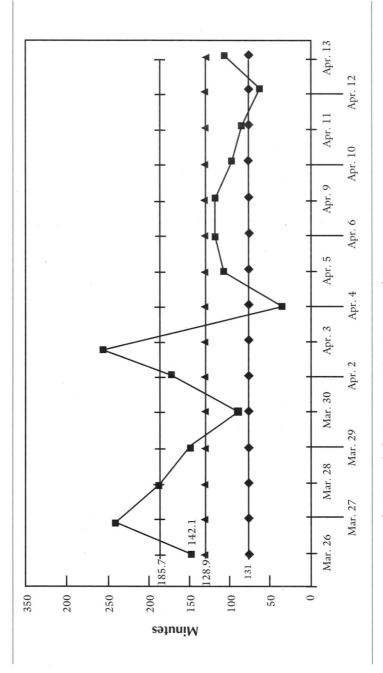

**Example:** Control chart representing turnaround time

### 6. What are the contributing factors? Use a *fishbone diagram.*

A fishbone diagram is a visual representation of the relationships between a given effect and its potential causes. It can be used to identify, explore, and display the possible causes of a specific problem or condition (effect). A well-detailed cause and effect diagram will take the shape of a fishbone, hence its name. The problem or effect to be analyzed is written at the right, where the fish's head would be. The factors that contribute to the effect are written as branches directly attached to the main trunk. Smaller branches fanning out from them represent specific influences within each major cause.

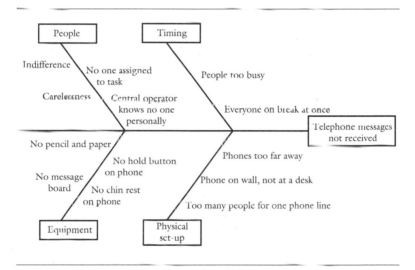

**Example:** Fishbone diagram representing missed telephone messages

### 7. Is there a correlation? Use a *scatter diagram.*

A scatter diagram is used to display what happens to one variable when another variable changes. It can be used to test a theory that the two variables are related. Scatter diagrams cannot be used to prove that changes in one variable cause changes in another variable, but they can identify whether a relationship exists and indicate the strength of that relationship.

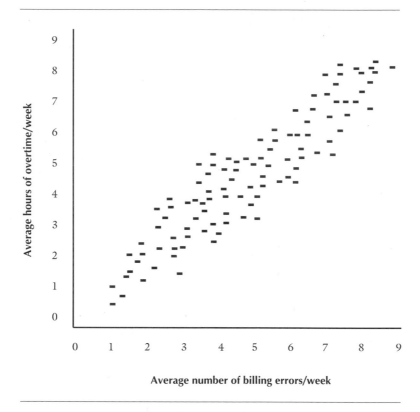

**Example:** Scatter diagram

## 8. What does the process look like? Use a *process flow diagram.*

A process flow diagram is a pictorial representation of the steps in any work process. It is used to investigate opportunities for improvement in any process, including production processes, administrative processes, or the flow of information or services. By examining how various steps in a process relate to each other, you can uncover potential sources of trouble. A process flow diagram is used to identify actual and ideal paths that any product or service follows, allowing deviations to be highlighted. It can be applied to any segment of a process to serve as the basis of process documentation.

**Example:** Process flowchart report delivery process

For more information:

*The Memory Jogger,* GOAL/ QPC, 2nd ed., 1988.

J. M. Juran, *Juran on Planning for Quality* (New York: The Free Press, 1988).

Geary A. Rummler and Alan Brache, *Improving Performance: How to Manage the Whitespace on the Organization Chart* (San Francisco: Jossey-Bass Publishers, 1990).

# APPENDIX E

# Systems Thinking Tools

## Glossary

**Archetypes** A causal loop archetype is a commonly encountered combination of feedback loops. Each archetype exhibits a particular pattern of behavior over time. Learning to recognize these structure/behavior pairs increases our ability to identify and recognize perceptual traps in the change process. By studying causal loop archetypes, we can turbocharge our intuition.

**Arrows** Arrows show the direction of influence between variables.

**Balancing feedback loop** A balancing feedback loop is a circular feedback relationship between two variables that resists change. It reflects goal-seeking behavior. A balancing loop is comprised of one *s* link and one *o* link. Example: As pressure to learn new skills increases, supervisors may feel more threatened (*s*). As supervisors feel more threatened, they participate less in the learning process (*o*).

**Causal loop diagram** A causal loop diagram is a combination of balancing feedback loops and/or reinforcing loops. Depending on the particular combination, different dynamic patterns of behavior emerge. Some combinations are more common than others. These are called *archetypes*.

**Delay** A delay is the time lag between cause and effect.

**"o" link** An *o* link is a causal relationship between two variables where the second variable moves in a direction *opposite* to changes in the first. Example: Higher customer satisfaction leads to fewer customer complaints.

**Reinforcing feedback loop** A reinforcing feedback loop is a circular feedback relationship between two variables that amplifies change in the same direction as the initial push. A reinforcing loop is comprised of two or more s links. Example: As interest payments accrue on a bank account, the balance increases. As the balance increases, the magnitude of the interest payment increases.

**"s" link** An *s* link is a causal relationship between two variables where the second variable moves in the *same* direction as changes in the first. Example: Higher customer satisfaction leads to more repeat purchases.

## Common structure/behavior pairs/archetypes

Archetypes are useful when you are just learning how to think in circles. In the real world, they are simplistic. They are simply the building blocks of far more complicated stories characterized by numerous balancing and reinforcing feedback loops among numerous variables. Once you get good at practicing these simple stories, you can take the training wheels off your bike and create your own,

## Limits to growth

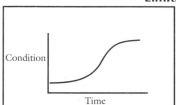

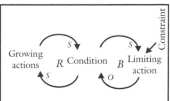

## Shifting the burden

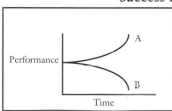

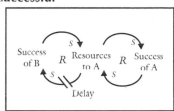

## Success to the successful

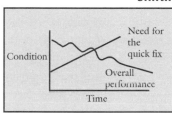

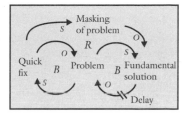

## Eroding goals

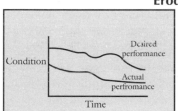

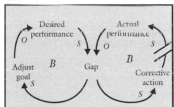

## Fixes that fail

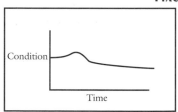

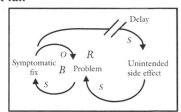

## Common management traps

more complicated causal loop stories. Remember, the map is not the territory. Too much detail can obscure the overall theme.

## Practice

Identify the archetype represented in each of the following situations.

1. We start our skills training thinking that we will gain competence in using analytical quality tools and the problem-solving process. We end up being satisfied if people learn how to draw fishbone diagrams.

2. Members of an executive team beginning to implement total quality management want to see immediate results so that they can feel good about their efforts. They spend money on training and consulting services to get things rolling "down in the trenches" rather than taking the time to get aligned among themselves before proceeding. Taking the time to educate themselves and align around shared mission, vision, and values seems to take too long. Many months later, they are dismayed at the level of confusion in their organization. They are unable to sustain early gains.

3. A company decides to implement an employee suggestion system. It invites all employees to submit suggestions on how they can "improve things around here." Suddenly, management is deluged with suggestions from all quarters. The response is overwhelming. Pent-up frustration with "the system" comes pouring forth in the form of suggestions requiring minor modifications to business as usual as well as suggestions that appear to be more complex and costly to implement. Management begins to sort through all the suggestions. At first management can keep up. But soon it finds that it is unable to implement the suggestions, let alone respond to them as quickly as they are coming in. Employees become discouraged and frustrated at the lack of response to their suggestions. "They asked us for suggestions, didn't they? Well, where are the results? Top management didn't really care after all. I am not going to submit any more suggestions. This was just a hoax."

**Answers:**

 1. Eroding goals archetype

 2. Shifting the burden archetype

 3. Limits to growth

## Systems modeling

Causal loop diagramming is quite useful for describing the key interrelationships that constrain our attempts to change. However, by itself, it has some limitations as an operational tool. While it can show what influences what and what's related to what, it does not show what causes what. Also, causal loop diagrams lack quantitative information. There are no numerical values included in a causal loop diagram to shed much light on "shifts in dominance" among various causal loop relationships.

There are some additional tools that are more operational in nature. These tools, including a mapping language and computer simulation, can assist you in your journey to becoming a systems thinker. For further information, contact the following.

Gould-Kreutzer Associates, Inc., River Court, 10 Rogers Street, Cambridge, Mass. 02142

High Performance Systems, Inc., 45 Lyme Road, Hanover, N.H. 03755

The Systems Thinker, Pegasus Communications, 1696 Massachusetts Avenue, Cambridge, Mass. 02138

# APPENDIX F

# Individual Learning Channels

A lot of instructors and managers dispense information in a purely linear fashion, ignoring the fact that everyone learns differently. To effectively communicate with people, you need to identify both your own and others' natural learning channels. Being able to recognize when you are in one channel and someone else is in another is critical to effective communication. You have not communicated until the other person has received the message. It is your responsibility to make sure that your message has been received. Effective communicators know how to appeal to the following learning modes.

• *Visual* people learn best through diagrams and pictures. When they speak, they often "paint pictures" with their words. They often draw pictures when describing things to others. Visual learners tend to think about and see relationships in a holistic, synthesizing way rather than in a linear fashion.

• *Auditory* learners like to have things explained to them. They would rather have a story read to them than to read it themselves. They like the sounds of words and often choose to communicate over the phone rather than in person.

• *Kinesthetic* people need action to learn. Rather than read diagrams or listen to instructions, they learn by walking through all the steps and trying it out for themselves. Action-based learning tends to be holistic.

• *Print-oriented* learners like to read instructions, books, and other printed material to learn. They would rather read the book than see the movie. Because words and language are primarily linear, print-oriented learners tend to view things logically.

• *Group-interactive* learners learn best through social group processes. They enjoy active dialogue and interchange with others. This type of learning is holistic in nature, not a linear, logical approach.

# Index